ing *with* **Stalinism**

Contending *with* Stalinism

Soviet Power & Popular Resistance in the 1930s

Edited by Lynne Viola

CORNELL UNIVERSITY PRESS

ITHACA AND LONDON

First published 2002 by Cornell University Press
First printing, Cornell Paperbacks, 2002

Printed in the United States of America

Library of Congress Cataloging-in-Publication Data

Contending with Stalinism : Soviet power and popular resistance in the 1930s / edited by Lynne Viola.
p. cm.
Includes bibliographical references and index.
ISBN 0-8014-3983-3 (alk. : cloth) — ISBN 0-8014-8774-9 (alk. : paperback)
1. Government, Resistance to—Soviet Union. 2. Soviet Union—History—1925–1953. I. Viola, Lynne.
DK267 .C66 2002
947.084'2—dc21
2002002764

Cornell University Press strives to use environmentally responsible suppliers and materials to the fullest extent possible in the publishing of its books. Such materials include vegetable-based, low-VOC inks and acid-free papers that are recycled, totally chlorine-free, or partly composed of nonwood fibers. For further information, visit our website at www.cornellpress.cornell.edu.

Cloth printing 10 9 8 7 6 5 4 3 2 1
Paperback printing 10 9 8 7 6 5 4 3 2 1

Contents

Preface

This is a book about resistance in the Soviet Union in the 1930s. A study of neither elite political opposition nor anti-Stalinism per se, it seeks to explore the ways in which resistance can serve as an analytical tool to inform our understanding of that curious amalgam of modifiers sometimes known as *Stalinism*, an "-ism" entirely lacking explanatory or causal force, a kind of syndrome, if you will, which is used here as simple shorthand for the not-unchanging face of the political culture of the times. That there was resistance under Stalin is not without interest, given past and present historiographical assumptions about the monolithic nature of the Stalinist state. Of greater interest to the authors of this book, however, are the ways in which resistance, broadly defined, casts light on formerly hidden social and cultural phenomena, long obscured by the towering formations of dictator, state, and police.

The opening, still partial, of formerly Soviet archives made this book possible. With few exceptions, these essays could not have been written without access to the archival record. Though archives form only one part of the source base of this book, it is the archival record that opens up new possibilities not only for finding and extracting information but for *seeing*. That the archives began to open precisely in the 1990s was a rather serendipitous circumstance for historians of modern Russia. The 1990s were rich in historical discourses and postmodernist sensibilities. The essays collected here represent a conjuncture between empirical possibilities and methodological innovation. They form a part of the changing historiographical paradigm of "Soviet studies" coming out of both cultural studies and present-day concerns with "modernity." Furthermore, most of them are based on material from regional archives and represent the new regional history in our field, demonstrating the possibilities of local studies as well as the riches of regional archival work.

The focus of our work is on the 1930s, with one important exception. The focus is natural, given historiographical preoccupations to date and the early stage of postwar studies. More important, the 1930s was the era of greatest transformation under Stalin, a time of profound cultural clash and historical movement as the Stalinist state endeavored to establish hegemony in all spheres. Difference was contained or not tolerated. Competing and autonomous cultural or social space was marginalized or targeted for elimination. At the same time, alternative cultures and societies persisted, some working within the confines of Stalinism, others against its grain. It was arguably this very persistence that in part determined the state's experiments in modernity, shaping their impact, degree of success, and eventual hybrid formations. The exception to our chronological theme is the essay by James Harris, which I decided to include because it shows an interesting institutional dimension, one that carried over into later years. It also reveals the complexities of the state and, like the other essays in the collection, the problem of the state–society binary.

Several of the essays originated at a conference sponsored by the Stalin-Era Research and Archives Project of the University of Toronto, which was held outside Toronto in the Canadian woods in the fall of 1999. This conference had as its central focus the conjunctures between state and society under Stalin and, as the introduction seeks to show, it is no coincidence that several of the contributors to this conference discussed the problem of resistance. I am grateful to my colleagues in the Stalin-Era Research and Archives Project—Robert Johnson, Thomas Lahusen, Ron Pruessen, Peter Solomon, and Susan Solomon—and to the Social Science and Humanities Research Council of Canada for supporting this work, both intellectually and financially.

I am also grateful to the editors of *Kritika* for allowing me to reprint my essay "Popular Resistance in the Stalinist 1930s: Soliloquy of a Devil's Advocate" in chapter 1. Peter Holquist encouraged me to transform what had been a rough discussant's talk for an AAASS (American Association for the Advancement of Slavic Studies) panel into an article for *Kritika*. *Kritika* produced a splendid first issue on the problem of resistance in Russian history, which inspired us to put together the current volume as a complement and supplement focusing on the 1930s.

I would like to take this opportunity to thank John Ackerman, Louise E. Robbins, and the fine staff at Cornell University Press for supporting this project. Our copyeditor, Carolyn Pouncy, improved the manuscript in immeasurable ways. Cornell's readers made a signal contribution to this work through their thoughtful and thorough commentaries. I would also like to thank the authors who participated in this volume for truly making this a collective and pleasurable enterprise. I also thank Serhy Yekelchyk for commenting on my introduction.

I thank and acknowledge the *Journal of Social History* and *Slavic Review* and the AAASS for granting permission to reprint the essays by Tracy

McDonald and Douglas Northrop. These essays first appeared as: Tracy McDonald, "A Peasant Rebellion in Stalin's Russia: The Pitelinskii Uprising, Riazan 1930," *Journal of Social History* 35, 1 (2001): 125–46; and Douglas Northrop, "Subaltern Dialogues: Subversion and Resistance in Soviet Uzbek Family Law," *Slavic Review* 60, 1 (2001): 115–39.

Finally, I am grateful to my partner, Colleen Craig, for providing me with a model of work discipline and *trudoliubie* that has allowed me to enjoy writing Russian history again. Sharik, George, and Monty also did their part.

LYNNE VIOLA

Toronto

Contending *with* Stalinism

Introduction

LYNNE VIOLA

The fall of the Soviet Union and the end of the cold war ushered in a wide variety of new studies of politics, culture, and society in the Stalinist 1930s, enriched by multidisciplinary, comparative, and theoretical perspectives and based on archival research. One of the most exciting areas of study and, indeed, empirical discovery has been that of popular resistance.[1]

Although the story of popular resistance in the Soviet Union in the 1930s is not entirely new, a clearer sense of its size and content is only now emerging. The very dimensions of popular resistance—the explosion of rebellion during the First Five-Year Plan and the chronic and malignant "everyday resistance" that followed—have startled researchers long spellbound by myths of Russian fatalism, passivity, and docile submission. This fact in itself may serve to alter traditional notions of the realities of living under the Stalinist dictatorship as well as the limits of that dictatorship's abilities to control, intervene, and transform. Yet, from a scholarly perspective, the significance of resistance resides in the light it sheds on its historical surroundings as much as, if not more than, in the topic itself. The wider story of resistance reveals an entire world within the Stalinist dictatorship, a semi-autonomous world of many layers, cultures, and languages of existence, experience, and survival that coexisted with, evolved within, interacted with, and at times bypassed the larger and seemingly omnipresent reality of Stalinism.

Resistance was only one part of a wide continuum of societal responses to Stalinism that also included accommodation, adaptation, acquiescence, apathy, internal emigration, opportunism, and positive support. Moreover, it was a part that the state chose to see everywhere at certain

[1] For further discussion, see Lynne Viola, "The Cold War in American Soviet Historiography and the End of the Soviet Union," *Russian Review* 61, 1 (2002): 2–11.

times, consequently highlighting the inherent subjectivities and ambiguities of the term that, fortunately for the historian, illuminate the ways in which the Stalinist state perceived society, reacted to social pressure, and acted on and interacted with specific elements of society. The subject of resistance is therefore as important for what it can tell us about the Stalinist dictatorship as for what it reveals about society.

The topic of resistance presents a rich field of problems for pondering larger questions of Soviet history in the 1930s. How do we understand such concepts as state and society under Stalin? What are the precise boundaries, if any, between state and society, dominant and subordinate? How homogeneous was the Soviet body politic? Was there one? How does the omnipresent Stalinist source lens shape realities and interpretations?[2] And, finally, what is resistance within the context of what has for so long been perceived as a monolithic and unitary politics and culture that obstructed access or outlet to alternative sources of knowledge, understanding, and expression?

What Is Resistance?

Resistance can be highly ambiguous. In this volume, the notion is refined, and some contributors prefer to speak of social and economic disobedience or strategies of self-protection and survival. Perhaps it would be best to speak of resistance*s*, a series of acts of varying dimensions, contours, and content, with multiple meanings and significance. Yet it is the very ambiguity of the term that opens up the richest possibilities for political, social, and cultural analysis and reconceptualization. Emphasizing the problem of resistance leads us to think more deeply about the Soviet experiment in modernity, its efforts at and impact on transformation, and the persistence and survival of other, often antithetically opposed, sometimes just different or previously hidden, Soviet practices, discourses, and cultures.

Chapter 1 serves as both a cautionary tale and an invitation to approach the problem of resistance, offering a discussion of the range of types of resistance, the opaqueness of popular motivations, the centrality of context, and the difficulties and subjectivities of interpretation. We see that resistance can encompass a wide range of acts, behaviors, and atti-

[2] The term *source lens* refers to the particular biases that are inherent in a source and shape the way in which a text is read. It is important to note, however, that the sources used in this collection have various provenances that do not always include the Stalinist administrative filter, or at times have an attenuated relationship to it.

tudes momentarily, intermittently, or persistently resistant to some object or measure of the official Soviet polity. We see that the determination and definition of resistance are contextual, situational, relative, and contingent. Once unhinged from its surroundings or factors of causation, resistance is not a stable and enduring concept. Moreover, as Michael Geyer notes in another, not totally dissimilar context, not all resistance is equal.[3] Besides the obvious range of types and languages of resistance, there is the question of intent, and intent varies widely from the clearly political to more economically motivated opposition to some combination of the two (see Rossman and McDonald); and from religious, cultural, or gender motivations (see Northrop and Healey) to the economic disobedience of the black market (see Osokina) and strategies of self-protection and survival (see Harris).

Resistance is not fixed and should not be fixed, lest we risk repeating traditional simplifications and reducing state and society formations to unitary, monolithic, and homogeneous entities rather than the complex and highly unstable structures that they were—mired in contradictions and exhibiting hybridity; multiple, conflicting, and coexisting identities; and blurred boundaries. We leave the ultimate definition and consideration of the utility of the notion of resistance to the reader, making of resistance a problem to be discussed and debated. However, in the lines that follow, I sketch out some ways in which resistance can be deployed to shed light on otherwise opaque dimensions of Soviet history in the 1930s and to break down certain overly reified analytical structures basic to our approaches to Stalinism.

Social and Cultural Fields

Neither state nor society were uniform, unitary, homogeneous entities; nor were the two separate and exclusive. Instability, constant flux, division, conflict, and multiple roles and identities characterized each, while interaction, interconnectedness, hybridity, and overlap characterized the whole. The study of resistances penetrates and breaks down this duality, bringing into play the equally unstable and borderless categories of dominant and subordinate.

Societies are complex formations, built on sometimes incongruent ele-

[3] Michael Geyer, "Resistance as an Ongoing Project: Visions of Order, Obligations to Strangers, and Struggles for Civil Society, 1933–1990," in *Resistance against the Third Reich, 1933–1990,* ed. Michael Geyer and John W. Boyer (Chicago: University of Chicago Press, 1994), p. 334.

ments. Acts of resistance uncover these elements, exposing aspects of their formation to the historian. The societies under investigation in this collection show through their resistances something of their internal political, social, and cultural dynamics. Society does not exist as a reified absolute in the study of resistances; instead our focus here is on societ*ies.* Each society, moreover, is the host of multiple and sometimes conflicting forces. For example, active forms of collective resistance—mass demonstrations, riots, strikes, and so on—seem to reveal at first glance a unitary mass aligned in opposition to its source of subordination. On closer examination, however, it becomes clear that such solidarity is as much created by the pressures of outside dominant forces as it is generated from within. Only the combination of shared interests under threat from a common foe in the context of extreme and generally sudden and short-term duress could serve to paper over the normal everyday divisions that run through a society.

The essays in this volume by Jeffrey Rossman and Tracy McDonald each describe at a microhistorical level instances of active, collective resistance. Each focuses on the shared interests of and threats against their social actors. And although normal, everyday divisions are rendered weaker by the pressure of outside force and shared duress, they are not altogether invisible even amid the inherent drama of the Vichuga strike or the Pitelino uprising. We see, for example, in Rossman's essay how the striking textile workers used threats and violence to force other workers to join them; how communist and Komsomol workers remained loyal to the regime in the main; and, perhaps most interestingly, how the highly skilled metalworkers—the regime's favorites—refused to endorse the strike, thus revealing the internal skill and occupational divisions that continued to differentiate workers into the 1930s.

In McDonald's essay, the vulnerability of the dissident *within* village society becomes apparent as we observe the precarious nature of the largely peasant *sel'sovet*'s role in the politics of collectivization. To go against the community carried with it, to paraphrase one of McDonald's peasant women, the smell of murder. If we look at the "victims" of peasant violence during collectivization, we also see that they were primarily "of the village"—peasant activists, who violated village norms of politics.[4] And although we know a fair amount about internal divisions within the working class, we know next to nothing about the village's socio-economic divisions and how or if they were manifested politically (that is, outside of

[4] See Lynne Viola, *Peasant Rebels under Stalin: Collectivization and the Culture of Peasant Resistance* (New York: Oxford University Press, 1996), chap. 4.

mostly theoretical Marxist paradigms of the 1920s). The peasant supporters of regime politics have most often been reduced to *bezdel'niki* and *lodyri*[5] in the Western literature as a response to decades of Soviet falsification, a range of source and interpretational difficulties, and the prejudices of the cold war. However, there *was* an internal politics within working class and peasant societies. These politics, moreover, were embedded in the everyday life of village and factory, feeding into the play of hierarchies of gender, generation, and local authority structures that rent societies in multiple directions.

Douglas Northrop's essay illustrates clearly the absence of a unitary voice within Uzbek society. Uzbek communists, for example, combined multiple roles in their lives and work. They were caught between their native culture and a political identity they had chosen to assume. Many continued to support Uzbek practices, but their intent is likely to have been less outright insubordination than, as Northrop puts it so well, "translation" and "negotiation" between the cultures they straddled.

Engagements with resistance should not obscure but rather illustrate the complexities of societies, their internal and sometimes politically unappealing divisions, their own dominants and subordinates, and the fact that resistance could be coerced from within just as compliance with the regime could be.[6] Nevertheless, these points should also not minimize the extent to which there were widely varying degrees of domination and subordination within societies and between society and state formations.

Gender is an interesting case in point. Although even among village women there were hierarchies of power and status, women tended to have the lowest social standing.[7] Yet in collective acts of resistance in the village, gender hierarchies were reversed and women played the dominant role. The officially classified "backward *baba*" could act with relative immunity in those infrequent moments of village turmoil and uprising when the men of the village were most politically vulnerable and forced into quiescence.[8] And the Uzbek "surrogate proletarian" could voice her solidarity with Uzbek cultural practices without consequence, since in the eyes of

[5] *Bezdel'niki* and *lodyri* were peasant terms of opprobrium for lazy, generally poor peasants.

[6] See, for example, the discussions in Sherry B. Ortner, "Resistance and the Problem of Ethnographic Refusal," *Comparative Studies in Society and History* 37, 1 (1995): 173–93; and Susan Gal, "Language and the 'Arts of Resistance,'" *Cultural Anthropology* 10, 3 (1995): 407–24.

[7] On social hierarchies among village women in the prerevolutionary period, see Christine Worobec, *Peasant Russia* (Princeton, N.J.: Princeton University Press, 1991).

[8] Although the topic has not been mined exhaustively, it is my guess that peasant women's relative political immunity did not continue into later years, especially the famine years, when women played a major role in foraging for food to keep their families alive, an activity

the regime her "resistance" to Soviet-imposed emancipation could be the result only of backwardness, not "counterrevolutionary" politics.[9] From the opposite vantage point, the woman who sided with the regime and consequently went against village norms was subject to a pitiless retribution. Peasant women activists could face beatings and even murder, often adorned with symbolic content—cutting off of braids, rape, for example—to signify clearly the gender hierarchies that had been violated. Perhaps nowhere is this ugly internal political violence of the "subordinate" so clearly in evidence as in the widespread wave of murders of Uzbek women who dared to counter native ways and loyalties.

Generation also surely played an important role in divisions of village status and power, though we know relatively little about these issues. In the village context, the official view was that youth sided with the regime. If and when this was the case, generational antagonisms were certain to be fierce. However—and this is also according to the official view (for empirical research is lacking)—when youth did not side with the regime but with their parents, they became, in most cases, "hooligans," demonstrating, as in the cases of the *baba* and the surrogate proletarian, the regime's unwillingness to negatively politicize its theoretical allies.[10]

In addition to multiple divisions within societies, there were also vastly differing languages of resistance, some rooted in specific cultures, others embedded within the dominant–subordinate nexus. Religious, national, gender, and class determinants (among others) were of signal importance in shaping the contours of resistance, whether we look at the religious metaphors of peasant rumor, the national otherness of colonized social actors, the gendered textures of the scenarios of rebellion, or the class traditions of the strike. The language of resistance also varied in direct relation to the power, proximity, and threat of dominant forces. The presence of force determined whether resistance would or could be clear and direct, or whether it would have to be artfully disguised in one of the languages of the weak (subterfuge, feigned obedience, manipulations of official language, and so on).[11] And, of course, these differing languages as-

---

the regime often classified in criminal terms. (On the *baba*, see Lynne Viola, "*Bab'i Bunty* and Peasant Women's Protest during Collectivization," *Russian Review* 45, 1 [1986]: 189–205.)

[9] The term "surrogate proletariat" as an appellation for Uzbek women derives from Gregory J. Massell's important book, *The Surrogate Proletariat: Moslem Women and Revolutionary Strategies in Soviet Central Asia, 1919–1929* (Princeton, N.J.: Princeton University Press, 1974).

[10] The "kulak son" is, of course, the exception and provided an outlet for the regime in cases when it was desirable to "politicize" the actions of youth.

[11] "Languages of resistance" could be quite literally different languages. As Douglas Northrop suggested to me, "languages, especially non-Russian tongues, some of them new literary languages devised in the 1920s, created vast syntactic spheres in which discourses

sumed many different forms, ranging from active and/or collective resistance to passive resistance to the myriad practices of everyday social and economic disobedience.

At this point, the important question of the motivations and intent underlying resistance arises. In chapter 1, I discuss the opaque nature of popular motivations and the dilemmas a historian faces in interpretation. Elsewhere in the collection, we can see as wide a variety of intents behind resistance as there are types and definitions of resistant activities. McDonald's Pitelino villagers run the gamut from a group that called for soviets without communists—an echo of 1917—to a female choir singing "God Save the Tsar." In the village context, intent can generally be judged only through action, and it is clear that intent varied widely across the diverse geographical and economic topographies of the Soviet countryside, from calls for a "genuine" Soviet government (generally meaning without communists) to "object-oriented" economic acts of resistance (e.g., breaking into barns to appropriate socialized seed grain or to take back socialized livestock) to the reinstatement of the prerevolutionary institution of the village elder. A precise determination of intent is difficult to apply to peasants, who had vastly different ways of seeing. However, motivation is clearer—peasants engaged in resistant acts, often violently, as a result of the policies, practices, and consequences of collectivization, dekulakization, and religious persecution.

While the intent informing cases of active, collective resistance described in McDonald's and Rossman's essays was a highly unstable mix of the economic and the political—the latter further complicated by a mix of anti-regime and anti-local official sentiments—the resistances described in Northrop's and Healey's essays were still more complex. Although some of their social actors may have held anti-regime sentiments, their resistant acts and behaviors were rooted in the very different soil of cultural–national difference and gender variation. Elena Osokina's subjects are perhaps the most interesting and complicated of all. Although she documents a range of acts of what she dubs "economic disobedience" rather than resistance per se, she notes that these sorts of behaviors could easily coexist with other attitudes and beliefs more clearly in line with the Soviet experiment.[12] James Harris's essay is also highly instructive in this regard. In his study of the mechanisms of self-protection practiced by Urals provincial officials (representing social actors of yet another variety)

---

could be generated that were under shaky (at best) control by Moscow" (correspondence with Douglas Northrop, 13 July 2001).

[12] On this point, see Sarah Davies, *Popular Opinion in Stalin's Russia: Terror, Propaganda, and Dissent, 1934–1941* (Cambridge: Cambridge University Press, 1997), pp. 185–86.

struggling to fulfill the plan, he emphasizes that it was only the official mentality of Stalinism that recast these officials' actions as "resistance" (that is, "wrecking" and "sabotage"), whereas their intent was political survival, often in the most literal sense.

The range of social and cultural complexities informing the problem of resistance reminds us that Soviet society was neither homogeneous nor unitary. It was for precisely this reason that resistances of varying types *could* evolve within the harsh climate of Stalinism. Jochen Hellbeck has urged that studies of resistance not result in the resistant individual's becoming "detached from [his/her] social and political environ," while Anna Krylova also warns against the "resisting subject [being] posited heroically against and outside historical forces."[13] These are significant points of criticism, derived chiefly from the historiographical lessons of the study of Nazi Germany, and should serve as especially instructive signposts for the still largely unstudied area of resistance, especially *political* resistance, to Stalinism.[14] Yet these arguments are based on the presumption of the existence of a monolithic Soviet culture in which it was difficult, if not impossible, for Soviet citizens to detach themselves from and to be at odds with the revolutionary collective.[15] Perhaps in the mind and consciousness of the mostly urban (and young) diarists that Hellbeck analyzes such a culture did exist. Yet it is important to keep in mind that the Soviet Union was made up of many different cultures in the highly unstable 1930s; Soviet society did not exist in the singular, and the individual could reside in one or several different societies or cultures.[16]

By broadening the historiographical gaze beyond intellectual history and beyond the insular urban centers of Sovietdom, it is possible to see the multidimensional dynamics of Soviet societies and cultures within and sometimes beyond the official culture. Although many, perhaps most, So-

[13] Jochen Hellbeck, "Speaking Out: Languages of Affirmation and Dissent in Stalinist Russia," *Kritika* 1, 1 (2000): 73; and Anna Krylova, "The Tenacious Liberal Subject in Soviet Studies," ibid., 144.

[14] See, for example, Geyer, "Resistance as an Ongoing Project," and Peter Fritzsche, "Where Did All the Nazis Go? Reflections on Resistance and Collaboration," *Tel Aviver Jahrbüch für deutsche Geschichte* 23 (1994): 191–214.

[15] Hellbeck, "Speaking Out," 94. Although Hellbeck writes of his disagreement with Stephen Kotkin regarding the latter's supposed argument that "individuals remained bound in the official parameters of identification because of their inability to think themselves out of the Soviet world" (ibid., 95), one could argue that Hellbeck makes the same point in a more generalized fashion, while Kotkin refers first and foremost to the articulation of a broad, organized *political* resistance against the Soviet regime. See Stephen Kotkin, *Magnetic Mountain: Stalinism as a Civilization* (Berkeley: University of California Press, 1995).

[16] See Hellbeck, "Speaking Out," 92 n. 52, for examples based on the writings of Raisa Orlova, Roy Medvedev, and Andrei Sakharov.

viet citizens did evolve politically within official Soviet culture, speaking and thinking its language and identifying with it on one level or another, and popular resistance often made use of the emancipatory language of the 1917 Revolution, that does not mean that the Soviet Union in the 1930s was monolithic or that the 1917 Revolution itself was not variously interpreted and heatedly contested. The essays in this collection do not endeavor to make heroes out of resistors or to set them apart from their societies. Yet, as Sherry Ortner has written, "the answer to the reified and romanticized subject must be an actor understood as more fully socially and culturally constructed from top to bottom."[17] Our task, then, must be to situate both the actors and their resistances within their social and cultural historical contexts, untidy and contradictory as they may be.

State Powers

The state is central to our understanding of resistances in this volume, and it is perhaps the very centrality of the state that sets apart Stalin-era resistance studies from studies of resistance in other times and places. In the context of Stalinism, the state defined the terms and set the parameters of resistant behaviors, acts, and even intent. The state also created much of the political and situational context for resistance through its interventions, repressions, and everyday politics. Finally, the state produced most of our sources on resistances.

Yet to talk of *the* state is as meaningless as to talk of *the* society, without definitions and conceptual qualifiers. The "state" was more complex than the traditional state–society binary would suggest; it was neither monolithic nor external and alien to "society."

Michel Foucault demonstrated the pervasiveness and diffuseness of power in modernity through the formation and evolution of discipline.[18] With the advent, for example, of the legal, medical, psychiatric, and educational professions, whose "gaze" made of "society" an object for transformation, power reached everywhere. Yet in Foucault's world, the state becomes amorphous and loses responsibility and agency, while society is reduced to a mere object of compliance.[19]

In the case of the Stalinist 1930s, there is little doubt of the overwhelming power of the state, its retention of many of the powers diffused

[17] Ortner, "Resistance and the Problem of Ethnographic Refusal," 186.

[18] See, in particular, Michel Foucault, *Discipline and Punish: The Birth of the Prison*, trans. Alan Sheridan (New York: Vintage, 1995), esp. part 3, chap. 1.

[19] See P. Steven Sangren, "Power against Ideology: A Critique of Foucaultian Usage," *Cultural Anthropology* 10, 1 (1995): 4.

through disciplinary powers in West European bourgeois polities, and even its "take-back" of certain powers (here I have in mind primarily, but not only, the market and economic sphere).[20] As Laura Engelstein has written in her seminal critique (and appreciation) of Foucault's work in the Russian context, the professional disciplines in Russia remained dependent on the state. Relatively lacking in autonomy, they tended, at least in the prerevolutionary period, to develop a more emancipatory stance toward their "populations" of study as a consequence of the powers of the tsarist administrative state and the absence of legal context.[21]

Yet, as Engelstein notes, the differences in the Russian case do not translate into an argument for a unitary state. While it is true, for example, that "the discursive authority of the professional disciplines . . . functioned only as a dependency of the state,"[22] even in the Stalinist 1930s, the "state-ized" professions—legal, medical, psychiatric, and other—retained and developed some measure of space for their own discourses of expertise and control, of competing professional cultures and allegiances. Dan Healey's essay offers a glimpse into these diffusions of power as he navigates among the legal, medical, and secret police authorities and their differing understandings and approaches to homosexuality. Healey succeeds in demonstrating that the Stalinist source lens was not unitary; it, too, was diffused with the sometimes very different views of alternative discourses.[23]

In the end, though, the Stalinist state still looms large in the world of the 1930s. And although the state assumed the powers of many traditional subdominants (e.g., factory owners, landlords, etc.) now lost in the Soviet nationalized economy, its powers were "diffused" in other ways. Elena Osokina, for example, shows the extent to which black-market economic formations emerged, as it were, "in symbiosis" with state economic practices, as a hybrid structure "shadowing" the official economy. Moreover, there was a range of dominations coexisting within the Soviet polity. Some, like Osokina's black-market actors, straddled the traditional state–society binary; others more clearly emerged from within societies, based on gen-

[20] Even this must be qualified, as we see in Elena Osokina's discussion of the market.

[21] Laura Engelstein, "Combined Underdevelopment: Discipline and the Law in Imperial and Soviet Russia," *American Historical Review* 98, 2 (1993): 338–53. See also her *Keys to Happiness* (Ithaca, N.Y.: Cornell University Press, 1992).

[22] Engelstein, "Combined Underdevelopment," 353.

[23] For other examples, see Kendall E. Bailes, *Technology and Society under Lenin and Stalin* (Princeton, N.J.: Princeton University Press, 1978); Peter Solomon, *Soviet Criminal Justice under Stalin* (Cambridge: Cambridge University Press, 1996); and Kiril Tomoff, "Creative Union: The Professional Organization of Soviet Composers, 1939–1953," Ph.D. dissertation, University of Chicago, 2001.

der, generation, and local power formations (the latter, which the state had tried desperately and not always successfully to extirpate, especially during the headlong assault on authority structures during the First Five-Year Plan).[24] Finally, the state presented itself locally through what we could arguably label an "administrative diffusion"—that is, an array of official actors, situated in the vast and unwieldy bureaucracies that sat astride and within what was largely an agrarian country. Whether this last feature represents a "diffusion" of state or central power or simply its division, representation, and possibly distortion is problematic, but it is nonetheless a further demonstration of the layered nature of what we know as the state.

The first type of division is hierarchical. State power was dispersed to the provinces through a long chain of subordinate agencies from the center to the republic and provincial levels to the county level to the local level (and further, if we include other types of officials within economic institutions like factories and state and collective farms). The second type of division involved bureaucracies and constituted parallel and perhaps multiple diffusions as different powers—party, soviet, police, commissariat—assumed and played multiple roles and functions, often overlapping and competing, in the generation and representation of power. Studies of resistance aid in the conceptualization of these powers as we look at their relations and interactions with societies. For instance, resistance at times assumed the aspect of a "collaboration" or alliance with one part of the state against another, whether it was a case of peasants or workers claiming loyalty to Stalin and the center against erring local officials (e.g., after publication of Stalin's "Dizziness from Success," which led to a retreat from collectivization and scapegoating of local officials) or alliances with local officials against unpopular or unrealistic central policies and practices (e.g., grain procurements). And the import or significance of these "alliances" could be multiple, formed as they were from above, below, and sometimes the "middle" (provincial or local officials). Similarly, although as in other alliances not necessarily articulated, popular alliances with one branch of the bureaucracy against another were always possible, as social actors attempted to use, say, the judiciary or the local soviet against party or police. In any of these cases, moreover, central state politics could easily be subject to absorption, adaptation, and alteration by local politics and local circumstances as, for example, Northrop demonstrates in the case of Uzbek officials reshaping Soviet law or as I have dis-

[24] See, for example, Sheila Fitzpatrick, ed., *Cultural Revolution in Russia, 1928–1931* (Bloomington: Indiana University Press, 1978); and Viola, *Peasant Rebels*, chap. 1.

cussed elsewhere in the case of the evolving hybridization of collective farming.[25]

Local officials represent an interesting socio-political formation. Caught between state and society, so to speak, they of necessity became translators of policy, language, and needs. They disseminated and enacted policy. In many cases, they more closely resembled the societies in which they were situated than the Communist Party of the Soviet Union (Bolshevik)—or an interesting combination of each. Here we see the possibility of local powers absorbing local—that is, community—politics, resulting in a kind of hybridization of Soviet policy. Local officials also had to deal with local societies, which themselves were capable of absorbing, transforming, and/or manipulating official policy, language, and representations to suit their own needs, whether through popular denunciations or through class war enmity grafted onto everyday community divisions not necessarily of a socio-economic nature.[26] All Soviet politics (official and unofficial, from above, below, or the "middle") was constantly contested—practiced, shaped, and altered in what was a highly ambiguous borderland between state powers, societies, and socio-political actors.

State agents, especially local ones, are often more easily understood if taken from their official capacities and reinserted in their social context, for they remain social actors even within the confines of their official roles. They, too, were shaped by their environments as well as their recently assumed political beliefs. They came from somewhere: most had home villages and grandmothers who were hardly inured to the great Soviet project. Many possessed hybrid identities within multiple cultures. McDonald demonstrates how sel'sovet officials were "of the village" and/or forced to play by community rules if they were to survive. Northrop's Uzbek communists are prime examples of local agents caught in the middle—working for the state yet remaining (or becoming) Uzbek and all that stood for. Professionals of many kinds—judges and doctors in Healey's case—operated within tangled professional community networks distinguished from the state by professional knowledge and skills and at times caught between professional identity and state power. In all these cases, the "state" cannot easily be distinguished from its social and cultural surroundings. Borders break down; binaries dissolve; and hybrid formations evolve.

[25] Viola, *Peasant Rebels*, pp. 231–40.

[26] On denunciations, see Sheila Fitzpatrick, "Signals from Below: Soviet Letters of Denunciation of the 1930s," in *Accusatory Practices: Denunciation in Modern European History, 1789–1989*, ed. Sheila Fitzpatrick and Robert Gellately (Chicago: University of Chicago Press, 1997).

At times, state elements engaged in resistant behaviors, themselves assuming the role of subordinate or subaltern or, at the very least, spokesmen of the same. In the countryside, largely out of their own desperation and the desperation all around them, rural officials were sometimes forced to speak out against excessive grain procurement plans, especially in the famine years, and other policies and practices of excess. In the judicial system, legal authorities often used their discretionary or other powers to soften the enforcement of "draconian" laws, as Healey shows in the case of homosexuality and as Peter Solomon has demonstrated in the case of the infamous law of 7 August 1932 against the theft of socialist property.[27]

James Harris identifies an institutional component in the generation of what we might classify as resistance, revealing a systemic aspect to the phenomenon. The logic of plan fulfillment, provincial funding competition, and center-periphery relations made it incumbent on many provincial officials to attempt to disguise plan underfulfillment in a variety of not so ingenious ways. This was increasingly true as the 1930s progressed and the center resorted more and more to the enemy label in cases of plan shortfall. In response, according to Harris, provincial officials in the Urals "resisted" by repeatedly offering the center an explanation for plan problems rooted in the worst explanatory mechanism of paranoid Stalinism and diverting the enemy label ("wrecker," "saboteur," and so on) downward to lower-level officials. Here the system itself generated the lens and language of resistance; for as Harris clearly points out, these officials were not engaged so much in acts of insubordination or "resistance" as in "strategies of self-protection." That is, the harsh lens of Stalinism recast these officials' actions as "resistance," whereas their intent was political and institutional survival, often in the most literal sense.

The issue of complicity and resistance arises at this point as an interpretational and perhaps even an ethical question.[28] To what extent can we, should we, extend the concept of resistance to regime participants—be they McDonald's local Soviet officials, Northrop's Uzbek communists, Healey's judges, or Harris's regional officials? It goes without saying that there were officials who resisted regime measures. But they were surely in the minority and likely to be operating within the context of the terms and conventions of political discourse created by the revolution. Moreover, there was a vast distance between, say, a Riutin who was willing to

[27] Solomon, *Soviet Criminal Justice under Stalin,* chap. 4.

[28] For a discussion of these issues as they relate to the historiography on Nazi Germany, see Fritzsche, "Where Did All the Nazis Go?"

put his political convictions and objections to Stalin in writing and an Uzbek official who preferred his wife veiled.[29] The greater part of official "resistance" consisted of a series of *acts* of resistance that could be described as survival strategies, cultural and religious customs, opportunism, and, at times, sheer common sense, transformed into resistance by the Stalinist lens.

The study of resistance redraws our picture of the Stalinist state in the 1930s. The real power of the state and its repressive organs is *not* diminished; power lay in definition, attribution, intervention, and force. In the 1930s, the state permeated society and culture as it attempted to "map" its populations in efforts at what James Scott calls "high modernism," or the control, ordered legibility, and transformation of populations.[30] (In this respect, the secret police's omnipresent reporting through *svodki* [see chapter 1] represents a figurative attempt at panopticism.) Highlighting the vast range of resistances forces us to think more deeply about the Soviet experiment in modernity, its efforts and success at transformation, the social and cultural realities of the "field" of transformation, the persistence and endurance of alternative and sometimes competing Soviet societies and cultures, and how and why they survived in spite and sometimes *because of* Soviet transformational efforts.

Conclusion

Peter Fritzsche, a historian of modern Germany, has written that Western studies of resistance in the Soviet Union of the 1930s are "unusually sensitive to the possibilities and limitations of the concept of resistance."[31] We have benefited from the "law of combined historiographical development," if I may borrow and transplant Trotsky's magnificent turn of phrase. As relative latecomers to this topic, largely due to source and access problems but also due to cold war and Western prejudices, historians of the Stalinist 1930s have learned from the study of resistance in other times and places.

[29] See chapter 2 for a discussion of Riutin.

[30] James C. Scott, *Seeing Like a State* (New Haven, Conn.: Yale University Press, 1998). On modernity in the Russian context, see Peter Holquist, " 'Information Is the Alpha and Omega of Our Work': Bolshevik Surveillance in Its Pan-European Context," *Journal of Modern History* 69 (1997): 415–50; David L. Hoffmann and Yanni Kotsonis, eds., *Russian Modernity* (London: Macmillan, 2000); David L. Hoffmann and Peter Holquist, *Cultivating the Masses: The Modern Social State in Russia, 1914–1941* (Ithaca, N.Y.: Cornell University Press, forthcoming); and Stephen Kotkin, "Modern Times: The Soviet Union and the Interwar Conjuncture," *Kritika* 2, 2 (2001).

[31] Peter Fritzsche, "On the Subjects of Resistance," *Kritika* 1, 1 (2000): 147.

Our studies are not and should not become platforms for the creation of a usable past for present-day politics.[32] We have no intention of mythologizing "resisters," an endeavor made unlikely by our own reluctance to reify resistance or reduce the intent informing resistances to a single factor. Nor do we view the complex of forces that make up the state as external or alien; instead we stress the interconnectedness and hybridization of state and society formations as well as the evolving range of popular responses to Stalinism. Given these factors, Western studies of resistance in the Stalinist 1930s are not likely to repeat the exaggerations and rationalizations of some of the studies on resistance in Nazi Germany, studies frequently rooted in the search for a usable past and describing societies vastly different from those of the Soviet Union.[33]

Postcolonial and subaltern studies may be of much greater use than studies of Nazi Germany, given the agrarian and colonial structures of the prewar Soviet Union. Moreover, these studies present sophisticated discussions of the state–society binary without losing sight of the real play of powers in such unequal relationships.[34] There was a state; there were societies; there were dominants and subordinates; not everything was equal. And in the Stalinist 1930s, state violence was extensive, in many ways unprecedented. To forget or to diminish the realities of power relations under Stalin would be shortsighted as well as historically inaccurate.[35]

Finally, the study of resistance in this volume is decidedly not about "the triumph of the resisting self" or the projection of a liberal self onto our subjects.[36] This is neither a study of elites, focused on intent and motivation, nor a study of *anti-Stalinism* per se. These essays instead explore collectivities within the context of environments that often do not conform to what we know of tsarist, bourgeois, or even Soviet society. They are grounded in the methods and practices of social and cultural history, making use of a variety of approaches, ranging from peasant and labor studies to cultural theory and *Alltagsgeschichte* to postcolonial and subal-

[32] Dan Healey does argue for the creation of a usable past in his essay in this collection. However, his is a slightly different agenda, and one that I support.

[33] See Geyer, "Resistance as an Ongoing Project," and Fritzsche, "Where Did All the Nazis Go?"

[34] See, for example, Bill Ashcroft, Gareth Griffiths, and Helen Tiffin, eds., *The Post-Colonial Studies Reader* (London: Routledge, 1995).

[35] In many ways, this is a plea for the acceptance of nuance in the historiography. Resistance does not cancel out support—or the reverse—and we make no claims for assessing *all* of the people *all* of the time. On support for the Stalinist project among certain categories of workers, see, for example, Lynne Viola, *The Best Sons of the Fatherland: Workers in the Vanguard of Soviet Collectivization* (New York: Oxford University Press, 1987).

[36] See Krylova, "The Tenacious Liberal Subject," 140–41.

tern studies to queer theory. To a great extent, this work builds on the Western revisionist historiographical foundations erected in the 1980s. These sought to produce a more nuanced and professional approach to historical understanding of the complexities of Stalinism in the 1930s and were shaped, in part, by an unwillingness to accept the facile binaries of state–society, support–resistance, and belief–disbelief.

The study of resistances demonstrates the extent to which the Stalinist 1930s was rich in discourses and cultures. Further and perhaps of greater import, visiting the sites of resistance provides a gauge for measuring and analyzing the degree and depths of transformation achieved by the great Soviet experiment in the 1930s.

CHAPTER ONE

Popular Resistance in the Stalinist 1930s

Soliloquy of a Devil's Advocate

LYNNE VIOLA

In the last fifty years, the Western historiographical map of the Stalinist 1930s has expanded topically and conceptually, albeit incrementally and sometimes reluctantly. From cold-war fixations on totalitarian control, repression, and societal atomization, attention first shifted in the 1980s to revisionist arguments that illuminated the social base of Stalinism, center–periphery conflicts, and the administrative weaknesses of Stalinist governance; and then in the 1990s to, among other concerns, an interest in the subject of resistance. Recent work on popular resistance to the Stalinist dictatorship derives chiefly from new evidence available in previously classified archival holdings, although to ignore or dismiss altogether the potential for historiographical virtue in these recent excavations would be, perhaps, shortsighted. An entrenched historiographical tradition that divided Soviet history into a Manichean world of good and evil and derived from cold-war and Stalinist mentalities (the latter seeping into the former all too often and, more recently within Russia, the opposite as well) should serve as a cautionary tale, for it highlights the potentially ahistorical pitfalls of either valorizing resistance or focusing on resistance to the exclusion of the rest of the historical record. If we ignore this lesson, we risk projecting our own cold-war, anti-Stalinist tropes onto the popular classes of the 1930s.[1]

[1] In "The Tenacious Liberal Subject in Soviet Studies," *Kritika* 1, 1 (2000): 119–46, in an otherwise novel and, I think, stimulating discussion of the historiography, Anna Krylova misreads the current literature on resistance, stating: "Refashioning manipulation and pursuit of self-interest as resistance, contemporary scholars liberate the Stalinist subject from moral condemnation for complicity with Stalinism, imposing 1990s notions of moral agency on the

Popular resistance is best treated as a kind of prism that refracts and reveals what otherwise might be opaque dimensions of the social, cultural, and political history of the 1930s. And at the same time that we highlight a new and largely salutary trend in recent scholarship, it is important to recognize the inherent subjectivities and blurred outlines of the nature of resistance, and to question when, under what circumstances, and from what angle of vision resistance is resistance and when it is merely resident in the eye of the beholder.[2]

The Devil's Suit

What is resistance? This is a difficult question which evades an easy answer, perhaps any answer, as we endeavor to situate the term and its vast range of practices within a larger body of questions and untidy qualifiers. At its core, resistance involves opposition—active, passive, artfully disguised, attributed, and even inferred. That our topic is popular resistance in the context of the Stalinist 1930s makes the task of definition all the more difficult in that we must rely, with few exceptions, on a single (though not necessarily unitary) source lens shaped by the rhetorical devices and administrative structures of Stalinism.

Ostensibly, active opposition is the most clear-cut type of resistance. Active forms of resistance may include rebellions, mutinies, and riots; demonstrations and protest meetings; strikes and work stoppages; incendiary or oppositional broadsheets (*listovki*), threat letters, and petitions; and arson, assaults, and assassinations. The major wave of active resistance in the 1930s was centered in the years of the First Five-Year Plan (1928–32). On the eve of and during collectivization, particularly in the breakthrough year of 1930, the peasantry engaged in a massive rebellion, resulting in 1930 in 13,754 mass disturbances, over a thousand assassinations of officials, countless eruptions of protest or violence at collectiviza-

---

Stalinist transformations of the 1930s. Contemporary scholars of the 1990s relieve themselves from their moral mission; the resisting subject now rules supreme throughout the Soviet years" (141). This kind of statement evokes older patterns of cold-war historiographical thinking that simplified and reduced currents in the historiography to an accessible black and white. The current literature on resistance is concerned far less with these older patterns than with perspectives from comparative history and other historical methodologies and *in no case posits the existence of a society resistant to Stalinism to the exclusion of anything else.* Of equal importance, current studies of resistance, *very* variously defined, are rooted within their social and political environment, understood in this perspective to be varied, layered, and heterogeneous and existing within and beyond the official Soviet political culture.

[2] Merle Fainsod's classic *Smolensk under Soviet Rule* (Cambridge, Mass.: Harvard University Press, 1958) provided many instances of popular resistance.

tion meetings, and a wide variety of other kinds of resistance.[3] Workers also resorted to active forms of resistance during the First Five-Year Plan, as the recent work of Jeffrey Rossman has demonstrated. The textile workers of the Ivanovo region took part in widespread and varied acts of open opposition, culminating in the strike at Teikovo and the uprising in Vichuga in 1932.[4] Whether Rossman's findings are unique to Ivanovo and its textile workers or indicative of a broader phenomenon requires further regional archive-based investigations, though the possibility of some repetition of these kinds of activities elsewhere is far from unlikely.

Passive resistance, an endemic and deeply rooted behavior of subaltern classes, was widespread throughout the 1930s, becoming a virtual way of life. Somewhat murkier in identification than most active types of resistance, passive resistance may include foot dragging, negligence, sabotage, theft, and flight among its many forms. Although the manifestation of passive resistance is subject to multiple interpretations and qualifications, its objective reality, at some level, cannot be doubted, given the context and result of popular behavior at the work site and elsewhere.

Motivated by a variety of not always clearly defined causes, both peasants and workers availed themselves of the many forms of passive resistance. Sheila Fitzpatrick has described to great effect the subaltern strategies of peasants in the 1930s as they confronted work, life, and survival within the new collective-farm system.[5] She has also documented the "push" and "pull" factors, including resistance, that motivated peasants to leave the countryside in the millions in the course of the 1930s.[6] Donald Filtzer and others have illustrated the many tactics of passive resistance employed by industrial workers, demonstrating the transnational as well

[3] Lynne Viola, *Peasant Rebels under Stalin: Collectivization and the Culture of Peasant Resistance* (New York: Oxford University Press, 1996), esp. pp. 105 and 136. See also McDonald's essay in this collection; and, for the eve of collectivization, D'Ann Penner, "Pride, Power, and Pitchforks: Farmer-Party Interaction on the Don, 1920–1928," Ph.D. dissertation, University of California at Berkeley, 1995.

[4] See Rossman's essay in this collection. Also see Jeffrey John Rossman, "Worker Resistance under Stalin: Class and Gender in the Textile Mills of the Ivanovo Industrial Region, 1928–32," Ph.D. dissertation, University of California at Berkeley, 1997; Rossman, "The Teikovo Cotton Workers' Strike of April 1932: Class, Gender and Identity Politics in Stalin's Russia," *Russian Review* 56, 1 (1997): 44–69; and Rossman, "Weaver of Rebellion and Poet of Resistance: Kapiton Klepikov (1880–1933) and Shop-Floor Opposition to Bolshevik Rule," *Jahrbucher für Geschichte Osteuropas* 44 (1996): 374–407.

[5] Sheila Fitzpatrick, *Stalin's Peasants: Resistance and Survival in the Russian Village after Collectivization* (New York: Oxford University Press, 1994).

[6] Sheila Fitzpatrick, "The Great Departure: Rural-Urban Migration in the Soviet Union, 1929–33," in *Social Dimensions of Soviet Industrialization*, ed. William G. Rosenberg and Lewis H. Siegelbaum (Bloomington: Indiana University Press, 1993), pp. 15–40.

as the customary and habitual ways of dealing with bosses and with the work regimen created and imposed from above.[7]

The category of passive resistance can be expanded to encompass what James C. Scott has labeled the "weapons of the weak," or "everyday forms of resistance," among which he includes all those elements of passive resistance noted above as well as the still more subjective terrain of popular discourse(s), ritual, feigned ignorance, dissimulation, and false compliance.[8] For Scott, these are the popular "arts of resistance," a category of analysis that broadens the scope of resistance to admit an autonomous or semi-autonomous popular culture or cultures existing alongside and interacting with the dominant culture. The expression of the arts of resistance presupposes a "shared worldview"[9] on the part of the social actors, developed within a larger "backstage" culture of resistance, whether that backstage be the "social spaces" provided by the hush arbors of American slaves; taverns, fairs, and markets; or, in the Soviet case, the *skhod* (peasant council) and church.[10]

The many "arts" of this kind of popular resistance in Stalin's Soviet Union are now surfacing from documents as historians employ new ways of seeing (or reading) borrowed from other disciplines. In 1986, I explored women's revolts (*bab'i bunty*) as a text on which was written a series of ritualistic codes derived from peasant women's sense of politics, survival, and outside images of themselves.[11] In 1990, I made use of peasant rumors from the collectivization era as a way of accessing peasant mentalities and exploring the widespread apocalyptic metaphors afield in those troubled times.[12] More recently, Sheila Fitzpatrick has analyzed denunciations and letters of complaint as sources of popular discourse that transmit ritualistic forms of expression and at times may manipulate official

[7] Donald Filtzer, *Soviet Workers and Stalinist Industrialization: The Formation of Modern Soviet Production Relations, 1929–1941* (London: Pluto, 1986). See also Vladimir Andrle, *Workers in Stalin's Russia: Industrialization and Social Change in a Planned Economy* (New York: St. Martin's, 1988); and Hiroaki Kuromiya, *Stalin's Industrial Revolution: Politics and Workers, 1928–1932* (Cambridge: Cambridge University Press, 1988).

[8] James C. Scott, *Weapons of the Weak: Everyday Forms of Peasant Resistance* (New Haven, Conn.: Yale University Press, 1985), p. xvi.

[9] Ibid., p. xvii.

[10] James C. Scott, *Domination and the Arts of Resistance: Hidden Transcripts* (New Haven, Conn.: Yale University Press, 1990), p. xi; and Viola, *Peasant Rebels*, pp. 38–42.

[11] Lynne Viola, "*Bab'i Bunty* and Peasant Women's Protest during Collectivization," *Russian Review* 45, 1 (1986): 189–205. This work owed much to the influence of Daniel Field's wonderful *Rebels in the Name of the Tsar* (Boston: Houghton Mifflin, 1976).

[12] Lynne Viola, "The Peasant Nightmare: Visions of Apocalypse in the Soviet Countryside," *Journal of Modern History* 62 (1990): 747–70.

discourse to express criticism or oppositional sentiment.[13] Sarah Davies, Leslie Rimmel, and Elena Zubkova, among others, have explored Communist Party and secret police *svodki* (sequential reports) as a repository of evidence on popular critical opinion in the 1930s and after.[14] Expression in these sources ranges from clear-cut and straightforward, through formal officialese and/or the seeming manipulation thereof, to language cloaked in peasant vestment. The last category can be identified both in terms of form, as in the humble, collective letter of petition, and in terms of content, as workers and peasants alike cast their sentiments in shades of "backwardness," "darkness," or "*nekul'turnost'*." These "arts of resistance"—if, indeed, that is what they are—are disguised for safety and effectiveness, reflecting Scott's maxim that "the more menacing the power, the thicker the mask."[15]

Other actions are still more difficult to evaluate as resistance per se, yet clearly reveal elements of deviance or antisocial behavior. Is there a place on the spectrum of resistance for crime, the black market,[16] *blat*,[17] and banditry, or, for that matter, the alternative subcultures and identities expressed in religious sects, the world of traditional healing, homosexuality, or non-Russian nationalities? Do we identify critical expression in personal diaries or kitchen table conversations as brands of resistance?[18] Does

[13] Sheila Fitzpatrick, "Readers' Letters to *Krest'ianskaia gazeta*, 1938," *Russian History* 24, 1–2 (1997): 149–70; Fitzpatrick, "Supplicants and Citizens: Public Letter-Writing in Soviet Russia in the 1930s," *Slavic Review* 55, 1 (1996): 78–105; and Fitzpatrick, "Signals from Below: Soviet Letters of Denunciation of the 1930s," in *Accusatory Practices: Denunciation in Modern European History, 1789–1989*, ed. Sheila Fitzpatrick and Robert Gellately (Chicago: University of Chicago Press, 1997), pp. 85–120.

[14] Sarah Davies, *Popular Opinion in Stalin's Russia: Terror, Propaganda and Dissent, 1934–1941* (Cambridge: Cambridge University Press, 1997); Davies, "The Crime of 'Anti-Soviet Agitation' in the Soviet Union in the 1930s," *Cahiers du monde russe* 39, 1–2 (1998): 149–68; *Davies*, " 'Us against Them': Social Identity in Soviet Russia, 1934–41," *Russian Review* 56, 1 (1997): 70–89; Lesley A. Rimmel, "Another Kind of Fear: The Kirov Murder and the End of Bread Rationing in Leningrad," *Slavic Review* 56, 3 (1997): 481–99; and Elena Zubkova, *Russia after the War: Hopes, Illusions, and Disappointments, 1945–57*, trans. Hugh Ragsdale (Armonk, N.Y.: M.E. Sharpe, 1998).

[15] Scott, *Domination and the Arts of Resistance*, p. 3.

[16] See Osokina's essay in this collection.

[17] Although the Russian term *blat* defies a simple English translation, it can best be understood as the informal exchange of favors, goods, or services between individuals and outside official state networks and institutions. For further discussion, see the remarkable work of Alena V. Ledeneva, *Russia's Economy of Favours:* Blat, *Networking, and Informal Exchange* (Cambridge: Cambridge University Press, 1998).

[18] See the provocative articles of Jochen Hellbeck for an emphatic argument against the notion of resistance: "Speaking Out: Languages of Affirmation and Dissent in Stalinist Russia,"

the very existence of alternative social space (see below) signify, within the Stalinist context, an inherent act of resistance?

As we list these categories, or possible categories, of resistance, it becomes clear that we are no closer to a definition of resistance and perhaps even in danger of losing sight of the term. Any understanding of resistance is situational and contingent, and the factors of analysis are highly subjective, all the more so within the context of the hegemonic official culture of Stalinism. Avoiding or evading any single definition, it seems more useful to continue the discussion by exploring acts of resistance in terms of several signal factors of analysis, including motivation, context, and source lens.

Oppositional motivations are most explicit in cases of active resistance. The working-class strikes of the First Five-Year Plan and the peasant revolts of collectivization are the clearest examples of popular active resistance in the 1930s. Yet having stated the seemingly obvious, how then do we further characterize such resistance? Unlike the factory inspectors' reports on strikes of the tsarist era, Stalin-era reports do not explicitly differentiate economic from political motivations in strikes or other forms of collective action. Nor do they necessarily differentiate between localized protest and anti-regime protest, instead generally tarring the whole with the counterrevolutionary brush. It seems clear, however, that the protest of Rossman's Ivanovo workers began as localized discontent over economic issues. Workers in Vichuga even requested the intervention of Moscow, sending a telegram to Kalinin, seemingly an expression of faith in the central authorities. While one might question the sincerity of the appeal to the good tsar in Moscow against the evil local officials violating his will, it seems nonetheless clear that the protest of most Ivanovo workers was not initially political. It was only when the central authorities intervened—and not in the style of the mythical good tsar—that the protest most clearly accelerated along the continuum from economic to political revolt.[19]

In the rural context, the mask is often too thick, to paraphrase Scott, to enable us to disaggregate motives, even in acts of open resistance. The resort to *bab'i bunty*, for example, served to cloak motivation in peasant riots by playing upon elite social constructions of benighted peasants, especially female peasants. Even in revolts that did not so obviously involve tra-

---

Kritika 1, 1 (2000): 71–96; and "Fashioning the Stalinist Soul: The Diary of Stepan Podlubnyi, 1931–9," *Jahrbucher für Geschichte Osteuropas* 44, 3 (1996): 344–73.

19 See Rossman's essay in this collection; and Rossman, "Worker Resistance under Stalin," pp. 530–32.

ditional rituals and scenarios of rebellion, it is often unclear what precisely the mix of political and economic motives was. Peasant revolt, by nature, is local and localized, and to expand its political significance often requires either a historian or a regime inclined to politicize, or depoliticize, peasant resistance.

Motivation is, perhaps, clearer in cases when peasants paraded with placards calling for the ouster of communists or equating the regime with the Antichrist. Yet, as D'Ann Penner reminds us, peasants could call for the removal of communists and still be loyal—or claim loyalty—to the institution of the soviets. This pattern appears to have been widespread in the Don.[20] In Riazan county, according to Tracy McDonald, peasants called for reelection of village soviets in cases when such soviets failed to represent their constituencies, instead participating in the worst of the state's collectivization atrocities.[21] In parts of Ukraine and elsewhere, however, reports of peasants dismantling village soviets and reinstating the institution of the peasant elder were not infrequent. In other cases, peasants simply chased out local officials and activists, communist and Soviet alike.[22] Were these actions aimed solely against local officials or were they emblematic of an anti-regime sensibility? The answer likely resides in the eye of the beholder—historian, local official, police agent, or central authority. The same issue arises when we attempt to make sense of the wave of arsons, physical attacks, and assassinations aimed at local officials and activists on the eve of and during collectivization. The problem is compounded by the fact that these officials and activists, many of them peasants themselves, were deeply enmeshed in village politics, thus making it difficult to separate out personal and community politics from the larger canvas of collectivization and class politics. What this means in practice is that any arson could be a simple fire, or—and especially from official perspectives—any fire an arson. Likewise, attacks on officials could be (or could be said to be) the result of drinking bouts or deals gone bad, while from an official perspective, drinking bouts or deals with local officials could become dangerous, politicized terrain. Here is a good example where context is central to analysis. The context of collectivization and the

[20] Penner, "Pride, Power, and Pitchforks," chaps. 7 and 10; Penner, "Electric Trains and Remote Archives: The Art of Working in Provincial Russia," Stalin-Era Research and Archive Project Working Paper (Toronto: Centre for Russian and East European Studies, University of Toronto, 2001); and Penner, "Stalin and the *Ital'ianka* of 1932–1933 in the Don Region," *Cahiers du monde russe* 39, 1–2 (1998): 27–68.

[21] See McDonald's essay in this collection.

[22] Viola, *Peasant Rebels*, chaps. 5–6; Valerii Vasil'ev, "Krest'ianskoie vosstaniia na Ukraine, 1929–30 gody," *Svobodnaia mysl'*, 1992, no. 9: 71–76.

increase in peasant violence in this period balances out the argument in favor of resistance. Even so, resistance remains a slippery concept and may not be so easily disentangled—and perhaps should not be—from community politics, long-standing feuds, and village social conflict.

The question of motivation becomes even more distorted by official perspectives and popular defense mechanisms when we turn our attention to passive resistance. At first glance, the political context of passive resistance seems scant. Hunger, survival, and desperation appear central, the primary motivational factors leading peasants and workers to engage in theft, foot dragging, absenteeism, and the like. The ever-present sabotage described in official texts seems as likely, if not more likely, to have been the result of lack of skill, incompetence, or fatigue as malice. Peasant flight was occasioned by the rural economy of scarcity and the lure of urban employment possibilities. Yet, having muddled the issue of resistance, we must refer back once again to context. In the case of peasants, the context was what some peasants described as a "second serfdom." Peasants pilfered to survive, but they stole from a state entity that many viewed as alien and unjust. Peasants left for the cities in search of jobs and a better life, but they left behind the detested collective farms. This is not to say that all motivations behind passive resistance were clearly oppositional, and it is certainly not to argue the existence of a homogeneous, resistant peasantry or the absence of a minority of rural beneficiaries of the regime. Rather, it is to draw attention to the difficulties and subjectivities of disaggregating the motives behind what could be viewed as resistance.

The motivations behind other acts are still more difficult to interpret. The "arts of resistance" are a fairly subjective array of popular behaviors which are objectively impenetrable from our outsider's vantage point. Did peasants and workers manipulate official discourse in their letters and petitions to higher authorities, or did they believe what they wrote? Did peasants and workers write to Kalinin because they saw him as their "all-union elder" and needed a traditional source of authority, or was it all just a ploy? Did peasants and workers cloak themselves in the mantle of backwardness to depoliticize their demands for reasons of safety? Or was this kind of rhetoric a ritualized discourse? Or did peasants truly see themselves in this way? How clever were the popular classes? Surely not as clever as historians and official observers. What was the mix of belief, fear, opportunism, and ritual? Interpretations of popular discourse are inextricably tied to our ways of seeing as historians, which are inevitably relativistic, presentist, and perhaps political. Our main remedies for myopia are context and comparison, across a range of sources and across cultures, in order to gauge the universality of popular defenses against domination.

The arena of crime and criminality is also subject to the interpretational vagaries of relativity and observational stance. Was the vast range of black-market activities so skillfully described by Elena Osokina a manifestation of everyday resistance, or of everyday crime, or was it simply the reality of everyday life?[23] Was the crime wave of the middle 1930s that David Shearer details so well a result of the social disruption and chaos of the times, or was it a reflection of mass social disobedience?[24] If the latter, how do we understand the full meaning and ramifications of "mass social disobedience" in the context of the Stalinist 1930s? And perhaps criminals were just criminals. Need we romanticize Ostap Bender (Ilf and Petrov's hero in *The Twelve Chairs*)? The same range of questions arises in the case of the emergence or continuation of certain alternative subcultures or identities, be they religious, national, or personal. Did individuals or groups assume alternative identities in a posture of resistance, or were such alternative identities simply unavoidable and sometimes culturally transmitted ways of being? Did such ways of being develop into resistant behaviors in response to regime definition and repression, going underground and evolving into inherently oppositional subcultures?

Finally, the question of intent becomes a central problem in approaching the topic of resistance. Does intent matter? If the intent behind an act of resistance is not oppositional, is the *act* resistant? Can we ever really get at the subject of intent when discussing subordinate groups? What is the range of resistant or oppositional intents? We must recognize the unequal nature of different kinds of resistances and the intents behind them, ranging from the most clearly politically oppositional to those based on immediate economic contingency and the petty, individualistic economic survival techniques of the everyday. The interpretational extrapolations that result from acknowledging such differences matter profoundly to our understanding of the history of the Stalinist 1930s.

The questions surrounding the ever-evasive definition and identity of resistance are mounting. Yet several useful common denominators in the equation of resistant behavior emerge: the opaque nature of popular motivation, the centrality of context, and the subjectivities of interpretation. At this point, we must add to these the unavoidable intrusiveness of the Stalinist source lens. This factor in the equation is perhaps central, given its omnipresence and omnipotence. The Stalinist mentality of enemies

23 See Osokina's essay in this collection.

24 David R. Shearer, "Crime and Social Disorder in Stalin's Russia: A Reassessment of the Great Retreat and the Origins of Mass Repression," *Cahiers du monde russe* 39, 1–2 (1998): 119–48.

universally present, whether feigned or believed, tended to generalize dissonant acts into subversion and counterrevolution. It allowed for exceptions of political convenience only when it was necessary publicly to minimize the extent of discontent, as in the case of the collectivization-era peasant rebellion. In such cases it recast resistant behaviors as the actions of the backward and apolitical masses, thus falling back on earlier elite social constructions of benighted peasants and unconscious workers.[25] While ignoring the last point for the moment, let us move on to explore this highly questionable source lens.

Evidence of resistance, or the possibility thereof, may be found in an almost endless variety of sources, both published and archival, the latter including most notably the records of the Commissariat of Justice, the Commissariat of Internal Affairs and the militia, Rabkrin (the Workers' and Peasants' Inspectorate), the Communist Party, the Soviet hierarchy, and so on. In part, it is simply a matter of that evasive definition: how and where one sees resistance determines how and where one looks for it. Unquestionably, however, the most logical and compatible domain of resistance is the police file, in our case, the secret police, variously titled through the 1930s as OGPU (Ob"edinennoe gosudarstvennoe politicheskoe upravlenie, or Unified State Political Administration) and NKVD (Narodnyi komissariat vnutrennykh del, or the People's Commissariat of Internal Affairs). Some of the most detailed and revealing information on resistance has surfaced in the archives of the FSB (Federal'naia sluzhba bezopasnosti, or Federal Security Service) and its regional affiliates, all notoriously difficult to access.[26] Secret police files (usually svodki) also appear sporadically in state and Communist Party archives within related record files.[27]

[25] There is considerable continuity with prerevolutionary stereotypes. See Stephen Frank, *Crime, Cultural Conflict, and Justice in Rural Russia, 1856–1914* (Berkeley: University of California Press, 1999); and Frank, "Confronting the Domestic Other: Rural Popular Culture and Its Enemies in Fin-de-Siècle Russia," in *Cultures in Flux: Lower-Class Values, Practices, and Resistance in Late Imperial Russia,* ed. Stephen P. Frank and Mark D. Steinberg (Princeton, N.J.: Princeton University Press, 1994), pp. 74–107; and Yanni Kotsonis, "How Peasants Became Backward: Agrarian Policy and Co-operatives in Russia, 1905–14," in *Transforming Peasants: Society, State, and the Peasantry, 1861–1930,* ed. Judith Pallot (New York: St. Martin's, 1998), pp. 15–36.

[26] See A. Berelovich and V. Danilov, eds., *Sovetskaia derevnia glazami VChK-OGPU-NKVD. Dokumenty i materialy,* vol. 1: *1918–1922* (Moscow, 1998); V. Danilov and A. Berelowitch, "Les documents des VCK-OGPU-NKVD sur la campagne Soviétique, 1918–1937," *Cahiers du monde russe* 35, 3 (1994): 633–82; and V. P. Danilov, R. T. Manning, and L. Viola, eds., *Tragediia Sovetskoi derevni. Kollektivizatsiia i raskulachivanie. Dokumenty i materialy. 1927–1939,* 5 vols. (Moscow, 1999–2003) for examples of svodki from FSB archives.

[27] For some examples of such OGPU svodki, see Lynne Viola, Tracy McDonald, Sergei Zhuravlev, and Andrei Mel'nik, eds., *Riazanskaia derevnia v 1929–1930 gg. Khronika golo-*

The secret police, or punitive (*karatel'nye*) organs, as a senior FSB archivist insisted on calling them during one rather frustrating semantic debate,[28] constituted the proverbial "state within a state" from at least the period of the first Five-Year Plan. Its massive bureaucracy, both central and regional, boasted many subdivisions responsible for an incredible array of administrative functions—including many not traditionally within the parameters of a secret police.[29] Above all, the secret police had certain vested interests in "the counterrevolution." After all, counterrevolution was its specialty, presenting unlimited opportunities for the secret police to enhance its power and prestige as well as its personnel and operating capital.[30]

Scholars of other national histories have long been aware—and critical—of the problematic nature of police records as sources of social history.[31] As the Genoveses reminded us over two decades ago, police records are "shaped by the intentions of the observer, not the observed."[32] The "observer"—itself a highly problematic entity, as we see below—was, moreover, constrained by his or her audience, in our case, a hierarchy of superiors extending all the way to the Kremlin. This was an audience existing in dangerously thin air. It could be expected, assumed, or inferred by the observer that a certain kind of reporting was necessary, replete with exaggeration, understatement, or cover-up depending on concrete circumstances and fears. All this reporting, moreover, was encoded in the requisite Stalinist parlance. Additionally, as reports made their way up the regional police hierarchy, they moved from the pens of observers to the

---

vokruzheniia. Dokumenty i materialy (Moscow: Rosspen, 1998); Nicolas Werth and Gael Moullec, eds., *Rapports secrets Soviétiques, 1921–1991* (Paris: Gallimard, 1994); A. Graziosi, "Collectivisation, révoltes paysannes et politiques gouvernementales à travers les rapports du GPU d'Ukraine de février–mars 1930," *Cahiers du monde russe* 35, 3 (1994): 437–631; and (for general information) Nicolas Werth, "Une source inédite: les *svodki* de la Tcheka-OGPU," *Revue des études slaves* 66, 1 (1994): 17–27.

28 This debate took place at the June 1998 business meeting of the *Tragediia Sovetskoi derevni* collective, at which time the FSB archivist took issue with the Russian translation of "secret police" used in our editorial foreword to the first volume of *Tragediia*. The archivist apparently assumed that the English term and the Russian translation were dictated by political or ideological considerations. He insisted that the OGPU was a punitive organ. I did not disagree.

29 See the very useful *Lubianka. VChK-KGB. Dokumenty* (Moscow: Mezhdunarodnyi fond "Demokratiia," 1997) for an indication of the administrative structure of the secret police.

30 Viola, *Peasant Rebels*, conclusion. See also James R. Harris's pioneering essay "The Growth of the Gulag: Forced Labor in the Urals Region, 1929–31," *Russian Review* 56, 2 (1997): 265–80.

31 A useful example is R. C. Cobb, *The Police and the People: French Popular Protest, 1789–1820* (Oxford: Oxford University Press, 1970).

32 Elizabeth Fox-Genovese and Eugene D. Genovese, "The Political Crisis of Social History: A Marxian Perspective," *Journal of Social History* 10, 2 (1976): 211.

pens of compilers, police scribes who sat in offices assembling regional data, summarizing its content, and providing selected examples, statistical compilations, charts, and maps.[33] The scribe-compiler often had the task of creating summary reports on an annual, semiannual, or monthly basis, thereby removing what began as secondhand data from its point of observation by yet one more level.

Who the initial observers were, and who their sources were, let alone who the scribe-compilers were, are central questions of source analysis. Were we so fortunate and confident as to be circumscribed by the totalitarian model in its heyday, we might well assume a monolithic worldview (whether of belief, mindlessness, or fear) and dispense with the torture of countless and invisible variables. Certainly, it is fair and logical to assume that many administrative officers of the secret police (and other institutional entities for that matter) believed in the system which they managed. Yet the exact blend of belief, fear, naïveté, opportunism, and bureaucratic correctness is impossible to disaggregate. Moreover, observers and scribe-compilers alike depended on informants for much of their raw material. This was especially the case for the ever-popular svodki, a source much prized in the repertoire of archival researchers. Who were the informants, what were their motivations, how were they chosen for their roles, and how did they transmit their information? These are central questions, not the least reason being that most informants were local people who, it could logically be assumed, were enmeshed in the politics of their own communities, be it the village, collective farm, factory shop, or communal apartment, as well as in the larger political world of Stalinism. I raised the important question of the informant with a senior FSB archivist in 1997, suggesting that this issue is central to a fuller understanding and interpretation of the many exquisite documents the FSB had contributed to the five-volume documentary history of the Soviet countryside, *Tragediia Sovetskoi derevni.*[34] The FSB archivist all but dismissed the question, relegating the issue to the realm of *deloproizvodstvo*[35] and giving the distinct impres-

[33] An excellent example of this type of summary report is Sekretno-Politicheskii otdel OGPU, "Dokladnaia zapiska o formakh i dinamike klassovoi bor'by v derevne v 1930 godu," *Tragediia Sovetskoi derevni,* vol. 2 (Moscow, 2000), pp. 787–808; excerpts from this document are also published in Danilov and Berelowitch, "Les documents des VCK-OGPU-NKVD sur la campagne Soviétique, 1918–1937," 671–80. The document is analyzed in detail in Viola, *Peasant Rebels.*

[34] At the June 1998 business meeting mentioned above.

[35] *Deloproizvodstvo* can be defined in short as the practices of institutional recordkeeping and archival organization. For a more complete discussion, see Lynne Viola, "Archival Research in the USSR: A Practical Guide for Historians," in *A Researcher's Guide to Sources on Soviet Social History in the 1930s,* ed. Sheila Fitzpatrick and Lynne Viola (Armonk, N.Y.: M. E. Sharpe,

sion that the FSB itself (and its predecessors) had, in a sense, bureaucratized its own source, objectifying and reducing it to a simple matter of record keeping.

The "organs," as they were familiarly known, produced reams of paper of interest to the historian—much of it no doubt indirectly derived from their own slave laborers in the forestry industry. Certain categories of their sources are more accessible than others. Among these are the svodki, which fortunately have tended to surface outside the FSB archive. The svodka is a valuable source of information on the possibilities of resistance, not the least reason being its apparent spatial and synchronic proximity (especially lower down the regional hierarchy) to the scene of action.[36] Yet it is important to maintain critical distance from these sources. Working on the postwar period, Elena Zubkova reminds us that the compilers of svodki—and especially of police svodki—emphasized "examples that deviated from consensual opinion."[37] Setting aside the intriguing question of the nature of "consensual opinion," we should note that Zubkova also reminds us that the svodki bear an "ideological imprimatur"[38] that glosses their evidence with a thick and sometimes opaque filter. The British historian Sarah Davies notes that the subjects of the svodki are encumbered by the questions asked and, in many cases, circumscribed by the confined structures of presentation imposed from above.[39]

The secret police regularly issued instructions on how to assemble svodki, prescribing the types of information and forms of presentation expected from what, to begin with, may have been less than highly educated or creative scribes. Questions about the inevitable shortcomings (*nedochety*) of campaigns and policy implementation were often central in the formulation of reports of all kinds. Svodki on rural campaigns during the First Five-Year Plan, for example, revealed their "ideological imprimatur," as Zubkova so nicely put it, by the prescribed division and categorization of political moods on any number of topics according to the social division of peasants into poor, middle, or strong peasants and kulaks. The term *kulak* was quite regularly paired with phrases like "anti-Soviet elements" or "anti-Soviet activities" in instructional directives (generally memoranda), thus again impairing the already highly unlikely possibility

1990), pp. 68–69. (This article is now largely a somewhat quaint, antiquarian essay, but it still contains a few useful sections.)

[36] See McDonald's article in this collection for a note to this effect and an empirical demonstration.

[37] Zubkova, *Russia after the War,* p. 7.

[38] Ibid.

[39] Davies, *Popular Opinion in Stalin's Russia,* p. 13.

of objective social reporting. The svodki and other similarly constructed reports became "standardized forms," structured from the center and allowing relatively little leeway for information to escape a densely packed political filter.[40]

In a sense, then, the filter distilling the information of the svodki assumed the existence of resistance and subversive political moods as a natural consequence of the Marxian laws of social order. This assumption is not helpful in the attempt to sort out popular motivations and mentalities, although the context from on high of fear and distrust is suggestive. Furthermore, as Sarah Davies reminds us, the emphasis on dissonance should not necessarily be interpreted as opposition, not only because of the problematic nature of the source but because dissonant discourses could and did coexist with "consensual" discourse, depending on time and context.[41]

Perhaps the svodki (and other types of police sources) reveal more about events and cases than motives, leaving the all-powerful historian to attempt to remove the ideological filter. Police sources are an invaluable repository of evidence, full of detail, description, and data. Still, the historian must wade through a thick marsh of Stalinist terminology and imagery to reach even a fleeting reality. I have discussed the problems of Stalinist semantics elsewhere, but it may bear repeating that the terminology of counterrevolution is as reflective of regime mentality as of popular behavior. In categorizing peasant disturbances, for example, the state and its agents used a series of different terms, some with distinct meaning, others without, and almost all heavily laden with official perceptions, obfuscation, and condescension. The most frequently used word was *vystuplenie,* which could mean any act of public defiance unless prefixed by "mass" (*massovoe*), in which case it was an angry demonstration or riot. *Vystuplenie* on its own, however, comes from the verb *vystupit',* which means "to step out." A *vystuplenie,* then, is a stepping out of line, an outbreak of some kind. In a sense, *vystuplenie* became a generic code for peasant unrest; it was an "incident" or a "disturbance," code words used by many politically repressive regimes to describe and depoliticize popular

40 For examples of such instructional documents, see *Tragediia Sovetskoi derevni,* vol. 1, pp. 736–37. Of equal interest are two documents that somehow failed to appear in that volume: "Tsirkuliar OGPU o podgotovke i vypuske nedel'nykh spetssvodok, osveshchaiushchikh khod khlebozagotovok, v sviazi s nachalom novoi khlebozagotovitel'noi kampanii. 20 iiulia 1929 g.," TsA FSB (Tsentral'nyi arkhiv Federal'noi sluzhby bezopasnosti), f. 66, op. 1, d. ?, l. 243; and "Tsirkuliar OGPU ob osveshchenii khoda osennei posevnoi kampanii 1928 g. i kontraktatsii posevov zernovykh kul'tur. 7 avgusta 1928 g.," TsA FSB, f. 66, op. 1, d. ?, l. 262.

41 Davies, *Popular Opinion in Stalin's Russia,* pp. 185–86.

acts of protest. The phrase *massovye vystupleniia* (mass disturbances) appears more frequently in documents, especially those of OGPU provenance, and like *vystuplenie,* generally served as a generic term for mass disturbances of all kinds. The word *volnenie* was another frequently used term for unrest. Literally translated, *volnenie* means a disturbance or agitated state, and is therefore again a slightly sanitized term for revolt, containing more than a hint of elite condescension and capturing the official view of "dark masses" rising up in senseless mayhem. Like *vystuplenie, volnenie*—without the "mass" prefix—could be used generically to refer to any manifestation of collective unrest. *Bunty* (riots), *volynki* (riots in the diminutive), and *svalki* (melees) were much clearer terms for riots, each signifying a spontaneous outburst carried out by "irrational" and "backward" peasants. These terms joined *vosstaniia* and *miatezhi,* meaning uprisings and mutinies, which were much clearer, less sanitized descriptions of collective acts of peasant rebellion. They were sometimes modified by the adjective *povstancheskii,* signifying a large and serious insurrection with organized and well-armed participants, spanning several districts and explicitly treasonous in intent. Despite the clarity of the terms, *bunty, svalki,* or *volynki* might be forgiven by the authorities; *miatezhi, vosstaniia,* and *povstancheskie vystupleniia* were most certainly considered counterrevolutionary acts, with an implicit kulak adjective and the attributes of conspiracy. We depend on local officials' reporting and higher officials' interpretations for the choice of descriptive term. Labels may have corresponded to the size, dynamics, and danger of a disturbance, or they may simply have reflected the effect the official interpreter intended to have on his audience of superiors. Some combination—contradictory, to be sure—of official denial, rationalization of political opposition, and paranoid exaggeration also filters into the reporting as well as the reception.[42]

Having raised several key issues of interpretation, we might reverse gears and ask whether the Stalinist source lens was simply a deadly, exaggerated, and highly ideological variation on universal themes of dominant discourses. If so, we are led in several possible directions. First, it is necessary to confront Peter Holquist's fascinating thematic reconceptualization, which situates "Bolshevik surveillance" and the police state within a "pan-European" context.[43] This then moves the historian onto a broader and perhaps more significant terrain: the consideration of the meaning of the (police) inquiry. For our more immediate purposes, however, the

[42] Viola, *Peasant Rebels,* pp. 134–35.

[43] Peter Holquist, " 'Information Is the Alpha and Omega of Our Work': Bolshevik Surveillance in Its Pan-European Context," *Journal of Modern History* 69, 3 (1997): 415–50.

question of comparison should aid us in refining the questions we use to interrogate our sources and in examining the extent of our own "otherness" as we attempt to interpret secret police sources and their reflections of the popular classes.

Opposing Arguments, or The Case for Resistance

Although we have managed a partial and rough excavation of the territory surrounding resistance, emphasizing the problematic nature of the phenomenon, we are no closer to an exact definition of the term. It is, perhaps, ultimately more important to explore the meaning of resistance against the larger historical canvas of the Stalinist 1930s, for the sheer fact of resistance is less historically significant than its explication.

Let us begin by attempting to turn what earlier was described as a weakness into a strength, or at least an imaginative possibility. As David Warren Sabean has pointed out in another context, "what is a fact about sources is not necessarily a weakness. Documents which perceive peasants [and subaltern classes in general—LV] through the eyes of rulers or their spokesmen begin with relationships of domination. The issue is to examine the constitution of peasant [or other subaltern—LV] notions within the dynamics of power and hierarchical relations."[44] It is within the interstices of the generally rather one-sided state–society dialogue that we may locate, or attempt to locate, what James Scott calls the "hidden transcripts" of domination.[45] The interstices are an opening onto official discourse; elite social constructions of the popular classes; and the language and mentality of Stalinism, which could transform peasants and workers into enemies and distort the realities of popular politics. Words like *counterrevolutionary, kulak, class enemy, sabotage, incorrect excesses, bab'i bunty,* and *volynki* complicate our work by partly obscuring popular voices and practices. Yet a semiotic approach to the use of this terminology can yield valuable understanding about relationships of domination. If the regime casts a shadow over the popular classes in the study of resistance, it is because the popular resistance of the 1930s depended on the regime for its existence. It evolved both within and against the grain of Stalinism.[46]

Popular resistance rebounds on the state. Its very existence as a hermeneutical concept in the sources means that the state chose to clas-

44 David Warren Sabean, *Power in the Blood: Popular Culture and Village Discourse in Early Modern Germany* (Cambridge: Cambridge University Press, 1984), pp. 2–3.

45 Scott, *Domination and the Arts of Resistance,* esp. pp. 4–5.

46 Viola, *Peasant Rebels,* p. 11.

sify certain events, phenomena, practices, or categories of actions as resistant or oppositional or dissonant, regardless of exact terminology or phraseology. Regime fears of instability are often mirrored in the sources by reflections of resistance. These fears surface in descriptions of events and in the events themselves. Rossman's work on the Vichuga uprising and the Teikovo strike demonstrates elite fears of the "masses" on both the national and local levels. The temporary collapse of authority in Vichuga and the center's resort to unbridled force provide testimony to these fears.[47] Doubtless, such fears were vastly magnified in consequence of the rebellions of the collectivization era when peasants succeeded (temporarily) in chasing out local representatives of power and brought (again temporarily) central policy to a halt.[48] In addition, even if we set aside the question of crime as resistance per se, David Shearer's study of crime in the middle 1930s reveals an explosion of "social disobedience" that instilled fear into political and especially secret police elites.[49]

Each of these phenomena assumed at a micro or macro level the proportions of a crisis that both revealed and compounded the regime's vulnerability, or perception of vulnerability, before the popular classes. Regime fears, however, could as easily lead to the depoliticization or denial of resistance as to its magnification. This was most often the case in examples of what Rossman calls "gendered" resistance,[50] meaning, I think, the resistance of women. When women engaged in mass acts of disobedience—whether blatantly in *bab'i bunty* or covertly in, for example, illegal abortions after 1936[51]—the regime turned a blind eye to the significance of the phenomena, resorting instead to traditional explanations of women's affairs that relied on social constructions of laboring women as "backward," "irrational," and "hysterical." The very silence of the sources is indicative of this "gendered" blind eye. For example, while Rossman is able to delve into the lives and mindsets of several of his most important male worker activists, the occasional woman leader (through no fault of Rossman's) appears and disappears almost simultaneously.[52] What other

[47] See Rossman's essay in this collection; and Rossman, "Worker Resistance under Stalin," chaps. 7–8.

[48] Viola, *Peasant Rebels*, chap. 5.

[49] Shearer, "Crime and Social Disorder in Stalin's Russia," 121–22, 136.

[50] Rossman, "Worker Resistance under Stalin," 18–19, 27–29.

[51] On abortion, see Wendy Goldman, *Women, the State, and Revolution: Soviet Family Policy and Social Life, 1917–1936* (Cambridge: Cambridge University Press, 1993), chap. 7; and Goldman, "Women, Abortion, and the State, 1917–1936," in *Russia's Women: Accommodation, Resistance, Transformation*, ed. Barbara Evans Clements, Barbara Alpern Engel, and Christine D. Worobec (Berkeley: University of California Press, 1991), pp. 243–66.

[52] Rossman, "Worker Resistance under Stalin," 230, 468.

instances of resistance may be buried by social perception, denial, or conscious disregard can only be conjectured and creatively reconfigured. When the state chose, peasants became *muzhiki* and *baby*, and workers were labeled "unconscious" or simply "peasants." Political convenience was the bedfellow of social bias and stereotype. The state, then, was a vital actor in the definition, discovery, or obfuscation of resistant behaviors; what it chose to label as resistance and in what context reveals much about official motivations and relations of domination.

Whether expressed through violent suppression or documentary denial, official fear of popular resistance had other definite short- and long-term consequences for state policy. Accommodation and repression alternated as regime responses to popular resistance. The "March fever" of 1930 led in large part to Stalin's temporary retreat from collectivization, announced in his cynical and accusatory article "Dizziness from Success."[53] The worker protest of 1932 in Ivanovo and perhaps elsewhere may well have formed a part of the background to the modifications in economic policy that followed in the protest's wake.[54] And Sheila Fitzpatrick has described a constant interplay of peasant resistance and regime accommodation through the 1930s, a process that she labels "negotiation."[55] Needless to say, such retreats, accommodations, and negotiations served state ends, and while they occasionally involved manipulations of a grotesque and sometimes dangerous form of "Stalinist populism" to deflect structural problems from the center onto local officials and enemies, they were seldom democratic or genuinely conciliatory responses to popular grievances.

Ultimately, resistance led to repression. The greater the real or perceived instability of the regime, the more deeply entrenched repression became as a systemic mechanism of governance. While policy was sometimes moderated in the center in response to popular resistance, the latter more often elicited direct reprisals. Furthermore, the wave of popular resistance in the early 1930s fed directly into the regime's expanding use of repression as an "everyday" tool of governance. The mass deportations of peasants as kulaks that accompanied collectivization led to a vast expansion of secret police personnel, assets, and prestige; the secret police emerged from the experience at the head of a huge and powerful police-run economic empire based on unfree labor.[56] Shearer has argued that

[53] Viola, *Peasant Rebels*, chap. 5.

[54] Rossman, "The Teikovo Cotton Workers' Strike," 68; and Rossman, "Worker Resistance under Stalin," 552.

[55] Fitzpatrick, *Stalin's Peasants*, p. 7.

[56] Lynne Viola, "The Role of the OGPU in Dekulakization, Mass Deportations, and Special Resettlement in 1930," *Carl Beck Papers in Russian and East European Studies*, no. 1406 (2000);

the Stalinist leadership, most especially Iagoda, became "obsessed with the attempt to 'fix' dangerous populations" as a result of the crime wave of the middle 1930s.[57] This "obsession," surely predating the middle 1930s by at least five years, translated into, among other things, the introduction of internal passports and the increasing use of socially and ethnically based deportations of suspect populations.[58] These findings are important, for they suggest formative lines of continuity in the emergence of the Stalinist police state that help explain the administrative, institutional, economic, and, in part, political underpinnings of the machinery of repression, all too often associated mainly with the terrible year 1937.

Moving away from the state side of the equation, the manifestation of resistance also informs our understanding of society and popular culture in the 1930s. In the expression of resistance, we glimpse the persistence of autonomous or semi-autonomous cultures, subcultures, and identities surviving within the hegemonic political culture of Stalinism. The endurance of older languages of resistance among the popular classes reveals a cultural edifice long obscured by the Stalinist source lens and the ideological preoccupations of historians.

For illustration, we turn again to the work of Jeffrey Rossman. Rossman's excavation of worker protest in the Ivanovo region during the First Five-Year Plan, and especially in 1932, reveals a popular culture in which class and the ideals of the Russian Revolution were paramount. Although some scholars share Steve Smith's argument that "it was extremely difficult to advance counterhegemonic conceptions and strategies" because the regime had co-opted the language of class,[59] Rossman's work suggests that we reexamine the centrality of class in the consciousness of workers quite apart from the state's co-optation. At the risk of sounding facile, perhaps we would do well to ask whose class it was in the first place. We must also broach the question of the relationship between the ideals of 1917

Viola, "The Other Archipelago: Kulak Deportations to the North in 1930," *Slavic Review* 60, 4 (2001): 730–55; and Viola, " 'Tear the Evil from the Roots': The Children of the *Spetspereselentsy* of the North," *Studia Slavica Finlandensia* 17 (2000): 34–72.

[57] Shearer, "Crime and Social Disorder in Stalin's Russia," 121–22, 136.

[58] See Terry Martin, "The Origins of Soviet Ethnic Cleansing," *Journal of Modern History* 70, 4 (1998): 813–61. For a broad and conceptually brilliant analysis of the political and cultural underpinnings of this phenomenon, see Amir Weiner, "Nature, Nurture, and Memory in a Socialist Utopia: Delineating the Soviet Socio-Ethnic Body in the Age of Socialism," *American Historical Review* 104, 4 (1999): 1114–55.

[59] Steve Smith, "Russian Workers and the Politics of Social Identity," *Russian Review* 56, 1 (1997): 1–7. See also Lewis H. Siegelbaum and Ronald Grigor Suny, "Class Backwards? In Search of the Soviet Working Class," in *Making Workers Soviet: Power, Class, and Identity*, ed. Lewis H. Siegelbaum and Ronald Grigor Suny (Ithaca, N.Y.: Cornell University Press, 1994), pp. 19–20.

and the hegemonic culture of Stalinism, which may be somewhere at the root of the issue. To what extent did a consciousness of class continue, arise, or reappear within the material realities of the workplace and community, separate from official pontifications and varying in contour from industry to industry? Certainly, the social and cultural realities of class lost their moorings in the abstract and rarefied enclosures of regime pronouncements. The sense of class, class belonging, and solidarity was reinforced and strengthened—if only temporarily—as normally disparate elements in the Ivanovo textile mills (skilled and unskilled, men and women, etc.) came together as a community and a political force in their confrontations with the outside forces of the state. In this confrontation, moreover, workers revived older working-class traditions, including the strike, petitions, and other forms of collective action. Workers protested under the banner of 1917 not because of false consciousness or as an opportunistic discursive strategy, but because 1917 was rightfully their revolution, a revolution that they believed had become unhinged from its social base.[60]

Peasant resistance exhibited similar continuities with prerevolutionary traditions and similar evidence of the strengthening of identity and community.[61] During collectivization, peasant resistance became a form of peasant politics. As the only genuinely oppositional politics then available to peasants, resistance reflected a collective consciousness of intent, action, and hoped-for resolution, as well as a clear and sometimes even prophetic sense of national politics and goals. The peasant solidarity of the collectivization era was the direct manifestation of peasant agency and political consciousness. The base determinants of peasant resistance derived from reasoned concerns centered largely on issues of justice and subsistence and supplemented by the primary elemental responses of anger, desperation, and rage. Peasants' ideas of justice were integral to popular protest.[62] Collectivization was a violation—a direct assault on—customary norms of village authority and government, ideals of collectivism and neighborhood, and, often, simple standards of human decency. Support for collectivization *within* the community was equally a violation of the village ideal of collectivism, thereby making retribution a

[60] Rossman, "Worker Resistance under Stalin," 15, 31–32, 498.

[61] Here I largely repeat arguments from *Peasant Rebels*, pp. 9–10.

[62] On the importance of popular conceptions of justice, see Barrington Moore, Jr., *Social Origins of Dictatorship and Democracy: Lord and Peasant in the Making of the Modern World* (Boston: Beacon, 1967), p. 471; and Charles Tilly, Louise Tilly, and Richard Tilly, *The Rebellious Century, 1830–1930* (Cambridge: Cambridge University Press, 1975), p. 85. Also see McDonald's essay in this collection.

key derivative of justice in motivating acts of peasant resistance. Collectivization was also, just as importantly, a threat to peasant household and community survival. Subsistence was a primary determinant of the shape of peasant politics and relations with the state.[63] It surely was a chief concern and responsibility of the peasant women, who dominated so much of the peasantry's response to collectivization, as was also common elsewhere when peasant survival was at stake. The contents and causes of peasant resistance to collectivization were, to a great extent, "generic," while still manifesting specificity in derivation, context, and response.

Peasant *forms* of resistance were shaped by a set of customary concerns and ways of acting that, although frequently appearing irrational and chaotic to outsiders, had their own logic. In most cases, they also had a long-established history as approaches to challenging authority. Tradition itself became a resource for legitimacy and mobilization as peasants sought justification for their responses to state policy.[64] Peasants made use of a customary array of resistance tactics: rumor, flight, dissimulation, and other passive and active forms of resistance. Their choices were clearly and logically guided by the actions of the state and the issue of their resistance. Peasant forms of resistance were informed by pragmatism, flexibility, and adaptation, each a vital resource in opposing a powerful and repressive state. Peasants turned to violence only as a last resort, when desperation and retribution reached such a level as to provoke them into a direct challenge. Often violence came out of ordinarily nonviolent settings, such as meetings, demonstrations, and other interactions with Soviet power, when the violent actions of the authorities pushed peasants to answer violence with violence. The forms of peasant resistance transpired, in large part, in ritualized, customary scenarios, continually reenacted because of their organizational merit and tactical utility in responding to power.

The antithetical (to the regime) nature of peasant culture and resistance most clearly expressed itself through metaphor and symbolic inversion, which constituted a form within a form or a vehicle for many specific types of protest. The discourse of peasant rebellion surfaced in the world of rumor, in which symbols of apocalypse and serfdom provided dominant motifs used to categorize the behavior of the state and its agents. Apocalypse turned the communist world on its head by associating the

[63] James C. Scott, *The Moral Economy of the Peasant: Rebellion and Subsistence in Southeast Asia* (New Haven, Conn.: Yale University Press, 1976), p. 3.

[64] See Terence Ranger, "Peasant Consciousness: Culture and Conflict in Zimbabwe," in *Peasants and Peasant Societies*, 2d ed., ed. Teodor Shanin (Oxford: Blackwell, 1987), p. 313.

state with the Antichrist, while serfdom signified the ultimate communist betrayal of revolutionary ideals. The massive destruction and sale of peasant property (*razbazarivanie*) served as another form of inversion, as the peasantry seemingly engaged in a wholesale attempt to overturn "class" in the village through social and economic leveling. Terror aimed at officials and activists and the chasing out of state authority constituted literal inversions of political power. Dissimulation constantly juggled power and weakness in attempts to hoodwink, disguise, and evade. Perhaps most important of all, the central role of women in the peasant resistance of 1930 demonstrated not only an inversion of power relations between the state and the peasantry but also a subversion of the patriarchal order, indicating a complete denial of norms of obedience and submission. Reversals of power, inversions of image and role, and counter-ideology provided the legitimation required to bolster peasant resistance within a stark symbolism of binary oppositions between state and peasantry.[65]

For peasants, as for workers, the manifestation and expression of resistance were rooted in deeply ingrained social identities, community, and universal strategies of popular collective action, all of which failed to recognize the historical divide of 1917 and the regime's claim to the revolution. The same ideals, politics, and consciousness that formed the backbone of popular action in 1917 animated peasants and workers in their struggles for social justice in the 1930s. And although the dominant peasant discourse of collectivization appears to have been apocalyptic, D'Ann Penner reminds us that some peasants remained loyal to the idea of the revolution, their revolution, continuing to defend Soviet power against the communists, or, in hybrid form, to defend Soviet power against the Antichrists.[66]

Other forms of culture and identity persisted through the vehicle of resistance. Nationality, whether consciously and politically expressed as nationalism or simply evoked in customary behavior, dress, and speech, could be construed as resistance, depending on time and context. Douglas Northrop, for example, has explored the ways in which Uzbek women's bodies became, in his formulation, "mutually agreed ground[s]

[65] On symbolic inversion, see David Underdown, *Revel, Riot, and Rebellion: Popular Politics and Culture in England, 1603–1660* (Oxford: Oxford University Press, 1985), p. 111; Emmanuel Le Roy Ladurie, *Carnival at Romans*, trans. Mary Feeney (New York: George Braziller, 1980), pp. 189–92, 316; T. V. Sathyamurthy, "Indian Peasant Historiography," *Journal of Peasant Studies* 18, 1 (1990): 111–12, 119; and Scott, *Domination and the Arts of Resistance*, p. 44.

[66] Penner, "Pride, Power, and Pitchforks," chaps. 7, 10; and Penner, "Electric Trains and Remote Archives."

(if unspoken) of conflict" between Bolsheviks and Uzbeks.[67] Customary practices like polygamy, bride-price, and the veil became "crimes of *byt*"[68] from the state's perspective, turning "traditionalists" into cultural rebels. In spite of—one could argue because of—the state's hostility and myopia, Uzbek society demonstrated "remarkable resilience and strong, consistent resistance through the 1930s."[69] In a very real sense, the state transformed what it saw as objectionable aspects of national culture into resistance. In doing so, the state unintentionally facilitated the emergence or survival of nationality and nationalism in more recalcitrant forms by forcing objectionable aspects of national culture underground. This demonstrates both the irony of repression and the limits of state cultural intervention even under Stalin.

Byt crimes were not restricted to national groups. As the relatively progressive legislation of the 1920s gave way to the new, more conservative legislation of the 1930s, the state, with the stroke of a pen, criminalized activities which earlier had been unrestricted, whether by necessity, oversight, or emancipatory zeal. Although the 1936 restrictions on abortion were meant to reduce women's control over childbirth, in practice their effect was far less than intended. As Wendy Goldman has demonstrated, "[i]n mass defiance of the state, women refused to return to the childbearing practices of the patriarchal peasant family."[70] Instead, they often were able to rely on a preexisting network of doctors, midwives, and village wisewomen, who implicitly maintained an autonomous space, or subculture, for women's needs. The state also passed legislation recriminalizing male homosexuality in 1933. Homosexuality, however, did not disappear in Stalin's Soviet Union. As the innovative research of Dan Healey has revealed, homosexuality survived as an underground subculture with its own codes and rituals.[71] One could multiply many times the categories of behavior that fell under "byt crimes," but the significance of

[67] Douglas Taylor Northrop, "Uzbek Women and the Veil: Gender and Power in Stalinist Central Asia," Ph.D. dissertation, Stanford University, 1999, 474; see also Northrop's essay in this collection.

[68] *Byt* is a difficult term to translate into English, but it has usually been rendered as "everyday life." In this context, the term is, perhaps, better translated as "way of life."

[69] Northrop, "Uzbek Women and the Veil," 468.

[70] Goldman, "Women, Abortion, and the State," 266.

[71] See Healey's essay in this collection. Also see Dan Healey, "Moscow," in *Queer Sites: Gay Urban Histories since 1600*, ed. David Higgs (London: Routledge, 1999), pp. 38–60; Healey, "The Russian Revolution and the Decriminalization of Homosexuality," *Revolutionary Russia* 6, 1 (1993): 26–54; and Healey, *Homosexual Desire in Revolutionary Russia: The Regulation of Sexual and Gender Dissent* (Chicago: University of Chicago Press, 2001).

this category would remain the same. The category depended on state definition (and legislation) for its classification as criminal, inherently resistant behavior, and it endured as cultural practice at least in part because of the state's recalcitrant stance. Yet, as elsewhere, the force of Stalinist hegemonic culture was limited, at times achieving the unintended consequence of preserving what it sought to destroy.[72]

As the state's definitions of resistance expanded in direct correlation to its interventions, the manifestation of "social space" acquired increased significance. James Scott has described social space as sites "in which offstage dissent to the official transcript of power relations may be voiced. The specific forms (for example, linguistic disguises, ritual codes, taverns, fairs, the 'hush arbors' of slave religion) this social space takes and the specific content of its dissent (for example, hopes of a returning prophet, ritual aggression via witchcraft, celebration of bandit heroes and resistance martyrs) are as unique as the particular culture and history of the actors in question require."[73] In the Stalinist 1930s, this kind of space was everywhere, or could be perceived to be anywhere, as the state attempted to extend its reach into all areas of life. The location of such space can range from the kitchen table to the bazaar to the church, depending upon how one defines the term and the meaning of the space. Above all, though, the term only has meaning in juxtaposition to the state. The private sphere, for example, was in many cases strengthened as a result of the swelling and oppressive encroachments of the public sphere. The kitchen table became a backstage social space for successive generations of the intelligentsia. The state could do little about this phenomenon and, indeed, may not have even recognized its full significance.[74]

In other areas, the state led a veritable war on social space. Peasant culture—customs, institutions, and ways of life—represented peasant autonomy. These islands of autonomy threatened the state's plan of domination, for they enabled the peasantry to maintain social space. The campaign against religion and the church is the best known and most obvious facet of the assault on peasant culture and social spaces, yet these were not the only cultural institutions targeted for destruction. The closures of agricultural markets began with the imposition of extraordinary measures in grain procurement. The closures served not only to facilitate the creation of a centralized command economy in agriculture and to de-

[72] See Osokina's essay in this collection.

[73] Scott, *Domination and the Arts of Resistance*, p. xi.

[74] This dimension of the private sphere is suggested in Beth Holmgren, *Women's Works in Stalin's Time* (Bloomington: Indiana University Press, 1993), pp. 9–12.

prive the peasantry of economic independence but also to take away a major cultural thoroughfare for contacts with other peasants and urban society, for it was here that the reproduction of peasant culture took place, with the celebration of holidays and the abundance of peasant arts, crafts, and popular entertainment.

The abolition of the peasant land society on 30 July 1930 in districts of wholesale collectivization, and the transfer of many village responsibilities to rural soviets and new collective farm boards, constituted yet another dimension in the subjugation of the peasantry. With the end of the land society, and the consequent curtailment of the *skhod* (peasant council), the state removed from peasants the right even to a limited self-government, depriving them of administrative and fiscal autonomy and the right to independent political expression. The closing of mills and shops was also a part of the war on peasant social space. Not only did the closing of these peasant-run establishments increase village dependence on the state, it sealed off an important gathering place for sociability, discussion, and political expression, hence removing yet another site of peasant autonomy. The elimination of many village craftsmen and artisans as kulaks or "NEP-men," and the expropriation of their property, had a similar effect on the community. It forced peasants into greater dependence on the state and into becoming consumers of urban, machine-made products, while seriously harming the reproduction of peasant material culture. The removal of village authority figures constituted a final dimension of the state's attempt to destroy peasant cultural autonomy. All these measures were intrinsic to the Stalinist socialization of the peasant economy. Yet they were equally vital to the Stalinist cultural revolution in the countryside and absolutely prerequisite to the establishment of communist controls over the peasantry.[75]

The great irony of resistance—or what the state chose to see as resistance—is that its identification as such in combination with the state's repression led to the strengthening of older cultural formations, identities, and loyalties. As groups, subcultures, and entire cultures were forced to go underground, they retreated to the private sphere for survival and re-formed in order to provide social space and protection.[76] This phenome-

[75] Viola, *Peasant Rebels*, pp. 40–41.

[76] It was not just Soviet repression that impacted on the endurance of cultures and nations; Soviet interventions of various kinds could reinforce older practices in sometimes unintentional ways, whether we speak of national ways and customs or the peasant adaptation of the collective farm over time. See Tamara Dragadze, *Rural Families in Soviet Georgia: A Case Study in Ratcha Province* (London: Routledge, 1988); Yuri Slezkine, "The Soviet Union as a Communal Apartment," *Slavic Review* 53, 2 (1994): 414–52; Ronald Grigor Suny, *The Revenge of the*

non, in turn, sheds light on the apparently sudden recovery of nationalism and the rapid proliferation of other unofficial cultures with the demise of the Soviet Union. I do not mean to suggest here a state–society bifurcation or some kind of homogeneous and resistant social mass. Rather, I wish to emphasize the solidity and endurance of popular culture and customs, as well as the limits of state intervention. It was the persistence of these diverse and layered cultural and political environments *coexisting within and beyond the dominant Soviet political culture* that enabled some individuals to engage in acts of resistance, whether those acts were to oppose the regime or its officials, maintain cultural differences and other nonconformist predilections, or take part in an economic subculture that consistently broke the law.[77]

Summation

The refraction of resistance through a socio-cultural prism is not intended to deny the political import of popular resistance under Stalin. It is, of course, immensely significant that peasants, workers, and other ordinary citizens would and could defy Stalinism. This fact in itself may serve to alter traditional notions of the realities of living under the Stalinist dictatorship and more recent views emphasizing a unitary, monolithic, and homogeneous political environment as well as the limits of that dictatorship's abilities to control, intervene, and transform. Yet there is a danger to the study of resistance for resistance's sake, and that is the danger of mythologizing or reifying resistance. The victors always have the advantage in historiographical mythmaking. The temptation for cold-war veterans and Russian revisionists alike is to reproduce the old state–society dichotomy, this time balancing out the repressive side of the equation with a resistant (rather than atomized) population, valorizing popular heroes, resurrecting old stereotypes, and creating new ones about resistant "masses." Present-mindedness in historiography provides an additional temptation to magnify and valorize resistance, through attempts to find historical antecedents for contemporary religious, national, and popular political movements. Resistance, however, was only one part, likely a small

Past (Stanford, Calif.: Stanford University Press, 1993), p. 115; and Viola, *Peasant Rebels*, conclusion.

[77] This is a point of no small importance when measured against recent views in the historiography that suggest that a monolithic Soviet political culture prevented the formation of alternative discourses; Krylova, for example, argues that "the resisting subject is posited heroically against and outside historical forces" in "The Tenacious Liberal Subject," 144; see also Hellbeck, "Speaking Out," 73–74, 82–83.

part, in a wide continuum of societal responses to the Stalinist state that included accommodation, adaptation, acquiescence, apathy, internal emigration, opportunism, and support. If we neglect this continuum, we risk reducing the regime, again, to the demonic and society to an undifferentiated whole.

We may also risk over-particularizing the Stalinist experience. While I have no doubt that Stalinism had tenacious roots in Russian historical soil, it is important not to lose sight of certain universals which, however distorted within the Stalinist context, lend themselves to comparative analysis and insight. Stalinist state building, a phenomenon rife with contradictions and perversions, implied cultural domination along with collectivization and industrialization. Like its predecessors in early modern Europe and elsewhere at other times, the Stalinist state sought to marginalize or eliminate anything that it viewed as counter to its own hegemonic cultural vision—whether that was religion and the church, officially defined deviants, "alien" social populations, traditional healers, or the Stalinist equivalent of the witch (those defined as enemies).[78] This process of cultural imperialism from top to bottom, though abhorrent in its very nature, was not an historical aberration. And, as elsewhere, subaltern classes fought cultural colonization with customary and traditional resources.

The significance of resistance, then, for understanding society, culture, and politics in the Stalinist 1930s is multidimensional. Yet we make this statement without offering an exact definition of the term. Perhaps this is a contradiction, a flaw in the argument of the devil's advocate. Perhaps we would be better served to speak of *acts* of resistance or resistance*s*. Yet there is no doubt that resistance existed. The real problem lies in identification. And here definition will always depend on the state and the historian as much as on objective reality. While we will always presume to speak for the popular classes, not to mention the state, in the end it is useful to recognize that we are the proverbial "other" of history, injecting ourselves into other worlds and cultures.

[78] Joseph Klaits, *Servants of Satan: The Age of the Witch Hunts* (Bloomington: Indiana University Press, 1985), pp. 3–7, chap. 2. More generally, see Keith Thomas, *Religion and the Decline of Magic* (New York: Scribner's, 1971).

CHAPTER TWO

A Workers' Strike in Stalin's Russia

The Vichuga Uprising of April 1932

JEFFREY J. ROSSMAN

If they gave us power, then we'd tear all those damn communists to pieces.

—Vichuga demonstrator Ignat'ev

We didn't destroy the soviet, but the [O]GPU, the civil police, and the district party committee.

—Vichuga strikers

In April 1932, Nikolai Shvernik, the head of the All-Union Central Council of Trade Unions, informed Stalin and L. M. Kaganovich (Politburo member and Stalin's troubleshooter extraordinaire) that workers in a number of regions were rebelling against the severe food shortages and the sharp cut in rations that had been implemented on the first of the month at all but the nation's most privileged industrial enterprises.[1] In the Ivanovo Industrial region (IPO), Lower Volga region, the Urals, Western Siberia, Ukraine, and Belorussia, workers were refusing to operate machines, openly denouncing supply officials, looting food-storage facilities, publicly demonstrating against the new "starvation" rations,

The author thanks Reginald Zelnik, Lynne Viola, and Corinne Field for their comments, and the Department of History of the University of California at Berkeley, the Social Science Research Council, the International Research and Exchanges Board, the Fulbright-Hays program, and the Mellon Foundation for financial support.

1 The epigraph comes from Rossiiskii gosudarstvennyi arkhiv sotsial'no-politicheskoi istorii (henceforth, RGASPI), f. 81, op. 3, d. 213, ll. 3–15, 72–76.

and flooding into those towns rumored to have even meager supplies of bread. Shvernik did not offer details about the most serious episode of unrest—a wave of violent and prolonged strikes by over sixteen thousand workers in four IPO mill towns—because Kaganovich, accompanied by a trainload of reinforcements, had descended upon the region himself to restore order. In a coded but ominous conclusion to his memorandum, Shvernik warned the main proponents of the regime's disastrous economic policies that the recent unrest was marked by political overtones: "In all the above-cited cases, counterrevolutionary and Trotskyite elements attempted to exploit the temporary difficulties in worker supply."[2]

Although the IPO strikes were never publicized, they served as the subtext of speeches at the national trade-union congress that met that month in Moscow. In appearances before the delegates, Shvernik ridiculed officials from the towns where the strikes occurred; Ian Rudzutak, head of the Communist Party's Central Control Commission, admitted that workers were "steeped in foul moods"; Kaganovich attributed the crisis of morale to the "petit-bourgeois" attitudes of new workers and the persistence of "bourgeois influences" among veteran workers; and the auditing commission argued that "class-alien elements," including "kulaks, petty tradesmen, déclassé elements, etc.," had infiltrated Soviet enterprises, where they continued to "conduct their subversive work."[3] With such sweeping statements, the party leadership inadvertently conceded what it had been told in confidence by the secret police (Ob"edinennoe gosudarstvennoe politicheskoe upravlenie, or OGPU): oppositional moods permeated *all* strata of the labor force.

Meanwhile, rumors of the unrest sweeping the nation's fields and factories stoked the flames of opposition within the party. Even if they had once endorsed Stalin's policies, many communists now were deeply troubled by the widespread suffering that was their immediate legacy. Shortly before the events of April 1932, for example, Martem'ian Riutin completed the first draft of his two-hundred-page treatise "Stalin and the Crisis of the Proletarian Dictatorship," which argued that the public's mounting discontent necessitated a wholesale change in the leadership and direction of the party:

> Adventurous tempos of industrialization, involving a colossal drop in the wages of workers and employees, unbearable overt and hid-

[2] Gosudarstvennyi arkhiv Rossiiskoi Federatsii (henceforth, GARF), f. 5451, op. 42, d. 250, ll. 17–18.

[3] *IX vsesoiuznyi s"ezd professional'nykh soiuzov SSSR: stenograficheskii otchet* (Moscow, 1933), pp. 96–99, 194, 659–60, 708.

> den taxes, inflation, price increases, and the fall in the value of the ten-ruble bank note; adventurous collectivization attended by unbelievable violence, terror, and dekulakization—which, in fact, has been directed mainly against the middle and lower masses in the countryside—and finally, the expropriation of the countryside by means of all sorts of requisitions and forcible procurements have led the whole country to the most profound crisis, the monstrous impoverishment of the masses, and famine in both the countryside and the city. . . .
>
> Peasant insurrections in which party and Komsomol members participate have been spreading in an uninterrupted wave in recent years across the entire Soviet Union. Despite savage terror, arrests, dismissals, and provocations, strikes by workers are breaking out now here, now there. . . .
>
> Even the most daring and ingenious provocateur could devise nothing better for the destruction of the proletarian dictatorship, for the discrediting of Leninism, than the leadership of Stalin and his clique.[4]

Although Riutin and his supporters succumbed to repression by the fall of 1932, their platform, whose existence demonstrates that information about the state of civilian morale was accessible despite press censorship and the strict system of classification governing OGPU reports, reflected the profound concerns permeating the party's ranks.[5]

The labor unrest of April 1932 is significant for several reasons. First, it marked a turning point in the relationship between the Stalin regime and Soviet society. By organizing strikes, slowdowns, "hunger marches," and emergency assemblies, the textile workers of the IPO expressed their willingness to engage in collective action to change the policies that had reduced them to poverty and hunger. And by sending troops under the command of Kaganovich to suppress the demonstrations, Stalin laid bare the

[4] Cited in B. A. Starkov, "Delo Riutina," in *Oni ne molchali,* comp. A. V. Afanas'ev (Moscow, 1991), pp. 162, 164.

[5] On the Riutin affair, see Starkov, "Delo Riutina," pp. 160–70; and Stephen F. Cohen, *Bukharin and the Bolshevik Revolution: A Political Biography, 1888–1938* (New York: Oxford University Press, 1980), pp. 343–45. On disaffection within the IPO party apparatus, see Tsentr dokumentatsii noveishei istorii Ivanovskoi oblasti (henceforth, TsDNIIO), f. 327, op. 4, d. 449, ll. 92–93. For an account of various episodes of resistance to Stalin and the policy retreats of 1932–34, see O. V. Khlevniuk, *1937–i: Stalin, NKVD, i sovetskoe obshchestvo* (Moscow, 1992), pp. 10–45.

hypocrisy of the claim that he was building a socialist workers' state. Coming as they did in the midst of collectivization and famine, these events also had profound ramifications: they transformed the government's economic program, exacerbated the crisis of public morale, and, during the Great Terror, served as a pretext for the repression of numerous state and party officials.[6] It took years for all the repercussions to become manifest, but word spread quickly that something unprecedented had occurred. Indeed, it had. In Vichuga, Soviet power all but collapsed in the face of a violent, working-class rebellion. Like the strike that erupted in Teikovo at the same time, the Vichuga uprising illustrates the dynamics of working-class resistance under Stalin.[7]

Background

Situated sixty kilometers northeast of Ivanovo, Vichuga was an old mill town that boasted three cotton enterprises, a machine-building plant, and a brick factory; villages in the district were home to another five prerevolutionary mills.[8] Like most Russian factory towns, Vichuga grew rapidly

[6] On the policy retreats of 1932–34 and the relationship between the events of 1932 and the Great Terror, see Khlevniuk, *1937–i*, pp. 10–45. On Kaganovich's use in 1937 of the labor unrest of 1932 to justify the repression of current and former IPO officials, see RGASPI, f. 81, op. 3, d. 229, ll. 9–11, 16–17.

[7] This essay is based primarily on Russian archival sources, including the OGPU files of strike participants and materials of the Central Control Commission, the IPO Communist Party committee, and the trade unions. For more on the IPO strike wave, see Jeffrey J. Rossman, "Worker Resistance under Stalin: Class and Gender in the Textile Mills of the Ivanovo Industrial Region, 1928–1932," Ph.D. dissertation, University of California at Berkeley, 1997. On the Teikovo strike, see also Rossman, "The Teikovo Cotton Workers' Strike of April 1932: Class, Gender and Identity Politics in Stalin's Russia," *Russian Review* 56, 1 (1997): 44–69. Although space does not permit a thorough examination here of the historiography, my research calls into question the view that Soviet workers were "quiescent" during the First Five-Year Plan or enthusiastically embraced Stalin's revolution "from above." For contrast, see William Chase, *Workers, Society, and the Soviet State: Labor and Life in Moscow, 1918–1929* (Urbana: University of Illinois Press, 1987); Stephen Kotkin, *Magnetic Mountain: Stalinism as a Civilization* (Berkeley: University of California Press, 1995); Hiroaki Kuromiya, *Stalin's Industrial Revolution: Politics and Workers, 1928–1932* (Cambridge: Cambridge University Press, 1988); Lewis H. Siegelbaum and Ronald G. Suny, eds., *Making Workers Soviet: Power, Class, and Identity* (Ithaca, N.Y.: Cornell University Press, 1994); Kenneth Straus, *Factory and Community in Stalin's Russia: The Making of an Industrial Working Class* (Pittsburgh: University of Pittsburgh Press, 1997); and Lynne Viola, *The Best Sons of the Fatherland: Workers in the Vanguard of Soviet Collectivization* (New York: Oxford University Press, 1987).

[8] The factories in Vichuga included the Nogin Spinning and Weaving Mill (7,439 workers), the Krasnyi Profintern (Tezinskaia) Spinning and Weaving Mill (7,494 workers), the United Shagov Spinning and Weaving Mills (2,529 workers), Machine-Building Plant No. 6 (425

during these years: from 1926 to 1933, its population rose from 24,700 to 36,000. Half the town's residents worked in industry, and Vichuga's factories employed some twenty thousand workers, the majority of them women.[9]

The problems confronting Vichuga at the end of the First Five-Year Plan were not unusual. Living conditions in workers' barracks and dormitories were abysmal; rents were high and rising; child-care facilities for the predominantly female labor force were scarce; food and consumer goods were in drastically short supply; shop floors suffered from declining output and productivity; opposition to output quotas was strong; and real wages were low and falling. Another problem was morale. In September 1931, the OGPU reported on the situation at the Nogin Mill, where specialists and supervisors openly denounced the regime's production norms; white-collar workers attempted to send a delegation to M. I. Kalinin (titular head of the government in his capacity as Chairman of the Central Executive Committee of the Soviet Union) to protest differentiated rations; and communists agitated against compulsory loan subscriptions and served as "leaders of the workers' mass discontent" over the implementation of a night shift.[10] At the level of the factory cells and the district *(raion)* committee, the party lacked discipline: for instance, only

---

workers), and the housing cooperative's brick factory (43 workers). Employment levels at the mills fluctuated in 1932 as a result of changes in both production capabilities and the availability of labor. In terms of equipment and staff, the Nogin and the Krasnyi Profintern Mills were among the largest in the IPO. All of Vichuga's mills were constructed in the nineteenth century and were situated within several kilometers of one another. TsDNIIO, f. 327, op. 4, d. 603, pages showing mill employment levels as of 1 January and 1 October 1932; op. 5, d. 162, l. 9; *Raiony Ivanovskoi promyshlennoi oblasti*, part 1: *Ekonomicheskaia kharakteristika* (henceforth, *Raiony IPO*) (Moscow/Ivanovo, 1933), pp. 24–26; *Tekstil'nye fabriki SSSR* (Moscow, 1927), pp. 14–15, 38–39, 58–63.

[9] *Raiony IPO*, pp. 26, 250; *Ivanovskaia oblast' za 50 let* (Ivanovo, 1967), p. 27.

[10] TsDNIIO, f. 327, op. 4, d. 449, l. 7; Gosudarstvennyi arkhiv Ivanovskoi oblasti (henceforth, GAIO), f. 1276, op. 23, d. 7, ll. 253–55; GARF, f. 374, op. 27, d. 1988, ll. 58–59; 115–14 (in some instances, documents in GARF are numbered backward); RGASPI, f. 81, op. 3, d. 213, ll. 3–15. Many of the workers hired to staff the night shift were housewives whose child-rearing responsibilities hindered their performance on the shop floor, since child-care facilities were few. GAIO, f. 1276, op. 23, d. 7, l. 254. As of 1 October 1932, a majority of workers in the typical IPO mill were women, party members were a small minority, and rank-and-file communists were more likely to be men than women. In Vichuga, women constituted 73.6 percent of the labor force at the Nogin Mill, 66.5 percent at the Shagov Mill, and 63.9 percent at the Krasnyi Profintern Mill; communists constituted 9.1 percent, 7.1 percent, and 6.3 percent of the labor force, respectively; and men made up 61.4 percent, 62.5 percent, and 63.5 percent of the rank-and-file communists, respectively. TsDNIIO, f. 327, op. 4, d. 603, page showing mill employment levels as of 1 October 1932.

View of the exterior of the Nogin Mill in Vichuga, Ivanovo region, Russian Federation, 1994. (Photo by author.)

half the rank and file bothered to attend mandatory assemblies. Meanwhile, communists failed to carry out agitation among the mill's nonparty workers.[11]

As was the case in other industrialized parts of the IPO, about half of the Vichuga district's land and peasant households were collectivized as of 1 January 1933, and the high proportion of workers with ties to the land—51.5 percent of the Krasnyi Profintern Mill's payroll on the eve of the strike—explains why a rank-and-file communist, speaking at an assembly of Iaroslavl' party members, and an IPO official, speaking at a regional (*oblast'*) committee plenum, noted in the aftermath of the April 1932 uprising that "anti-Soviet moods" and discontent over collectivization were common on Vichuga's shop floors.[12] Such moods were reflected in a re-

[11] TsDNIIO, f. 327, op. 4, d. 449, ll. 2–7, 45, 130, 138–39; d. 507, ll. 29–30; GAIO, f. 1276, op. 23, d. 7, ll. 11, 255; GARF, f. 374, op. 27, d. 1988, l. 114.

[12] *Raiony IPO*, pp. 26, 250–51; TsDNIIO, f. 327, op. 4, d. 449, l. 7; d. 508, l. 34; op. 5, d. 162, l. 9. Of the 3,862 Krasnyi Profintern workers who reported ties to the land on 1 April 1932, 52 percent were collective farmers and 48 percent were *edinolichniki* (peasants who farmed privately, outside the collective-farm sector). While 51.5 percent of Krasnyi Profintern workers had ties to the land, the figure at the Nogin Mill was only 20 percent. TsDNIIO, f. 327, op. 5, d. 162, ll. 9, 20. Data for the region's other textile mills were collected in November 1932

mark made in late 1930 by a male Krasnyi Profintern worker: "How can the communists not be ashamed of going into the villages and seizing the last of the peasant's bread and potatoes? The only thing left to fleece off him is his skin!"[13]

If recent recruits from the countryside were disaffected, so too were workers with many years of experience on the shop floor. ("Cadre workers" were a majority in the mills: for instance, as of 1 January 1933, they comprised 63.1 percent of the Nogin Mill's labor force.)[14] A report by the OGPU indicated that the workers' spokesmen often were ex-communists or former members of non-Bolshevik parties—that is, the most politically active members of the labor force.[15] At a conference of Krasnyi Profintern workers in late 1930, a certain Moshkarev made no effort to conceal his opinion of the state: "The Soviet regime drinks the blood of the workers and the peasants more than any other government." The weaver Liubimova demanded that workers take action forthwith: "When this five-year plan ends, you'll be going to and from work on nothing but bread. We must insist that one of the rulers from the center sees what the worker has come to." A spinner named Kozlov called on workers to take matters into their own hands: "They haven't begun to supply us and they aren't giving us any money. Lenin taught us how to fight, so now we must fight and look after our own well-being." Others questioned the loyalty of Stalin and Kalinin and expressed support for "proletarian leaders of the party" such as Trotsky, Rykov, Bukharin, and Zinoviev, who suffered because they spoke "the truth" and defended "the proper line."[16]

Similar attitudes could be found in party cells. A male communist at the Krasnyi Profintern Mill condemned labor-intensification measures during remarks to a group of workers in January 1931: "We are in the fourteenth year [of the revolution]: we're starving, [and] there haven't been any improvements, but they make us work at accelerated tempos." Echoed a female party member: "Where are we headed? To the deterioration of the condition of the working class." The same year, three of the Nogin Mill's male party members denounced current labor policies: "All the measures

---

and included office personnel as well as workers: at the Shagov Combine, 11.3 percent had ties to the land; at the Krasin Mill, 25.7 percent; at Krasnyi Oktiabr', 26.4 percent. GARF, f. 5457, op. 23, d. 199, l. 59.

[13] GAIO, f. 1276, op. 23, d. 7, l. 13.

[14] TsDNIIO, f. 327, op. 5, d. 162, l. 9.

[15] Significantly, the Socialist Revolutionaries had a strong following on Vichuga's shop floors in 1917. TsDNIIO, f. 2, op. 12, d. 74, l. 167.

[16] GAIO, f. 1276, op. 23, d. 7, ll. 13–14.

being carried out now are an unnecessary burden for the workers." A male communist fitter concurred: "It's become very difficult to live. It's worse than under the [former] mill owner, Konovalov."[17]

The collapse of shop-floor morale had a deleterious effect on production. In 1931, the OGPU recorded about a dozen episodes of unrest in Vichuga's mills.[18] In early 1932, rates of absenteeism and turnover escalated, which along with myriad production problems (most importantly, high levels of equipment idleness) made it impossible for the mills to fulfill production goals.[19] As wages fell further into arrears, fraud and incompetence in the cooperatives, cutbacks by central and regional supply organs, compulsory transfers of regionally cultivated potatoes to centers of heavy industry, and the failure of grain shipments to arrive on time precipitated the unauthorized cancellation or reduction of rations for many families, who soon found themselves relying on friends and relatives for support—or teetering on the brink of starvation.[20] As for the town's stores and cooperatives, Kaganovich reported in April 1932 that they were "virtually empty."[21]

Although their options were limited, local authorities made few efforts to ameliorate the suffering. According to a regional party committee official, Fomenko, lower party organizations underestimated the significance of keeping workers adequately supplied: "People don't understand that a

[17] GAIO, f. 1276, op. 23, d. 7, ll. 11, 254.

[18] GAIO, f. 1276, op. 23, d. 7, ll. 8–14, 57–59, 83, 91–94, 97, 106, 113, 146, 230, 288, 293, 296, 330, 357.

[19] GAIO, f. 1283, op. 1, d. 459, ll. 52–54; f. 2888, op. 1, d. 49, ll. 70–72.

[20] TsDNIIO, f. 327, op. 4, d. 516, l. 25; GARF, f. 374, op. 27, d. 1988, l. 84; RGASPI, f. 81, op. 3, d. 213, ll. 3–15, 21, 23–24, 26, 28, 48–49, 51–56, 59–61. The hardest hit were the labor force's one hundred or so single parents, mostly women, who were given no advantages by the supply agencies and who therefore found it all but impossible to support their dependents. Exacerbating the suffering was the fact that kindergartens started to give children only half their daily ration of 100 grams of bread. After the strike, Kaganovich estimated that single parents with three to four dependents were receiving "less than half a pound of bread per day" per family member. Families with several wage earners and few children were somewhat shielded from the shortages, as were those fortunate enough by virtue of either their ties to the land or forethought to have reserves on hand. RGASPI, f. 81, op. 3, d. 213, ll. 3–15, 90–92.

[21] RGASPI, f. 81, op. 3, d. 213, ll. 3–15, 26, 28. For a breakdown of items sent to Vichuga and the IPO as a whole by central supply agencies, see RGASPI, f. 81, op. 3, d. 213, ll. 19–20, 26. Other documents (ll. 21, 23–24, 28) reveal that cooperatives never received many of the shipments for which they paid and misappropriated or squandered a fair portion of the rest. Despite much official rhetoric about the abuse of ration cards, a "verification" carried out in March 1932 (l. 24) by the Nogin cooperative found that only 3.5 percent of cards in circulation were illicit.

political mood forms around a bowl of soup, that a political mood forms around an empty thermos."[22]

The Vichuga Uprising

On 12 March 1932, a student at Vichuga's Textile Technical College, Kholshchevnikov, contradicted official assertions about popular living conditions during a session of his "Current Politics" study circle: "The condition of the working class isn't improving, as was stated in the decisions of the Seventeenth Party Conference, but is deteriorating. As a result of the intensifying food difficulties, the workers' real wages are falling. The workers are beginning to starve." The civics teacher at the school, Aristov, validated Kholshchevnikov's assertions and, in lectures to his classes, reiterated them. Not only was mortality rising as a result of falling living standards, he declared, but the party's misguided efforts to build socialism were to blame.[23]

Not surprisingly, such remarks created a stir both at the college and on shop floors, where "the starving existence of the workers" had become the major topic of conversation among students, engineering-technical workers, and the rank and file. Remarks that P. S. Borisov made to his fellow teachers at Factory School No. 1 show that the erosion of faith was advanced even among those charged with mobilizing support for Moscow's program. Borisov argued, "What Aristov said is the truth, and I fully share his thoughts. I won't go to the workers to lead discussions and to convince them of something in which I myself don't believe. You won't build socialism in one country—Lenin himself wrote about that—and what is more, foreigners are convinced that the Soviet Union can be broken without a war, that they can wait quietly for a revolution in Russia itself, without an intervention on their part." Borisov concluded with a prescient analysis: "The condition in Russia is so tense now that one tremor is enough to detonate the atmosphere that has been created."[24]

When party secretaries finally assembled their members to combat the proliferation of such "Trotskyite" moods, they found some of the rank and file unwilling to toe the line. Declared the communist I. V. Zatroev of the Shagov Combine, "The third decisive year of the five-year plan was critical, and, having endured it, we thought 'supplies will improve,' but it turned out exactly the other way around. Last year we received fish and meat,

[22] GARF, f. 374, op. 27, d. 1988, ll. 84–83; TsDNIIO, f. 327, op. 4, d. 449, l. 6.
[23] RGASPI, f. 81, op. 3, d. 213, ll. 72–76.
[24] Ibid.

even if only a little, but now we see nothing. We've reached the point where there's not even anything with which to grease the lampions. We have to improve centralized supply, and not rely on the laying-in of our own supplies [*samozagotovki*]." Although few party members openly supported his speech, Zatroev claimed to be representing their views: "Many are in agreement with me, you know, but are afraid to speak. I'm afraid of nothing at all and will always say what I think."[25]

Meanwhile, the "discontent" of the nonparty labor force manifested itself in rumors that workers with ties to the land would be removed from the ration rolls and the escalation of complaints among the six hundred Nogin employees who failed to get any flour from the cooperative in February. Although the shop floor's frustration culminated in scattered slowdowns and work stoppages on 25 March, the district party committee ignored OGPU reports detailing "the signals of swelling discontent."[26]

Frustrated by the stonewalling, a crowd of Nogin workers marched to the center of town on 31 March and demanded that district authorities give them their back rations immediately. Upon being rebuffed, the demonstrators elected a delegation of workers to go to Moscow to complain. Notified of the conflict, OGPU agents promptly intercepted the delegates, preventing them from leaving town.[27]

During the first week of April, the Vichuga district committee belatedly responded to Moscow's order to cut rations by 31 to 47 percent for workers and 50 percent for dependents by convening closed assemblies of party, Komsomol, and trade-union cells. In response to the "discontent" that rumors of the cutback had aroused—manifested in a one-hour strike among the Nogin Mill's white-collar employees—party officials chose not to convene general assemblies, which were notoriously difficult to control. Instead, the reduction in ration levels was to be explained during special assemblies held at the level of the brigade or workshop.[28]

Ironically, it was officialdom's refusal to convene general assemblies that triggered the first protests. On Sunday, 3 April, a group of 150 workers stormed out of an assembly at the Nogin Mill's club, "burst into the factory, and demanded the summoning of an all-factory conference on food supply." The next day, two worker assemblies at Shagov Mill No. 1 ended in the same manner. In an indication of the role that official stonewalling

25 Ibid.

26 RGASPI, f. 81, op. 3, d. 213, ll. 3–15, 72–76; TsDNIIO, f. 327, op. 4, d. 449, l. 145. One reason for the district party committee's inaction was that the local supply organization had grossly underreported the number of families for which it lacked flour.

27 RGASPI, f. 81, op. 3, d. 213, ll. 3–15, 72–76.

28 RGASPI, f. 81, op. 3, d. 213, ll. 3–15, 50–51, 62, 72–76; GARF, f. 374, op. 27, d. 1988, l. 92.

played in the escalation of the conflict, agitation in favor of a strike and unauthorized shop-floor assemblies proliferated as soon as it became clear that the workers' demand to deal collectively with the crisis was being rebuffed.[29]

On Tuesday, 5 April, weavers from Shagov Mill No. 1 continued to condemn managers' efforts to keep workers isolated from one another: "Why are you assembling us in small groups? Convene general worker assemblies, where we, too, [will] speak." Overwhelmed by the discontent, their superiors finally relented and allowed several departments to meet jointly. As feared, however, the assemblies became "very noisy" as soon as the reduction in ration levels was announced. At one such meeting, moreover, the fitter Tezin and the weaver Zabelkina pointedly asked their colleagues "to organize a strike."[30]

As a result of such agitation, weavers gathered outside the Shagov Combine at the end of work that day and agitated in favor of a strike and a general assembly. Not surprisingly, other workers immediately offered their support. Informed of the disturbance, the district committee dispatched several officials to explain the situation to the demonstrators, who eventually dispersed. Convinced that order had been restored, notwithstanding OGPU reports to the contrary, the district committee quickly turned its attention to "routine matters." Meanwhile, support for a collective response to the crisis mounted on shop floors and in working-class communities across town.[31]

Wednesday through Friday

Under the leadership of Zabelkina and Tezin, almost all the workers at Shagov Weaving Mill No. 1 struck from 9:30 to 11:00 A.M. on 6 April and demanded a factorywide assembly to discuss food supplies. Workers from the second shift struck from 1:00 to 3:00 P.M. in support of the same demand. Although agitation by district committee officials and the arrest of the organizers brought those job actions to an end, operations in Spinning Mill No. 1 ground to a halt at 4:00 P.M. as a result of anger over the new policy and officialdom's unwillingness to allow workers to act collectively.[32]

In an indication of the depth of support for a collective response, the secretary of the party cell in one of the Shagov weaving sheds—Buev, a communist since 1924—was an "instigator" of the strike there, and at least

[29] RGASPI, f. 81, op. 3, d. 213, ll. 3–15, 72–76.

[30] GARF, f. 374, op. 27, d. 1988, l. 92; TsDNIIO, f. 327, op. 4, d. 516, l. 23; RGASPI, f. 81, op. 3, d. 213, ll. 3–15, 72–76.

[31] GARF, f. 374, op. 27, d. 1988, l. 92; RGASPI, f. 81, op. 3, d. 213, ll. 3–15, 64–67, 72–76.

[32] RGASPI, f. 81, op. 3, d. 213, ll. 3–15, 64–67, 72–76; GARF, f. 374, op. 27, d. 1988, l. 92; TsDNIIO, f. 327, op. 4, d. 516, l. 24.

six rank-and-file communists supported him. As for those who opposed the job action—mostly Komsomol and party members—they were immediately threatened with reprisals. Meanwhile, "persistent rumors" that a general strike was being organized for 8 April spread through Vichuga's shop floors.[33]

No disturbances were reported on 7 April, which was a day off for most workers. Pressed by the OGPU, the district committee finally convened a meeting of party-cell secretaries and factory committee chairmen to discuss "the workers' moods" and settle on "the tactics of struggle against the strike." A representative from the OGPU reported that strikers from the Shagov Combine were poised to send delegations to other factories, or even to march on them, in an effort to expand their protest. In the first of a series of bad decisions and missed opportunities, however, the district committee concluded that "concrete measures" did not have to be taken because the disturbances were unlikely to spread "beyond the confines of individual enterprises." Despite their intimate familiarity with the "sharp forms" of conflict that had already taken place in the district, Vichuga's leaders dismissed the OGPU's warnings as "exaggerated," thereby sacrificing the initiative.[34]

Notwithstanding the district committee's faith in its ability to maintain order, the strike resumed on 8 April. At the start of the first shift, at 5:00 A.M., workers at the Shagov Weaving Mill No. 1 and Spinning Mill No. 1 refused to start their machines. In a sign of gender solidarity, moreover, the overlookers—all of whom were, by tradition, male—now served as the enforcers of the strike, forcibly idling production lines and threatening those who withheld their support. As for party members, those in the spinning mill supported the strike, while those in the weaving shed did not.

Early that afternoon, workers arriving for the second shift joined protesters at the gates of the Shagov Combine. At 1:00 P.M., workers at Shagov Mill No. 3 and both of the Krasin enterprises idled their machines. Eventually, so did those at the remaining two Shagov Mills, Nos. 2 and 4. In an indication of their close contacts with one another, moreover, strikers everywhere demanded that monthly bread rations be restored to sixteen kilograms for workers and eight kilograms for dependents.[35]

As rumors of the day's events spread, tensions rose sharply even in

33 GARF, f. 374, op. 27, d. 1988, ll. 89–88; RGASPI, f. 81, op. 3, d. 213, ll. 3–15, 64–67; TsDNIIO, f. 327, op. 4, d. 449, l. 5.

34 This and the following paragraph are based on GARF, f. 374, op. 27, d. 1988, l. 92; and RGASPI, f. 81, op. 3, d. 213, ll. 3–15, 64–67, 72–76, 77.

35 GARF, f. 374, op. 27, d. 1988, ll. 92–91; RGASPI, f. 81, op. 3, d. 213, ll. 3–15, 72–76. One source states that workers at the Krasnyi Oktiabr' Mill, situated eighteen kilometers north of Vichuga, also went on strike that day. RGASPI, f. 81, op. 3, d. 213, ll. 64–67.

those mills that had yet to join the strike. Meanwhile, notwithstanding the fact that a number of district committee officials went to the Shagov and the Krasin mills to organize countermeasures, the response of Vichuga's notables left much to be desired. Though he knew that trouble was brewing, the chairman of the city soviet, Filippov, proceeded with his long-planned vacation and checked into a sanitarium. The head of the district party committee, Vorkuev, conveniently "fell ill" with tonsillitis after attending an assembly of angry Krasin workers—and stayed home for three days. Having received an OGPU account of the disturbances soon after they began, the chairman of the district soviet executive committee, Aref'ev, nonetheless went to visit his wife in Rybinsk. Finally, the district prosecutor, Krutikov, disobeyed warnings from the Control Commission and "deserted" his post.[36]

By succumbing to panic and refusing to fulfill their duties, Filippov, Vorkuev, Aref'ev, and Krutikov revealed the depths of their alienation from the shop floor and ceded the initiative to the strikers. As a result, noted Kaganovich, "the district found itself to all intents and purposes without leaders," which paralyzed the organs of authority and rank-and-file party members. As for those officials who dutifully remained at their posts, they miscalculated the significance of the uprising, delayed placing the emergency call for help to the regional party committee, and quickly lost control of the situation.

Curiously, the chaos in the ranks of officialdom contrasted sharply with the cohesiveness of the shop floor. Although the Vichuga strike was the largest and most geographically dispersed of the April 1932 strikes, its organizers were no less nimble than their counterparts in other mill towns. Perhaps because there were so many leaders of the demonstrations, the sources reveal little about them. Nevertheless, a regional party committee official, Fomenko, later spoke enviously of their ability to mount "a counterrevolutionary organization" that won the loyalty of the town's workers. "You know," he said, "it's an established fact that they convened a conference in the forest. During the strike itself information was purveyed perfectly well, [and] they responded to our measures very flexibly. There were moments when they tapped into the [telegraph] wires, put forward their own Morse code signalers, and so on. Despite the fact that all the preconditions for exposing this organization had been met, the party organization slept through all this." In his report to Stalin, Kaganovich also

[36] This and the following paragraph are based on GARF, f. 374, op. 27, d. 1988, ll. 89, 91; TsDNIIO, f. 327, op. 4, d. 449, l. 145; d. 509, l. 68; op. 5, d. 162, l. 146; and RGASPI, f. 81, op. 3, d. 213, ll. 3–15, 64–67, 90–92.

noted that the strike's leaders enjoyed excellent "reconnaissance" and "the closest communication" with other mill towns—including, significantly, those engulfed by disturbances of their own.[37]

Saturday

On the morning of 9 April, two warp drawers from the Nogin Mill—Iurkin, a former communist who quit the party in 1922 on account of "political differences," and Komarov, who allegedly hailed from "prosperous peasants"—demanded that an all-factory conference be convened to deal with the crisis. Soon all their colleagues in the department and a number of dressers idled their machines and marched to the factory committee. "Give us bread!" they demanded. "We won't work for eleven kilograms!"[38]

At the Krasin Mill and Shagov Mill No. 1, meanwhile, weavers continued to strike. At the Shagov Combine, the strikers soon persuaded the spinners to join them. (Damage to equipment and attacks against party and nonparty opponents of the job action occurred after workers from Mills Nos. 1 and 3 broke into Mill No. 2.) By early afternoon, most of the Shagov Mill's 66,900 spindles and 2,158 looms lay idle.[39]

At 2:30 P.M., the Shagov strikers resolved to expand the movement and headed for the Nogin Mill. On the way, they eagerly invited passersby to join them. Twenty-nine-year-old Grigorii Simov, a heating engineer employed at the Krasnyi Profintern Mill, spotted an acquaintance in the crowd: "How did you wind up here?" he inquired. "So you really don't want to eat?!" came the response. "We're going to get workers from the [Nogin] Mill." Attempts were also made to agitate among Red Army troops, one of whom was threatened after he tried to intervene: "So it seems you're a communist? Well then, we should rough you up!" Likewise, brawls ensued when the strikers came upon a group of communists and Komsomol members who had been dispatched to intercept them.[40]

Upon reaching the Nogin Mill, the strikers cast rocks through the windows, broke through a line of Komsomol members stationed at the gates, and penetrated shop floors, where they demanded that everyone "stop work." Venting their anger, the intruders, under the leadership of Iurkin, also proceeded to smash equipment, destroy supplies, and beat their opponents. Outside, meanwhile, a crowd took control of the entrance to the

[37] TsDNIIO, f. 327, op. 4, d. 449, l. 5; RGASPI, f. 81, op. 3, d. 213, ll. 3–15.

[38] RGASPI, f. 81, op. 3, d. 213, ll. 3–15, 64–67, 93–95.

[39] GARF, f. 374, op. 27, d. 1988, l. 91; RGASPI, f. 81, op. 3, d. 213, ll. 3–15; *Raiony IPO*, p. 26.

[40] GARF, f. 374, op. 27, d. 1988, l. 91; Arkhivnoe podrazdelenie upravleniia federal'noi sluzhby bezopasnosti po Ivanovskoi oblasti (henceforth, APUFSBIO), d. 8537-p, l. 130b.; RGASPI, f. 81, op. 3, d. 213, ll. 64–67, 72–76.

mill and agitated among those scheduled to work the night shift, such as forty-five-year-old Pavel Korotkov, a nonparty warp drawer who lived in town with his wife and five children. Having asked two overlookers what they were doing, Korotkov was told that they intended to increase their numbers or, at a minimum, prevent anyone else from working.[41]

Most Nogin workers were sympathetic to the demands made by the Shagov strikers; indeed, some fifteen hundred of them (over half of those on duty) joined the protest that day. Although most dissenters maintained a low profile, a handful spoke out: "Comrade workers from the Shagov Mill!" shouted one party member. "There's nothing for you to do here! We won't join you, and we cast shame on you!" Just as he spoke, however, a large number of workers poured out of the mill in a show of support for the demonstration. During the next five days, most of the Nogin Mill's production lines lay idle.[42]

As soon as it became clear that the demand for a restoration of rations was popular and that most nonparty workers supported the strike, some women in the crowd demanded a further expansion of the protest: "Comrades!" they shouted. "Let's go to the Tezinskaia Mill!" Under the leadership of Iurkin, Komarov, and several of their female colleagues, the crowd of some three thousand strikers proceeded to march to the Krasnyi Profintern Mill, where Iurkin made a poignant appeal for solidarity: "Comrades, we'll die from hunger in the fifteenth year of the revolution, our children will die, and what will we do—be silent? If Stalin were put on

[41] RGASPI, f. 81, op. 3, d. 213, ll. 64–67, 72–76, 93–95; APUFSBIO, d. 8537-p, ll. 5, 7ob., 8ob.–13ob.–14, 17. Korotkov grew up in a poor peasant family in a village near Vichuga and entered the labor force at the age of twelve, when he landed a job as a warp drawer at one of the Morokin (Shagov) mills. His tenure on the shop floor was interrupted by compulsory military service (1909–12, 1914–17), and by the collapse of the economy in 1918. During the Civil War, he worked as a greaser in a grist mill in Khar'kov region. In 1921, he returned with his family to Vichuga, helped organize a workers' food cooperative, and was elected by mill hands to run their cafeteria for a year. During the rest of the NEP, he earned a living as a freelance stove setter. (His declining eyesight made it difficult for him to continue full-time in the weaving shed.) After dabbling briefly in trading, Korotkov was exiled in 1929 to Enisei region for purchasing stolen goods. Upon his return to Vichuga eighteen months later, he supported his family by working as a stove setter at the Shagov Combine and a warp drawer at the Nogin Mill. Despite his many years of service in industry, he was branded "a former tradesman" by OGPU investigators. Korotkov's wife worked as a weaver at the Shagov from 1902 to 1918 and sold bread after returning to Vichuga in 1921. She also purchased a trading license and opened a grocery shop, but in 1924 was deprived of her civil rights during a crackdown on "speculators." APUFSBIO, d. 8537-p, ll. 5–5ob., 8ob., 13ob., 17, 19, 33ob.–35, 37.

[42] GARF, f. 374, op. 27, d. 1988, l. 91; RGASPI, f. 81, op. 3, d. 213, ll. 3–15, 72–76; APUFSBIO, d. 8537-p, ll. 8ob., 12.

a ration of eleven kilograms, then he would probably leave the party. Eleven kilograms don't make sixteen, and four kilograms don't make eight. They lubricate the machine with oil, but what do they lubricate us with? Will the comrades be left behind and not support us?"[43]

Typically, workers responded by abandoning their machines. Even a small number of the Krasnyi Profintern Mill's communists—twenty-nine out of five hundred, to be exact—sided with the strikers. (After assuring them that they would not be docked pay, one candidate member of the party, Varentsov, led his coworkers out of the factory; another, Zakharov, galvanized support for the strike by conceding that "all the communists are self-aggrandizers" who "have forgotten the interests of the working class.") As for those who resisted—typically, either communists or Komsomol members—they were beaten with shuttles and their machines sabotaged. Gradually, the number of demonstrators outside the mill surpassed five thousand.[44]

In his speech to the crowd, Iurkin explained why he had joined the strike: "Comrades, I earn 200 rubles, I have a family of two, and no children. I have an adequate supply of bread, but I speak for the workers and the peasants, not for the briefcases and deceivers who drive the workers to the grave." His message was clear: those who had enough to eat, like himself, had a moral obligation to side with those who did not. Conscious of the dangers of speaking out, Iurkin won sympathy by refusing to be intimidated by the OGPU: "I know they'll seize me, but I hope that you'll support me." Inspired by his courage, other speakers vowed that the strike would continue until rations were restored. As for those who dared to condemn the protest, they were subjected to verbal and physical abuse.[45]

By the end of the day, almost every enterprise in Vichuga was on strike. Flush with success, several thousand strikers carried their protest to the district's only outpost of heavy industry: Machine-Building Plant No. 6 ("the metal factory"), whose 425 employees fabricated parts for textile equipment. In a sign of the gender- and sector-defined boundaries of class solidarity, however, the plant's (male) workers rebuffed every attempt to win their support.[46]

[43] GARF, f. 374, op. 27, d. 1988, l. 91; APUFSBIO, d. 8537-p, l. 8ob.; RGASPI, f. 81, op. 3, d. 213, ll. 3–15, 64–67, 72–76.

[44] GARF, f. 374, op. 27, d. 1988, l. 91; TsDNIIO, f. 327, op. 4, d. 449, l. 5; RGASPI, f. 81, op. 3, d. 213, ll. 3–15, 64–67, 72–76, 85, 90–92.

[45] RGASPI, f. 81, op. 3, d. 213, ll. 3–15, 64–67, 72–76.

[46] RGASPI, f. 81, op. 3, d. 213, ll. 3–15; GARF, f. 374, op. 27, d. 1988, l. 91; TsDNIIO, f. 327, op. 5, d. 162, ll. 137–38. The metalworkers' refusal to join the strike is barely illuminated by

As for Korotkov, he stayed behind at the Nogin Mill with two hundred other strikers, including a fellow warp drawer, Golubev. The demonstrators applauded speeches by a woman worker and a fitter employed at the Krasnyi Profintern Mill, Kostkin, both of whom called on management to come out and negotiate. The crowd also agitated among employees scheduled to work the night shift, and several who sought to enter the mill were beaten. The strikers' calls for negotiations were rebuffed, however, and by 9:00 P.M. just about everyone—including those scheduled to work overnight—went home.[47]

Having finally received word of the strike enveloping one of their most important centers of industry, the regional party committee dispatched a commission (the Ivanovo commission), whose members included El'zov, Fomenko, Gribova, Kisel'nikov, Kotsen, and Sever'ianova of the regional committee Secretariat; Koriagin and Postnova of the Control Commission; Semagin of the Council of Trade Unions; Andreev and Ivanov of the OGPU; and Novikov and Sulimov of the civil police. After nightfall, the secret police arrested Iurkin, one of the workers' most popular spokesmen, and conveyed him secretly to Ivanovo for interrogation. Little did they know that Iurkin's arrest would only increase his authority on the shop floor and provoke a violent escalation of the conflict.[48]

Sunday

At the crack of dawn on 10 April, groups of strikers appeared at the gates of Vichuga's mills in a coordinated effort to enforce the job action. Again, opponents of the strike were treated harshly. By 7:00 A.M. all production lines had been idled, at which point the strikers again turned their attention to the machine-building plant. Although the entrances were being guarded by communists, the strikers managed to break through the gates, penetrate shop floors, and clear them of workers. (So as to avoid "a slaughter," the plant's employees had been ordered by the party secretary not to resist.) Still, most of the metalworkers refused to en-

---

the sources. The fact that their rations were cut as much as the strikers' only deepens the mystery. What could have generated their sense of isolation? First, the machine-building plant was a tiny outpost of heavy industry in a light-industry town. Second, its product—spare parts for textile equipment—was in extremely high demand. Third, its employees were all men. Taken together, these factors probably created a sense of privilege that impeded identification with rank-and-file (mostly female) textile workers.

47 APUFSBIO, d. 8537-p, ll. 70b., 80b.–9; GARF, f. 374, op. 27, d. 1988, l. 91; RGASPI, f. 81, op. 3, d. 213, ll. 3–15, 64–67, 72–76.

48 GARF, f. 374, op. 27, d. 1988, ll. 31–30, 60; RGASPI, f. 81, op. 3, d. 213, ll. 3–15, 34–37, 90–92. Apparently, Iurkin was the only leader arrested during the strike. RGASPI, f. 81, op. 3, d. 213, l. 89.

dorse the strike, and operations resumed as soon as the plant's sabotaged boilers were repaired.[49]

Meanwhile, many bystanders enthusiastically joined the demonstration. "It's necessary for me to go," the former tradesman Ignat'ev explained to his friends. "As an unemployed person, I'm a member of the committee, you know." Ignat'ev's mysterious reference to "the committee" lent some credence to Kaganovich's assertion that "the strike was led by an underground organization." "The character of the speeches, the strikers' slogans, the rapid change of tactics, the individual composition of the ringleaders," Kaganovich noted in his report to Stalin—"all this testifies to the organized character of the strike."[50]

To the extent that it did exist, however, the "strike committee" was far less sinister than Kaganovich imagined. Essentially, it was an ad hoc and continually changing group of individuals who struggled to give shape to a spontaneous outburst of popular discontent.[51] More significant, therefore, was another remark made by Ignat'ev—one that reflected the mounting frustration and foreshadowed the day's dramatic events. "If they gave us power," he asserted, "then we'd tear all those damned communists to pieces."[52]

By 10:00 A.M. some five thousand workers fulfilled a pledge made to Iurkin the night before and gathered in the square in front of the city soviet to demand the restoration of ration levels. When it became clear that their leader had been arrested, however, they demanded that he be released immediately. Although a false rumor—that a representative from the party's Central Committee would give a speech—generated premature expectations of compromise, the strikers refused to let local officials address them.[53]

In a desperate attempt to restore order, the authorities finally sent in the mounted police. Unwilling to disperse, the strikers fought back with objects scavenged from the streets. Overwhelmed, the contingent of officers retreated. Enraged, the crowd marched to the police station and, in an effort to find Iurkin, laid siege to the building.

[49] RGASPI, f. 81, op. 3, d. 213, ll. 3–15, 64–67, 72–76; TsDNIIO, f. 327, op. 5, d. 162, ll. 137–38.

[50] RGASPI, f. 81, op. 3, d. 213, ll. 3–15, 72–76.

[51] After interrogating scores of witnesses, the OGPU conceded in its July 1932 report to Kaganovich that it had been unable, after all, to identify "a counterrevolutionary organization" as the organizer of "the Vichuga events." RGASPI, f. 81, op. 3, d. 213, ll. 93–95.

[52] RGASPI, f. 81, op. 3, d. 213, ll. 72–76.

[53] This and the following paragraph are based on GARF, f. 374, op. 27, d. 1988, ll. 31, 91–90; RGASPI, f. 81, op. 3, d. 213, ll. 3–15, 34–37, 64–67, 72–76; APUFSBIO, d. 8537-p, l. 9; and d. 8545-p, l. 20b.

After overpowering the guards at the entrance to the police station, the most active group of strikers confronted the chief of police, Mokhov, with their demand. Frustrated by the response—that Iurkin was not there and that his whereabouts were unknown—they proceeded to beat up every officer in the building, ransack offices, rummage through arrest files, and search for an entrance to the holding chamber. "What are you looking for?" a bystander asked two young men who led the assault. "Iurkin!" replied one of them: "I'm going to look for Iurkin until I find him!" "Iurkin must be here! He was seen only today!" Eventually, the invaders broke into the holding chamber and liberated those being held in custody, including the petty criminals. Iurkin, however, was not among them. (He was already in an Ivanovo OGPU cell.) Their plan foiled, the strikers vented their rage by smashing windows, tearing out doors and cabinets, and pummeling Mokhov and his deputy, Shantsev, to the point of unconsciousness.[54]

Outside, repeated attempts by a detachment of mounted police to disperse the crowd ended in failure. Unwilling to disperse, the workers defended themselves with rocks and sticks. After watching his men sustain "serious injuries," their commander, Chistiakov, ordered them to pull back to the railroad tracks and then to reassemble at the fire station. During their chaotic retreat, however, a junior officer was thrown from his horse and beaten unconscious with his own rifle by a group of strikers.[55]

Responding to a rumor that "a mass meeting" was underway at the district committee, the strikers now laid siege to the headquarters of the party and the OGPU, which were situated next to one another in the cen-

[54] RGASPI, f. 81, op. 3, d. 213, ll. 3–15, 34–37, 64–67, 72–76; GARF, f. 374, op. 27, d. 1988, ll. 31, 90; APUFSBIO, d. 8537-p, l. 9; 8545-p, ll. 2ob., 7ob., 8ob. According to Komsomol member Pavel Finoedov, the two young men who led the search for Iurkin were eighteen-year-old Nikolai Nikitin, a migrant from Kazan region who had briefly apprenticed as a chef at the Nogin Mill's factory kitchen, and a certain Sozin, a worker who lived in the same settlement, Gol'chikha, as Iurkin. Nikitin admitted that he had observed the assault but claimed that he had not participated. (Two other witnesses placed Nikitin outside the police station at the time of the uprising.) The sources do not clarify Nikitin's precise role, but he was an easy target for prosecution: young, orphaned, unemployed, and critical of Soviet power, he could easily be portrayed as one of the "class-alien and hooligan elements" who were predictably blamed for the uprising. APUFSBIO, d. 8545-p, ll. 2–2ob., 4ob., 5ob., 6ob.–7ob., 8ob., 10ob.; GARF, f. 374, op. 27, d. 1988, l. 90; RGASPI, f. 81, op. 3, d. 213, ll. 3–15, 72–76. Others in the crowd that day included workers from the Krasnyi Profintern Mill, such as Iakov Pankov and the weaver Pavel Sholev, and assorted bystanders, such as the petty tradeswoman Rozova. Because his wife was ill, which required him to look after their children, Korotkov missed the day's events. He received updates, however, from Pankov and his in-law Sholev; and he heard the clashes from afar. APUFSBIO, d. 8537-p, ll. 9, 34; RGASPI, f. 81, op. 3, d. 213, ll. 69–71.

[55] RGASPI, f. 81, op. 3, d. 213, ll. 34–37; APUFSBIO, d. 8545-p, ll. 7ob., 8ob.; d. 8537-p, l. 9. Fortunately, the officer's rifle was not loaded with ammunition.

ter of town. By now, the conflict was as much about visiting vengeance upon the detested organs of authority as it was about locating Iurkin. At the district party committee building, the strikers fulfilled the crowd's battle cry—"Beat the Chekisty and the communists!"—by pummeling the chairman of the local trade-union council, Rybakov, and the head of the regional party committee's Department of Cadres, El'zov. Three other regional party committee officials—Kotsen, Semagin, and Ivanov—fled the building in a panic just before the crowd took it over. Having been aroused from his "sickbed," meanwhile, the district committee secretary, Vorkuev, observed the assault from afar but still made no effort to defend his colleagues. (Questioned later by his superiors, Vorkuev lamely asserted that "a policeman kept me out" of the building.)[56]

Still hoping to find their leader, the strikers cornered the district head of the OGPU, Itkin: "Either give us Iurkin, or we'll kill you." After "negotiations" went nowhere, the crowd ransacked the OGPU building for two hours and set upon Itkin and his subordinates, some of whom burnt sensitive files before fleeing. Of all the officials targeted for revenge, Itkin came closest to losing his life. Dragged into the courtyard and beaten with bricks, he fell unconscious from multiple blows to the head. Fortunately, however, an unidentified worker spirited him to safety, which enabled plainclothes OGPU agents to get him into a cab, and then to a hospital.[57]

Meanwhile, a departmental chief from the Ivanovo OGPU, Golubev, "who had arrived in Vichuga the day before," appeared at the fire station and ordered the mounted police to recapture the OGPU building and liberate his subordinates. Arriving at the scene by automobile, ten officers—now under Golubev's direct command—met fierce "resistance" in the form of "a torrent of stones," resulting in "serious injuries" to some of them. After forcing their way inside and drawing their weapons, however, they managed to clear the building and secure the gates to the courtyard.[58]

Incensed by their treatment at the hands of the officers, the strikers promptly "surrounded the building from all sides," bombarded those standing in the courtyard with bricks and rocks, and began to ram the gates. ("*Ura!*" they shouted.) With only moments to spare before losing control of the building, Golubev ordered his men to fire their weapons into the air. Startled, the crowd pulled back. Seizing the moment, Gol-

[56] GARF, f. 374, op. 27, d. 1988, ll. 31, 90; RGASPI, f. 81, op. 3, d. 213, ll. 3–15, 34–37, 64–67, 72–76, ll. 90–92; TsDNIIO, f. 327, op. 4, d. 509, l. 68; op. 5, d. 162, l. 146.

[57] RGASPI, f. 81, op. 3, d. 213, ll. 3–15, 34–37, 64–67, 72–76; GARF, f. 374, op. 27, d. 1988, ll. 31, 57, 90. Besides Itkin, there were nine (male) agents and one (female) typist in the building when the strikers arrived.

[58] RGASPI, f. 81, op. 3, d. 213, ll. 3–15, 34–37, 64–67, 72–76.

ubev unlocked the gates and led his men outside. Although one worker lay dead in the street from a bullet wound, neither side backed down. Fearing a renewed assault on the building and still dodging projectiles, Golubev permitted his men to continue firing. Out of fear, panic, or lust for revenge, several of the officers aimed directly at the crowd. More shots were fired, and several more workers fell to the ground. The crowd fled for cover.[59]

By 4:30 P.M. Golubev's men had retaken all of Vichuga's administrative buildings. The strikers, meanwhile, regrouped in the square near the city soviet, at the train station, in cafeterias, and at the mills, where they again drove clusters of nonstriking workers from the shop floor and beat up communists, Komsomol members, and "even nonparty women" whose loyalty had come into question because, significantly, they wore red scarves. In an attempt to get the word out to workers in other districts and to deprive local authorities of communications with Ivanovo, the strikers even tried to occupy the post office. When that failed, however, they ingeniously found a way to tap directly into Vichuga's telegraph cables.[60]

After a meeting in the forest that evening, the strikers again descended on the mills, clearing shop floors of those who had remained at their posts, beating up party loyalists, plundering supplies, and—in a daring move that required penetration of several lines of defense—sabotaging the boilers that powered production lines. Later, eight members of "the strike committee," including the timekeeper and former party member Mironov of Shagov Spinning Mill No. 1, debated strategy at the home of Mironov's colleague, the flyer-frame spinner Surova. Having settled on a plan of action, they dispersed at 2:00 A.M. [61]

Within a matter of days, a strike whose goal was economic had turned into what IPO officials called "political banditism" and a witness described

[59] RGASPI, f. 81, op. 3, d. 213, ll. 3–15, 34–37, 64–67, 72–76; GARF, f. 374, op. 27, d. 1988, ll. 57, 90; APUFSBIO, d. 8537-p, l. 9. Kaganovich immediately ordered an investigation into the use of force; later, Central Committee investigators branded it "a great political mistake." RGASPI, f. 81, op. 3, d. 213, ll. 3–15, 90–92.

[60] GARF, f. 374, op. 27, d. 1988, ll. 31, 90; RGASPI, f. 81, op. 3, d. 213, ll. 3–15, 34–37, 64–67, 72–76; APUFSBIO, d. 8545-p, l. 3; TsDNIIO, f. 327, op. 4, d. 449, l. 5. On 11 April, strikers in Lezhnevo anxiously awaited delivery of a letter from their counterparts in Vichuga. RGASPI, f. 81, op. 3, d. 213, ll. 64–67.

[61] TsDNIIO, f. 327, op. 4, d. 449, l. 5; RGASPI, f. 81, op. 3, d. 213, ll. 3–15, 64–67, 69–71, 72–76. The sabotaging of the factory boilers was particularly dangerous because party cells had ordered their members to defend them "by all means" necessary—a task in which they were assisted by OGPU agents. In other instances, however, communists had been instructed not to resist the strikers. RGASPI, f. 81, op. 3, d. 213, ll. 3–15, 69–71.

as "a full-fledged revolt" against Vichuga's guarantors of order: the party, the OGPU, and the civil police.[62] The arrest of Iurkin, which the authorities later admitted was "a tactical mistake," infuriated the workers and gave the discontented among them a pretext for escalation.[63] Moreover, members of the social groups that the authorities referred to as "class-alien and hooligan elements"—that is, *lishentsy* (people deprived of civil rights, generally due to class origins), *byvshie liudi* (political, economic, and social elites from the old regime), the unemployed, juvenile delinquents, and so on—contributed to the radicalization of the strike by engaging in extraordinary acts of trespass and assault.[64] Still, most of the protesters were mill hands, and it was *their* rage that fueled the four-and-a-half-hour riot.[65]

As Kaganovich himself conceded in his report to Stalin, it was "significant" that the strikers attacked the district party committee, the OGPU, and the civil police, but spared the city soviet. Clearly, shop floors harbored no illusions about the loci of power. At the same time, they retained a modicum of allegiance to the main organ of state authority—specifically, "Soviet power"—which had sprung from the revolution and whose members remained subject to popular election. Two days later, several strike leaders confirmed Kaganovich's analysis: "We aren't against the soviets," they declared. "We gather[ed] on the square by the city soviet, and we sent a telegram to the TsIK [Tsentral'nyi ispolnitel'nyi komitet, or the Central Executive Committee of Soviets]. We didn't destroy the soviet, but the [O]GPU, the civil police, and the district [party] committee."[66]

A tally of the victims illustrates the extent of the violence that had descended upon Vichuga. Of the thirty to sixty rounds of ammunition fired by the police under Golubev's command, three broke flesh. The worker Polunin, who had a wife and child, died immediately; F. G. Dolgov, a twenty-five-year-old unskilled laborer in the Nogin Mill's storage facility and a recent peasant migrant from the Lower Volga region, succumbed to

[62] GARF, f. 374, op. 27, d. 1988, l. 90; Nina Dmitrievna Guseva, interview with author, Kineshma, Ivanovo region, 23 May 1994.

[63] GARF, f. 374, op. 27, d. 1988, l. 90; TsDNIIO, f. 327, op. 4, d. 449, l. 141.

[64] GARF, f. 374, op. 27, d. 1988, l. 90; RGASPI, f. 81, op. 3, d. 213, ll. 3–15.

[65] The siege of the organs of authority began at noon and was over by 4:30 P.M. APUFSBIO, f. 8545-p, l. 20b.; GARF, f. 374, op. 27, d. 1988, l. 31.

[66] RGASPI, f. 81, op. 3, d. 213, ll. 3–15. Such fine distinctions do not seem to have been shared by the district's deeply embittered peasants, two of whom—the twenty-five-year-old Reutskii and the forty-two-year-old Poliakov—led an assault during the strike against the Rep'evo sel'sovet in an effort to visit "reprisals" on its detested chairman. RGASPI, f. 81, op. 3, d. 213, ll. 93–95.

a blood infection while being treated in the hospital for a thigh wound; and a female worker suffered a slight graze.[67] Among the forces of order, the casualties were less serious, if more numerous: about thirty individuals, including half a dozen officials, sustained broken ribs, fractured skulls, and burst eardrums. As for those who opposed the strike and endeavored to keep production lines running, meanwhile, some seventy-two had been assaulted to date.[68]

As their behavior that day illustrated, regional party leaders were cognizant of the hostility that the population harbored toward the forces of order. The Ivanovo commission transferred its base of operations several times. On learning that the strikers were headed for the center of town, for example, they fled from the district party committee to the Krasnyi Profintern Mill. Later, hearing that a crowd was gathering nearby, they moved to the machine-building plant, whose shop floors remained immune to the calls for disobedience.[69]

To be sure, the highest-ranking official in Vichuga—Kotsen, the regional party committee's number two man—struggled to recapture the initiative. In response to the clashes, he eventually ordered Vichuga's "military commissar" to mobilize "a detachment of three hundred communists" and told the OGPU to "rescue" his Ivanovo commission colleague, El'zov, who had been stranded at the district party committee. After being assaulted by demonstrators, however, El'zov made it to safety on his own.

Kotsen's decisive actions could not conceal the fact that the local establishment, paralyzed by fear, had fallen into disarray. Not even the officials who remained on duty were effective: physically dispersed, they were unable to communicate with one another, which forced Kotsen to make decisions on the basis of "imprecise and exaggerated 'street' rumors." (For instance, he mobilized the three hundred communists after being

[67] RGASPI, f. 81, op. 3, d. 213, ll. 3–15, 34–37, 64–67, 90–92; GARF, f. 374, op. 27, d. 1988, ll. 37, 90. In response to Kaganovich's demand that the use of weapons against the crowd be thoroughly investigated, the OGPU reached three conclusions in a preliminary report filed four days after the clashes. First, confronted by an "extraordinarily tense" situation, the police had used their weapons only after "other measures to prevent the complete devastation of the building and the plundering of documents" had failed. Second, the three casualties probably were caused by bullets that ricocheted off a building on the other side of the street. Third, as the senior official on the scene and the author of the order to fire warning shots, Golubev of the Ivanovo OGPU bore responsibility for the tragedy. RGASPI, f. 81, op. 3, d. 213, ll. 3–15, 34–37.

[68] RGASPI, f. 81, op. 3, d. 213, ll. 3–15, 34–37, 89, 90–92. Overall, forty to fifty people were admitted to the hospital for strike-related injuries.

[69] This and the following two paragraphs are based on GARF, f. 374, op. 27, d. 1988, ll. 31–30; TsDNIIO, f. 327, op. 4, d. 449, l. 141; and d. 509, l. 68.

told that five thousand workers were headed to the OGPU to avenge the murder of three strikers. In fact, only one person was dead, and no one ventured near the building after the officers opened fire.)

Despite the confusion in his ranks, Kotsen did receive one piece of reliable information: the OGPU was in possession of a worker's bloody corpse. Realizing that the body could become a totem of the revolt, he ordered the agents to convey it secretly to the train station. Hoping to avert further bloodshed, he also instructed the civil police to pull back. An hour or so later, he convened an emergency meeting of mobilized communists beneath the semaphore. Although he forbade further applications of force against the strikers, he responded to a report that a crowd was on its way to the train station by ordering those with weapons to remain at his side. As for the rest, they were sent home without further instructions.[70]

Moments later, Kotsen fled to the station with his armed defenders, commandeered a train, and oversaw the removal of Polunin's "carefully wrapped" corpse from a delivery truck. The body was spirited into a makeshift coffin and onto the train. Loaded with corpse, armed communists, and four members of the Ivanovo commission (Kotsen, Ivanov, Semagin, and Kisel'nikov), the train departed shortly after 5:00 P.M. for Gorkino, a village situated twenty kilometers to the west of Vichuga. Despite all the commotion, Kotsen's macabre endeavor was successfully concealed.[71]

From Moscow's point of view, Kotsen's actions would have been acceptable had he communicated his plans to those left behind. His failure to do so, however, created the demoralizing impression that the Ivanovo commission "had retreated" and left the district "without leadership" at the height of the crisis. Worse, the confusion caused by the sudden departure of these officials was amplified when, at about 7:30 that evening, three other members of the Ivanovo commission fled town after mistakenly concluding that their base of operations had been transferred yet again.[72]

At the Gorkino station, Kotsen detached his wagon from the train and ordered the conductor to convey Polunin's body to Ivanovo. After reuniting with the other members of the Ivanovo commission, he learned that a "special train" of reinforcements—some 450 police officers and 17 OGPU agents—was en route from Kostroma; when it passed through the village, he attached his car to the rear. Shortly after 9:00 P.M., the seven most sen-

[70] GARF, f. 374, op. 27, d. 1988, unnumbered page between l. 31 and l. 30; RGASPI, f. 81, op. 3, d. 213, l. 79.

[71] Ibid.

[72] GARF, f. 374, op. 27, d. 1988, l. 30 and unnumbered page between l. 31 and l. 30; RGASPI, f. 81, op. 3, d. 213, l. 79.

ior members of the Ivanovo commission returned to Vichuga with fresh troops under their command. Although their cover-up succeeded, Kotsen and his colleagues displayed a lapse in judgment for which they would be reprimanded: aside from Fomenko, none was present in the aftermath of one of the most violent clashes ever between IPO workers and the Soviet state. Their authority still in question, they promptly convened a late-night session of the district party committee and outlined a "plan of action."[73]

Monday

On the morning of 11 April, a handful of workers who opposed the strike came into conflict again with strikers monitoring the gates of the mills, and it was not long before production ground to a halt. At 9:00 A.M., some two thousand strikers gathered on the square outside the city soviet and demanded that the day's meeting begin and a course of action be chosen. Most of the speakers were strikers who denounced the new ration levels ("We won't go to work until our demands are fulfilled!"), but several local and regional party leaders also addressed the crowd.[74]

Around 1:00 P.M., a member of the Ivanovo commission announced from a balcony overlooking the square that concessions could not be offered until everyone went back to work. The strikers rebuffed him ("Give a clear answer! What will you give us?"), and turned their attention to a weaver who recounted her latest experience of administrative callousness. A group of Shagov workers, she claimed, had summoned the chairman of the cooperative and complained about the new ration levels; instead of addressing their concerns, however, the official sarcastically dismissed them: "What sort of famine is *this* if we aren't eating our own children yet?" Not surprisingly, her story provoked further cries of indignation.[75]

Later, during his speech to the strikers, Korotkov ridiculed the portly official from Ivanovo: "The comrades have done no good at all. Look at him (I pointed to the provincial comrade). He's well fed, but we and our families are starving. Why shouldn't we yell at him? They get by and aren't as exhausted as the worker." A witness claimed that Korotkov also threatened violence against the official—"Down with him! Drag him off the rostrum! We should tear him to pieces!"—and told the crowd to go to the ma-

[73] GARF, f. 374, op. 27, d. 1988, l. 30; RGASPI, f. 81, op. 3, d. 213, ll. 69–71, 79.

[74] RGASPI, f. 81, op. 3, d. 213, ll. 3–15, 64–67, 72–76; APUFSBIO, d. 8537-p, l. 11ob.; d. 8545-p, l. 3. The OGPU claimed that its agents persuaded three hundred employees of the Krasnyi Profintern Mill (about 4 percent of its labor force) to return to work that day—which may explain why the most serious of the morning's clashes between strikers and nonstrikers took place there. RGASPI, f. 81, op. 3, d. 213, ll. 69–71, 72–76.

[75] APUFSBIO, d. 8537-p, ll. 9, 11ob.

chine-building plant and make yet another effort to engage its employees in the strike. More inflammatory speeches ensued, and the strikers demonstrated their anger by ignoring calls for order and refusing to let any other officials address them.[76]

Eventually, the deputy chairman of the district soviet executive committee, Smirnov, managed to win the crowd's attention with a proposal that a commission be elected "to settle the conflict." He then turned the podium over to the official from Ivanovo, who adopted a conciliatory tone and noted that such a commission would be allowed to investigate local food-supply organizations. In an appeal to the sentiments of the predominantly female labor force, he also called for a study of the nurseries, whose facilities left much to be desired.[77]

A long debate ensued, but the strikers were unable to overcome the gulf of hostility separating them from their superiors: "A series of speakers," noted an OGPU report, "insisted that proposals being put forth by representatives of party and soviet organizations not be accepted, and that [the workers] not go to work until all [their] demands were fulfilled."

A suggestion that the strikers send a delegation to Moscow—made by the recently "recovered" district committee secretary, Vorkuev—also was rejected.[78] Deeply suspicious, the workers feared that it was merely an attempt to decapitate their movement. Having fought so hard to meet collectively, they were unwilling to be driven apart in the absence of concrete achievements. "We'll withdraw everyone from work," the strikers declared, and "we're going to discuss everything together."

Convinced that local and regional bureaucrats would only betray them, the strikers decided to send a telegram to Mikhail Kalinin. After pausing long enough for a group to go to the Nogin Mill to drive a cluster of nonstriking workers from the shop floor, the crowd elected a commission consisting of three women and two men, who promptly withdrew to the offices of the district soviet executive committee to draft an appeal. Apparently, there was some disagreement over the wording, for the male members of the commission stepped down and had to be replaced. Eventually, however, the reconstituted commission completed its task, returned to the square, and submitted the text to the crowd. (Smirnov of the district soviet executive committee, whose voice carried well and whom

[76] APUFSBIO, d. 8537-p, ll. 11ob., 14, 17ob.

[77] This and the following two paragraphs are based on APUFSBIO, d. 8537-p, ll. 11ob.; and RGASPI, f. 81, op. 3, d. 213, ll. 3–15, 64–67, 72–76.

[78] Curiously, several workers interpreted Vorkuev's proposal as a sign of support for their demand, as a result of which they suggested that he be elected to "the strike committee." RGASPI, f. 81, op. 3, d. 213, ll. 3–15.

workers seemed to trust more than other officials, was recruited to read it aloud.) At 7:00 P.M., the strikers voted to transmit their appeal to Moscow. As commission members rushed to the post office to complete their mission, speakers called on their fellow strikers to stand firm until their demands were met. Gradually, the crowd dispersed.[79]

Graphic, succinct, and devoid of slogans, the telegram underscored that the gulf separating regional elites from the shop floor was so wide that nothing short of direct intervention by Moscow could bring the conflict to an end:

> [To:] Moscow, the Kremlin, the TsIK. As a result of the reduction of the food ration, the mass of fifteen thousand workers has left their factories and ceased work for five days now. The laboring mass has clashed with the police and the organs of the OGPU, where a bloody clash—with several injuries and victims—has taken place. The workers demand that three representatives from the TsIK come immediately to the site for settlement of the present conflict. Work has been discontinued until your departure. Of the workers who have given speeches, one comrade Iurkin has been seized. The masses demand his immediate release.
>
> Signed: Bol'shakov (Shagov Mill No. 3), Obukhov, Golubev (the Nogin Mill), Kostkin (the Krasnyi Profintern Mill).[80]

That night, "the strike committee" met again at the home of the spinner Surova. Meanwhile, the rural areas in which many workers lived began to stir. "Tomorrow . . . the peasants from neighboring villages intend to go to Vichuga to demand bread," announced a female peasant selling milk at the bazaar. "We've already sent delegates to Fediaevo [her village] to teach the chairman of the sel'sovet a lesson. The trouble is, we don't have any weapons. We'll have to go with just pitchforks and axes."[81]

[79] APUFSBIO, d. 8537-p, ll. 9–10, 11ob.–12, 17ob.; RGASPI, f. 81, op. 3, d. 213, ll. 3–15, 64–67, 72–76.

[80] RGASPI, f. 81, op. 3, d. 213, ll. 3–15, 72–76. It is not clear why the women on the commission that drafted the telegram did not sign it. As for those who did, Golubev was a warp drawer at the Nogin Mill, Obukhov was a worker at the same enterprise and "a Trotskyite who had been excluded from the Party," and Kostkin was a fitter in the machine shop of the Krasnyi Profintern Mill. APUFSBIO, d. 8537-p, ll. 8ob., 12; RGASPI, f. 81, op. 3, d. 213, ll. 3–15. The sources do not further identify Bol'shakov.

[81] RGASPI, f. 81, op. 3, d. 213, ll. 3–15, 72–76.

Tuesday

After a night of hasty preparations intended to jump-start production and undermine the strikers' solidarity, management opened the gates of Vichuga's mills at 5:00 A.M. on 12 April. Exhausted by a week of demonstrations, some 30 to 40 percent of those scheduled to work the morning shift reported to their posts. Efforts to enforce the job action, however, quickly cut that figure in half. During the second shift, staffing levels reached no more than 15 to 20 percent. As a result, "all the streets were filled to overflowing with agitated workers."[82]

Notwithstanding the low turnout at the mills, the authorities began to gain leverage over the situation: Kotsen ordered the hundreds of police officers under his command to enforce an overnight curfew; Kaganovich, who arrived at 9:30 A.M., had them encircle the town in an effort to seal it off from the outside world; and dozens of OGPU agents set about securing state property, infiltrating the crowd, and combating "strike moods" in the district's collective farms. By blocking all access to the town, the authorities inadvertently made it harder for management to restore production, but also kept many supporters of the IPO strike movement—both workers and peasants—from reaching its capital.[83]

Despite the show of force, it was too late for the authorities to isolate the strikers completely, as Kaganovich noted in his report to Stalin: "The Vichuga strikers were in contact with other districts. They wrote letters there and sent their representatives. In turn, people came to Vichuga in large groups from other mills and districts—'To study how to do this.' On the day of our arrival, 12 April, dozens of visitors with suitcases walked about Vichuga. All of them attended our speech at the club. There were many railroad workers in the crowd." As if the involvement of the transportation sector was not alarming enough, it was reported that some strikers were agitating among the peasantry.[84]

Buoyed by the support of neighboring communities, Vichuga's workers

[82] GARF, f. 374, op. 27, d. 1988, l. 90; RGASPI, f. 81, op. 3, d. 213, ll. 3–15.

[83] GARF, f. 374, op. 27, d. 1988, l. 90; RGASPI, f. 81, op. 3, d. 213, ll. 69–71; Gennadii Shutov, "Delo 'Filosofii': Dokumental'nyi ocherk," *Ivanovo-Voznesensk: Regional'naia gazeta Rossiiskogo soiuza promyshlennikov i predprinimatelei*, 1994, nos. 2–3 (35–36): 15; Marco Carynnyk, Lubomyr Y. Luciuk, and Bohdan S. Kordan, eds., *The Foreign Office and the Famine: British Documents on Ukraine and the Great Famine of 1932–1933* (Kingston, Ontario: Limestone, 1988), p. 6; and Guseva, interview with author.

[84] RGASPI, f. 81, op. 3, d. 213, ll. 3–15. Perhaps in response to the appearance of railroad workers in the crowd, the OGPU placed "traveling agents" on all trains that passed through IPO strike regions, as a result of which the transportation system continued to function normally. RGASPI, f. 81, op. 3, d. 213, ll. 69–71.

persevered. In a reversal of the events of the strike's early days, a crowd of Nogin and Krasnyi Profintern workers marched to the Shagov Combine in an effort to enforce the job action. Although communists and Komsomol members blocked the entrances to two of the Shagov mills, agitators penetrated Mill No. 3, whose shop floors emptied for the second time in five days. Some of the strikers, meanwhile, responded to a rumor that Iurkin had been freed and was hiding in his apartment by heading to the nearby settlement of Gol'chikha. Before leaving, however, they pointedly vowed to descend again on the police station and the OGPU if they should fail to locate him.[85]

Eager to gauge the mood of the shop floor, Kaganovich spent the first part of the day meeting with groups of workers who had reported to their posts at the Nogin Mill. Accompanying him were three notables: Isidor Liubimov, the USSR commissar of light industry and a former chairman of the Ivanovo-Voznesensk regional soviet executive committee; Korotkov of the State Textile Trust; and Ivan Nosov, head of the IPO party committee. In a revealing display of the institutional hierarchy of power, however, not a single representative of the trade union accompanied Kaganovich.[86]

Although the workers with whom Kaganovich met had remained aloof from the strike, many sympathized with the demands made by their (more radical) colleagues on the streets. Later, Kaganovich summarized his impressions for Stalin: "We listened attentively, and the workers who spoke out complained about outrages with regard to provisions. A portion of the women workers cried hysterically. But there wasn't any strong pressure for the retention of the sixteen kilogram [ration]. The discontent was divided among a series of sore points, and mainly the shortages taking place because of bungling by local organs." Particularly noteworthy is the dismissive remark about the women, whose pleas, typically, were taken less seriously when delivered in an emotional manner.[87]

While Kaganovich tried to win over the labor force, the strike's leaders countered with agitation of their own. After failing to prevent all those assigned to the Nogin Mill's first shift from reporting to their posts, Obukhov attempted to undermine the credibility of the visitors from Moscow. "There's no point listening" to Kaganovich and Liubimov, he argued, because "the former" was an Armenian and "the latter" a Jew.[88]

[85] GARF, f. 374, op. 27, d. 1988, l. 90; RGASPI, f. 81, op. 3, d. 213, ll. 72–76. Iurkin's apartment was not far from the Shagov Combine.

[86] RGASPI, f. 81, op. 3, d. 213, ll. 3–15.

[87] Ibid.

[88] Ibid. In fact, the speaker confused "former" and "latter": Kaganovich was Jewish, and the speaker believed Liubimov to be Armenian.

Despite the agitation, some one thousand workers gathered on the square near the city soviet to hear Kaganovich speak. Around 11:00 A.M., an official emerged from the district soviet executive committee and announced that the meeting would be held at the Nogin Mill. The crowd went there, but the gates were locked and the police refused to admit them. Several women panicked after being rebuffed by armed guards, but Korotkov reassured them: "Don't be afraid, they won't shoot." As the crowd grew in size, some of its members became impatient. Within an hour, however, Kaganovich finished his meetings inside the mill and emerged to face the anxious crowd of three to four thousand strikers.[89]

Unable to make himself heard from where he was standing, Kaganovich led the strikers to a nearby club, from whose steps he and Liubimov spoke for ten minutes. In their remarks, they justified the cut in rations, explained why a strike was the "wrong path" to take, and sharply condemned the attack on Soviet institutions, as well as the incidents of assault and battery against certain workers and executives. After promising that complaints would be addressed within each enterprise and at a special citywide conference, they also called on the strikers "to disperse and go back to work."[90]

Although the workers treated Kaganovich and Liubimov "with respect" and "listened very attentively" to their remarks, several tried to respond with speeches of their own. Kaganovich denounced the attempt "to conduct a meeting and discussion on the street," however, and promptly departed. Exhausted from all the demonstrating and more or less satisfied that their concerns would be addressed, the strikers "quickly dispersed." The impact of the appearance by the Moscow dignitaries—and their display of force—is evident in reports that 65 to 85 percent of those scheduled to work the night shift, including Korotkov, reported to their posts.[91]

Having produced a turning point in the crisis with their stern remarks, Kaganovich and Liubimov quickly set about mobilizing rank-and-file party members, dispatching plenipotentiaries to the mills and agitators to the workers' barracks, and arranging for workers and women's delegates to vent their complaints in tightly controlled assemblies. That evening, they personally chaired two such meetings, attended by over one thousand workers, at the Krasnyi Profintern Mill, where they promised to improve the performance of supply agencies and collected petitions from individ-

[89] RGASPI, f. 81, op. 3, d. 213, ll. 3–15; APUFSBIO, d. 8537-p, ll. 10, 12, 17ob.

[90] RGASPI, f. 81, op. 3, d. 213, ll. 3–15; APUFSBIO, d. 8537-p, ll. 7ob., 10, 12–12ob.

[91] RGASPI, f. 81, op. 3, d. 213, ll. 3–15, 89; APUFSBIO, d. 8537-p, ll. 10, 12ob.; GARF, f. 374, op. 27, d. 1988, l. 90; Guseva, interview with author.

ual members of the audience. Afterwards, they went to a special session of the district party committee, where they received briefings from both party-cell secretaries and their own plenipotentiaries.[92]

Wednesday

Vichuga's mills were scheduled to rest on 13 April, so members of the Kaganovich commission spent the day chairing party assemblies and agitating among workers in their barracks and homes. In addition, they convened a general assembly of the machine-building plant, whose employees remained aloof from the strike and responded well to the speeches by both Nosov and Kaganovich.[93]

Kaganovich also chaired a meeting of the regional party committee, most of whose members were still in Vichuga. In his address, Kaganovich gave his view of "the essence of the event" that had just taken place and called for the identification and arrest of its "initiators." Despite the party's "successes," such as the elimination of unemployment, he noted, the current economic "difficulties" had made it necessary to reduce ration levels. At the same time, the "shortcomings" of local officialdom—including the squandering of foodstuffs, insensitive distribution policies, excessive reliance on central supply agencies, and inattention to the needs of children—were entirely to blame for the unrest.[94]

In its protocol, the regional party committee made it clear that it had heard the shop floor's message. After condemning the performance of local supply agencies, it ordered them to distribute rations earlier in the month, instructed provincial suppliers to increase allocations to the district, demanded that schools and child-care facilities honor existing ration commitments, gave urban workers the right to cultivate unoccupied strips of land near town, required local organizations to draft plans for the development of "supplementary resources" (including rabbit and pig breeding, suburban agriculture, and "Soviet bazaars"), and confirmed that the People's Commissariat of Light Industry would open a department store in town in the near future. Significantly, the regional party committee also called on authorities at every level—including the center—to review their policies on "independent kitchen gardens for workers," "the system of suburban agriculture," and "bread supply norms for workers with large

[92] RGASPI, f. 81, op. 3, d. 213, ll. 3–15; TsDNIIO, f. 327, op. 4, d. 506, ll. 1–4, 10–11, 20; op. 5, d. 162, l. 139; Shutov, "Delo 'Filosofii,' " p. 15; and Shutov, interview with author, Ivanovo, 28 March 1994.

[93] RGASPI, f. 81, op. 3, d. 213, ll. 3–15, 89.

[94] My summary of Kaganovich's speech is based on a brief handwritten outline from which he seems to have read. RGASPI, f. 81, op. 3, d. 213, l. 16.

families."[95] Given the similarity of these recommendations to the policies that were soon implemented by Moscow to improve urban food supplies, it seems that the IPO strike wave had national ramifications.

Thursday

On the morning of 14 April, Kaganovich proudly informed Stalin that "the first shift is working normally" and that shop floors were staffed at "close to 100 percent." Moreover, the level of absenteeism was "lower than usual." The second and third shifts also went smoothly. Indeed, the only incident reported that day was a "small hitch" at Kamenka's Krasnyi Oktiabr' Mill, "but it was quickly settled."[96]

At noon, Kaganovich oversaw a district party committee plenum that approved decrees enumerating the errors committed by the local organs of authority and relieving its secretary, Vorkuev, and the chairman of the district soviet executive committee, Aref'ev, of their duties. Two hours later, Kaganovich, Liubimov, Korotkov, and Nosov attended a joint session of the city soviet and the district trade-union council, where they and representatives from district supply organizations addressed an audience of fifteen hundred, including factory committee members, women's delegates, "spokesmen for the female workers," and eight hundred worker delegates who had been elected that morning.[97]

Although the workers chosen to respond to the official speakers carefully condemned the strike and the acts of violence committed by its participants, they also criticized "the abominable work of local supply and trading organs." Typically, the notes sent to the podium were blunter. Among other things, they revealed that most segments of the population, including peasants, textile and construction workers, and white-collar employees, found the supply situation "impossible"; that regional variations continued to arouse envy ("Why do they supply the center better than Vichuga? Are workers equal everywhere?"); that hostility toward local authorities, including party and supply officials and "those who shot into the crowd," was profound ("Rather than prosecute them, hang them"); and that grain procurements continued to provoke peasant discontent. Besides a restoration of rations, the notes also called for the creation of a bazaar in Vichuga, a reduction in the cultural tax, and the remedy of personal grievances. Another inquired poignantly of Kaganovich: "Before

95 RGASPI, f. 81, op. 3, d. 213, ll. 18–18ob.

96 RGASPI, f. 81, op. 3, d. 213, ll. 1–15, 89; GARF, f. 374, op. 27, d. 1988, l. 90.

97 RGASPI, f. 81, op. 3, d. 213, ll. 3–15, 31–32; GARF, f. 374, op. 27, d. 1988, ll. 90–89.

your arrival in Vichuga, did you know how and by what means they provision the workers here?"[98]

Although many critical views were expressed, the dignitaries from Moscow continued to command respect, which enabled them to secure passage of the lengthy official resolution, consisting of four sections. The first enumerated "the abuses and most serious deficiencies" of district supply organizations. The second demanded "a radical restructuring" of their operations, including top-to-bottom verification of staff members, rigorous supervision by the organs of worker control, and the development of local resources. Highlighting a reversal of long-standing efforts to "proletarianize" the labor force, this section also included a list of specific measures to be taken by the city soviet to strengthen workers' ties to the land.[99]

Having enumerated the concessions from above, the resolution then gave Moscow the signs of obeisance that it demanded. Its third section, for example, approved the cutback in ration levels that had initially sent workers into the streets. Still, in a reflection of the continued sensitivity of the matter, it emphasized that the measure was but a temporary one: "The united conference holds that the . . . temporary reduction (until the new harvest) of bread norms . . . , which was provoked by the failure of the harvest and the need for an urgent loan of seeds to the principal grain regions, is unavoidable, and considers the measures of the Soviet regime directed at the protection of sowings and the future harvest in the principal [grain-]producing regions of the Soviet Union to be correct."[100]

The fourth section, which bore the most obvious indications of Kaganovich's influence, focused on the unrest itself. Those who would "make use of the temporary difficulties" to incite workers to strike, it noted, were by definition "enemies of Soviet power, provocateur and kulak elements," or members of "the dying class enemy," whose "furious resistance" had been provoked by socialist industrialization and collectivization. Those "individual groups of workers" who engaged in violence, meanwhile, were "unworthy of the title of Soviet proletarian." To be sure, "the overwhelming majority of workers" deserved credit for recognizing their "error" and going back to work. By fulfilling the plan, embracing "socialist competition and shock work," "rallying around" the party, and rebuffing further attempts to disrupt production, they could yet "administer

98 RGASPI, f. 81, op. 3, d. 213, ll. 3–15, 33; GARF, f. 374, op. 27, d. 1988, l. 89.
99 RGASPI, f. 81, op. 3, d. 213, ll. 3–15, 31–32; GARF, f. 374, op. 27, d. 1988, l. 89.
100 RGASPI, f. 81, op. 3, d. 213, ll. 31–32.

a crippling blow" to "anti-Soviet elements" and "restore" their "glorious revolutionary traditions."[101]

Regardless of the use of such boilerplate, the presidium found it necessary to appease the shop floor by deleting some of the resolution's harshest passages, including two that virtually accused the strikers of treason:

> The united conference holds that the behavior of that portion of workers who yielded to the provocation of those elements who are hostile to the working class and Soviet power and suspended work in the mills was politically harmful, being in essence a betrayal of the cause of the working class of the Soviet Union.
>
> . . . Any toiler who yields to these provocations stands to all intents and purposes on the path of struggle against Soviet power.

Also excised was a passage that vowed to visit "the entire strength of the proletarian dictatorship" on those "provocateurs" and "counterrevolutionaries" who might yet seek "to infringe upon revolutionary order in Soviet factories and the town." Given the sympathy felt on shop floors for the victims of arrest, the elimination of such inflammatory declarations was prudent.[102]

In the end, however, Moscow got most of what it wanted. Satisfied that public order had been restored and that the delegates "went away in an uplifted mood," Kaganovich promptly informed Stalin that the conference "went well" and that he was ready to return to Moscow.[103]

Though flattered by Moscow's attentions, many workers remained skeptical. "With the arrival of officials from the center, we'll see how things change," some whispered after the conference ended. "Will the deficiencies that were disclosed be eliminated?" Signaling a willingness to compromise and fear for their livelihoods, however, most bit their tongues and reported to work the following day.[104]

Epilogue

Having learned a painful lesson from the arrest of Iurkin, party cells immediately flooded shop floors with denunciations of the strike's "ringleaders," thereby setting the stage for a roundup by the secret police. On

[101] Ibid.
[102] Ibid.
[103] RGASPI, f. 81, op. 3, d. 213, ll. 2–15.
[104] RGASPI, f. 81, op. 3, d. 213, ll. 3–15; GARF, f. 374, op. 27, d. 1988, l. 89.

the night of 14–15 April, fifteen persons were arrested; shortly thereafter, so were sixteen others, including Korotkov and Nikitin. Typically, the OGPU targeted individuals from the most vulnerable social groups: ex-communists who had records of "deviation"; former Socialist Revolutionaries and anarchists; tsarist constables, gendarmes, and manufacturers; and numerous others from the universe of "class-alien elements" whom Moscow blamed for the unrest (e.g., kulaks, tradesmen, bootleggers, *lishentsy,* the unemployed). Also vulnerable were those identified as having perpetrated acts of violence. As for the handful of women who were arrested, all were tainted by association with a "class-alien" husband or father.[105]

During the next few weeks, the OGPU interrogated its prisoners and deposed dozens of witnesses. In June, indictments were filed, as usual, under Articles 58(10) and 59(2) of the Russian Republic's Criminal Code, which forbade "anti-Soviet" and "counterrevolutionary" speech and behavior. Convictions were handed down by an OGPU court the following month: eight defendants deemed "fit for physical labor," including Korotkov, were sent to concentration camps, while twenty-four others, including Nikitin, were exiled. Most of the sentences carried a term of three years.[106]

Conclusion

Following months of scattered protests against the consequences of Stalin's revolution from above, the situation in Vichuga's mills was "tense," and the prevailing mood was one of "depression."[107] When starvation ra-

[105] RGASPI, f. 81, op. 3, d. 213, ll. 3–15, 69–71, 77–78, 80, 89, 90–92, 93–95; APUFSBIO, d. 8537-p, l. 42; d. 8545-p, l. 17.

[106] RGASPI, f. 81, op. 3, d. 213, ll. 3–15, 93–95; APUFSBIO, d. 8537-p, ll. 5, 7ob.–8, 11, 13, 16–17, 19–21, 42; d. 8545-p, ll. 2, 4–10, 12–14, 17ob. The OGPU sent Korotkov to the Murmansk concentration camp, part of the White Sea Canal project. In August 1932, Korotkov's wife received an OGPU sentence of five years for "speculation," which essentially orphaned their five young children. In an appeal to the TsIK on 1 December 1932, Korotkov claimed that his wife had broken the law only to get more food for the children, and asked for clemency on account of their "poverty," parental obligations, and many years of factory employment. Ten months later, Korotkov's sentence was suspended, and he finally gained his freedom in January 1934. As for Nikitin, he was ordered to serve his term of exile in Arkhangel'sk. In 1989, both Korotkov and Nikitin were rehabilitated. APUFSBIO, d. 8537-p, ll. 22, 32–35, 39–40, 42–42ob.; d. 8545-p, l. 15, 17–17ob. Others prosecuted included the peasants Reutskii and Poliakov, who posed as Vichuga "rebels" while leading an attack against their sel'sovet, but who apparently had no involvement in the strike. Iurkin also was convicted, but his fate is unknown. RGASPI, f. 81, op. 3, d. 213, ll. 93–95.

[107] Guseva, interview with author; TsDNIIO, f. 327, op. 5, d. 162, l. 139.

tions were implemented in April 1932, the shop floor erupted in rebellion. The strike was small at first, but distinguished itself from earlier episodes of unrest by expanding in size: on 6 April, 15 percent of the weavers at the Shagov Combine idled their looms; a few days later, most of the district's seventeen thousand textile workers were on strike.[108] The protests snowballed for two reasons: first, the shop floor's discontent was profound (officials believed, for instance, that reduced bread rations never would have triggered "a movement of this scale" had it not been for the chronic deterioration of conditions in the mills);[109] and second, the leaders of the protest included some effective and persuasive organizers.

Initially, the response from above exacerbated the crisis: the desertion of their posts by key officials meant that an effective strategy could not be implemented; the refusal to negotiate fueled popular hostility; the use of force sparked a violent uprising; and when the regional party committee's number two man (Kotsen) mobilized party members for duty, he inadvertently removed a vital source of stability from the shop floor. By all accounts, the authorities' response to the strike was deficient. "We [made] the most flagrant errors," conceded one official, "not only from a political standpoint but from a tactical one as well." The panic that characterized their behavior indicates that a deep-seated fear of the "unruly" masses was an obstacle to the restoration of order. "During the strike," conceded a rank-and-file communist from the Nogin Mill, "Party and soviet leaders became afraid of the workers: they hid beneath tables and behind corners." The violent clash between strikers and the forces of order generated an unprecedented collapse of authority. For a terrifying, if brief, moment, noted the head of the regional soviet executive committee, "there was no Soviet power in Vichuga."[110]

The strike was the largest to occur in the IPO in April 1932, but it was

[108] TsDNIIO, f. 327, op. 4, d. 449, l. 141; *Raiony IPO*, p. 26. The "overwhelming majority" of Vichuga's Komsomol members and communists did not participate in the strike. Instead, they reported for work or, in a handful of cases, served in brigades assigned to protect factory property. Lacking leadership and having been ordered by some officials not to clash with the strikers, most did little more than observe, even when their own machines and colleagues came under attack. At the same time, a substantial minority sympathized with the strikers and joined the demonstrations. (Those most likely to oppose the strike were the Komsomol members; those most likely to support it, party members who had three or more children to feed.) As for the nonparty working wives of rank-and-file communists, many—especially those employed in the weaving sheds—joined the protest. RGASPI, f. 81, op. 3, d. 213, ll. 3–15, 85, 90–92; GARF, f. 374, op. 27, d. 1988, ll. 89–88; TsDNIIO, d. 327, op. 4, d. 449, ll. 5, 93; d. 507, ll. 29–30.

[109] TsDNIIO, f. 327, op. 4, d. 449, ll. 93, 101.

[110] GARF, f. 374, op. 27, d. 1988, l. 89; TsDNIIO, f. 327, op. 4, d. 449, ll. 93, 141; op. 5, d. 162, ll. 139–40.

not the number of demonstrators so much as the violence, carried out by individuals on both sides of the conflict, that made it stand out. Although force—or the *threat* of force—was a factor in other episodes of unrest, only in Vichuga did it play as significant a role as speech in the interaction between workers and the state: it was used by Shagov workers who sought to bring production to a halt; by mounted officers who attempted to disperse peaceful demonstrators; and again by workers who sought to liberate their leader from prison. A teacher who was prevented by strikers from reporting to her post recalled their destructive rage: "My God, they spared nothing." The sabotaged looms in the mills, the piles of rocks and broken glass on the streets—and most dramatically, a worker's bloody corpse—were the consequences of the clash with the police. Its immediate result: a curfew and a cordon of police, whose siege prevented outside support from reaching the strikers and the virus of rebellion from spreading to adjacent mill towns.[111]

If the violence was purposive, it also was richly symbolic. The attack on peaceful demonstrators by mounted officers evoked dark memories of the prerevolutionary era—and, not surprisingly, provoked an extraordinary response. During their attempt to find Iurkin, the young, nonparty fitter who became a catalyst of the uprising, the strikers expressed their hostility toward the institutions that implemented the regime's policies and the men who ruled in their name.[112]

Still, it was a minority of workers—and an undetermined number of discontented bystanders—who engaged in violence. In fact, the majority eschewed radicalism and concentrated on the singular goal of the protest: to restore rations to their previous levels. Despite continued provocations from above, the strikers stepped back from the precipice of 10 April and pursued a moderate course of action. Whereas the Teikovo strikers veered in a radical direction upon determining that their voices were not being heard, Vichuga's steered a moderate course after learning that the center apparently had answered the plea for help.[113] The transition from radicalism to moderation highlights the contours of resistance in Vichuga. In their belief that the center would set things straight and their respectful

[111] Guseva, interview with author; Shutov, interview with author; and Shutov, "Delo 'Filosofii,'" p. 15. The violence may explain why Guseva recalled seeing adults of both sexes—but no children—on the streets during the strike.

[112] The important role played by rumors—about managerial callousness, executives' privileges, and the use of force—likewise illustrates the mobilizing effect of symbols.

[113] Having received no response to their telegram to Moscow, the Teikovo strikers launched a "hunger march" to the provincial capital, Ivanovo. (They were intercepted by the authorities just outside the city.) See Rossman, "The Teikovo Cotton Workers' Strike."

treatment of Kaganovich, the workers displayed their faith in the continued existence of a "good tsar."

Was it a symptom of their naïveté? Not necessarily. Most workers supported "Soviet power," or more precisely what the term stood for in their minds. If one official's claim that the strikers had not gone "against the party . . . [or] the government" was not inaccurate, neither was it complete.[114] Whatever "Soviet power" signified in the popular imagination, certainly it was not the regime's current economic program.[115] Keenly aware of the balance of forces, the workers knew that their lives would improve only if Moscow could be persuaded or compelled to modify its most unpopular policies. Thus, the shop floor's hostility was directed against those who *implemented* the regime's policies, and hopes for improvement were projected on those who authored, *and had the power to change*, them. In short, Vichuga's workers pursued a strategy that was goal-oriented and roughly calibrated to the prevailing asymmetries of power.

Was the uprising a failure? In terms of the demand for higher rations, certainly. The answer is more ambiguous, however, if we adopt a broader perspective. Taken together, these events contributed to the social pressures that compelled the dictatorship to soften its economic policies. In the weeks following Kaganovich's visit to Vichuga, a series of reforms were enacted by the Politburo: the People's Commissariat of Supply was allowed to use emergency grain reserves to supply minimum rations to workers; collective-farm markets were legalized; grain from the summer harvest was earmarked for industrial centers and the army; and supplies of nonrationed goods were increased in an effort to tame inflation. To boost living standards, moreover, investment in light industry was increased during the Second Five-Year Plan.[116]

Such reforms gradually alleviated some of the popular suffering: more consumer goods meant a better quality of life, at least in urban areas; and

[114] TsDNIIO, f. 327, op. 4, d. 449, l. 140.

[115] Studies of Russian labor unrest during the Civil War also conclude that workers generally supported the principles of Soviet power but opposed its implementation. See Jonathan Aves, *Workers against Lenin: Labour Protest and the Bolshevik Dictatorship* (London: Tauris Academic Studies, 1996); and William G. Rosenberg, "Russian Labor and Bolshevik Power after October," *Slavic Review* 44, 2 (1985): 113–31. Given the affinities between the policies of war communism and those of Stalin's revolution from above, we may conclude that Soviet workers consistently opposed the most radical (Bolshevik) versions of socialism.

[116] Kuromiya, *Stalin's Industrial Revolution*, 288, 304–5; R. W. Davies, M. B. Tauger, and S. G. Wheatcroft, "Stalin, Grain Stocks, and the Famine of 1932–1933," *Slavic Review* 54, 3 (1995): 651–52, 656; Alec Nove, *An Economic History of the USSR* (London: Penguin, 1984), pp. 227–28, 231; and Vladimir Andrle, *A Social History of Twentieth-Century Russia* (London: Edward Arnold, 1994), pp. 172–73.

more investment in the textile industry resulted in higher levels of employment, especially in the IPO.[117] If Stalin's policies deserve credit for the economic recovery that occurred in the mid-1930s, then so do the reforms enacted in response to the labor unrest of April 1932.[118]

Another achievement is difficult to measure but no less significant. Although the strike wave was suppressed rapidly, the rumor mill inspired a wave of sympathetic protests, not to mention soul-searching among those who failed to join the struggle.[119] Not surprisingly, the surge of unrest did not stop at the IPO's borders. The aloofness of Vichuga's 425 metalworkers notwithstanding, the willingness of thousands of textile workers to go on strike despite the overwhelming strength of their adversaries inspired other branches of industry to adopt a more militant stance vis-à-vis the regime. A June 1932 report to the People's Commissariat of Supply from the regional party committee of Udmurtskaia region—whose capital, Izhevsk, is 730 kilometers east of Ivanovo—starkly illustrates the capacity of collective action in one region to shape social dynamics in another:

> At present, the political mood among workers, ITR [Engineering-Technical Personnel], agronomists, and physicians has become considerably aggravated. If in previous months the workers' discontent manifested itself in an organized manner (in assemblies, by means of statements to shop and factory organizations) and bore a healthy disposition, then in recent days the workers' moods have been characterized by an increase in bitterness, a lack of faith in the possibility of securing improvement by such means, an increase in the frequency of . . . group protests [*gruppovye vystupleniia*], which are organized behind the back of shop organizations, *together with the simultaneous intensification of agitation by class-alien elements regarding the necessity of following the example of Ivanovo-Voznesensk.* The departure

117 After declining sharply between 1929 and 1931, employment in the textile industry increased steadily. By the end of the Second Five-Year Plan, Russian mills employed as many workers as in 1929—that is, before the squeeze on the industry's resources began. GARF (filial), f. 374, op. 20, d. 32, l. 105; d. 49, l. 16; d. 69, l. 1; d. 85, l. 63.

118 While Moscow's concessions undoubtedly made it possible for hundreds of thousands of working-class families to survive the Great Famine, they also stabilized the regime by shifting more of the burden of sacrifice onto the peasantry.

119 Workers in Ivanovo were particularly upset when they realized that they had ceded their traditional place of honor in the underground labor movement to second-tier mill towns such as Vichuga. Meanwhile, groups of workers in several towns made plans—which never materialized—to renew the strike movement on May Day. GARF (filial), f. 374, op. 27, d. 1988, ll. 70–60.

> of workers from the factory has increased, including something that did not occur before: basic, highly skilled cadres are leaving.[120]

Apparently, the myth of the IPO strike wave outlived many of its participants. When rations were reduced in 1943, discontent again swept Vichuga's shop floors. Remarked an employee of the Nogin Mill, succinctly and bitterly: "They've forgotten 1932!"[121]

[120] Rossiiskii gosudarstvennyi arkhiv ekonomiki (RGAE), f. 8043, op. 11, d. 57, ll. 285–90, emphasis added. (My thanks to Julie Hessler for this citation.) According to a British diplomatic cable of 4 May 1932, the Kremlin worried that disturbances would break out in other parts of the country: "Fleets of lorries are said to be held in readiness at various points in Moscow in case similar trouble should arise in the future." Carynnyk et al., eds., *The Foreign Office and the Famine*, p. 6.

[121] RGASPI, f. 17, op. 88, d. 177, l. 93.

CHAPTER THREE

A Peasant Rebellion in Stalin's Russia

The Pitelinskii Uprising, Riazan, 1930

TRACY MCDONALD

Let's go home. It smells like murder here. (*Poidem domoi, zdes' pakhnet ubiistvom.*)

—Wife of the sel'sovet chairman in Zabelino, 16 March 1930

On the night of 27 January 1930, Avanesov, a member of a collectivization brigade, raped a peasant woman in the village of Malye Mochily in Pitelinskii district, Riazan county. The woman's husband returned home to find Avanesov hiding in their cellar. According to the OGPU (Ob"edinennoe gosudarstvennoe politicheskoe upravlenie, or secret police) report on the incident, a "massive scandal resulted, which compromised the whole brigade."[1] The brigade, however, was in fact already compromised by its tendency to indulge in "tactless activities." Brigade members, for example, demonstrated a penchant for firing off their guns in the middle of the night; and the local peasants used these nocturnal gunshots as an excuse to stop attending meetings on collectivization. The incident in Malye Mochily set the scene for a rebellion against collectivization that would encompass more than twenty villages in

I would like to thank David Brandenberger, Robert Johnson, Stephen Kotkin, Denis Kozlov, Douglas Northrop, Jeffrey Rossman, and Lynne Viola for their helpful comments on earlier versions of this chapter. I would also like to thank Philip Kremer for generous assistance and editing on the earliest drafts.

[1] Quotation is from Gosudarstvennyi arkhiv Riazanskoi oblasti (henceforth, GARO), f. 5, op. 2, d. 5, l. 295 (OGPU, "Spetssvodka," 20 February 1930). See also l. 251 (OGPU "Spetssvodka," 14 February 1930); and l. 281 (OGPU, telegrams, 4–21 February 1930).

Pitelinskii district, rage openly for six days, simmer for months, and involve thousands of peasants.

The Communist Party launched a massive campaign to collectivize the peasantry in the winter of 1929–30. Industrial workers and urban activists were sent en masse to the countryside to aid local party and Soviet officials in the business of collectivization.[2] In the Moscow region, the zealous regional party first secretary, K. Ia. Bauman, directed collectivization, pushing Riazan especially hard to be a model and challenge to other districts in the race for the rapid collectivization of his region.[3] Perhaps even more than elsewhere in the Russian Republic, the implementation of wholesale collectivization in the Moscow region led to massive "excesses" (or *peregiby*, to use a Soviet euphemism). It also led to a peasant rebellion of major significance in Riazan's Pitelinskii district.[4]

The Pitelinskii Uprising

Pitelinskii district is located about 100 miles due east of the city of Riazan, which in turn is located 125 miles southeast of Moscow. In 1929, Riazan province (*guberniia*) had a population of almost two million people. In 1930, the province became a county (*okrug*) within the newly formed Moscow region (*oblast'*). Riazan county was subdivided into smaller administrative units or districts (*raions*). Pitelinskii district was one of the smaller of Riazan's twenty-seven districts. It was about 934 square kilometers in size, with one village or rural soviet (*sel'sovet*) located every 32 square kilometers on average.[5] The district was characterized by a fairly high population density: its inhabitants included 22,976 men and 26,593

[2] For information on the recruitment drive and collectivization in general, see Lynne Viola, *The Best Sons of the Fatherland: Workers in the Vanguard of Soviet Collectivization* (New York: Oxford University Press, 1987).

[3] For more on Bauman and his attitude to collectivization in Riazan, see R. W. Davies, *The Socialist Offensive: The Collectivization of Soviet Agriculture, 1929–1930* (Cambridge, Mass.: Harvard University Press, 1980), pp. 113, 215, 262–63; and V. P. Danilov, R. T. Manning, and L. Viola, eds., *Tragediia Sovetskoi derevni: Kollektivizatsiia i raskulachivanie. Dokumenty i materialy, 1927–1939* (Moscow, 2000), vol. 2, pp. 385–87.

[4] The rebellion was also the factual inspiration for the rebellion in Boris Mozhaev's *Muzhiki i baby* (Moscow, 1988).

[5] The sel'sovet was the lowest level of the state administrative structure. The Russian word, *sel'sovet*, is used throughout the chapter, rather than a translation, because of the key role of the sel'sovet in the argument developed here. The literal translation, "village soviet," is misleading since every village did not have a sel'sovet, but the other standard translation, "rural soviet," somewhat undermines the importance of the institution because it makes it sound remote and disconnected from the village.

A village lane in Riazan, 1920s. Courtesy Tracy McDonald.

women, virtually all classified as rural inhabitants rather than migrant workers or town dwellers.[6]

From January 1930, the relationship between collectivizers and the local peasantry in Pitelinskii district was tense as events moved relentlessly toward a violent confrontation. On 22 February, peasants from across the Pitelinskii district began to gather on the few narrow streets of the village of Veriaevo. Early in the day, rumors circulated to the effect that the collectivization brigade and the sel'sovet were "gathering cattle to slaughter and ship to Moscow."[7] Over the course of the day, more and more peasants filled the village streets. One version of events later claimed that in the days leading up to 22 February, brigade members had seized cattle to be redistributed to poor peasants. The gathered cattle escaped, and when the brigade members went chasing after the beasts a crowd gathered to watch the spectacle.[8] A second version of events claimed that the problems in Veriaevo occurred due to the "tactless conduct" of the plenipotentiaries involved in collectivization work. Furthermore, the unrest did not involve

[6] *Statisticheskii spravochnik po Riazanskomu okrugu za 1927–28–29* (Riazan, 1930), pp. 2–3. The male/female discrepancy can be attributed to losses in World War I and the Civil War, and to an exodus of migrant labor from the region.

[7] GARO, f. 5, op. 2, d. 5, l. 404 (OGPU, "Opersvodka," 25 February 1930).

[8] Ibid., ll. 286–286ob. (OGPU, telegram, 23 February 1930).

cattle, but rather the collection of seed grain. Whatever the case may be, there is no doubt that the brigade and the sel'sovet members were indeed "tactless." They went from door to door in the villages of the district and emptied the barns, most belonging to "middle" peasants, of *all* remaining grain.[9] Thirty of these middle peasants were then fined for not contributing to the grain reserve collection. Brigade members and sel'sovet officials combed the homes of villagers in their relentless search for hidden grain, even breaking open the locked trunks in which peasant families kept their most treasured possessions. The collectivizers seized not only seed grain reserved for the next planting but baked bread, which they often took by force. When women resisted, the brigade members dragged them around by their braids.[10] According to an OGPU report, the local sel'sovet told peasants that they had twenty-four hours to turn over their grain. Those who failed to do so were subject to fines and searches. Locks were broken on storehouses which were then "picked clean" (*vygrebalo vse do chista*). The report went on to note that livestock was collectivized without adequate preparation, and with no thought given to shelter or fodder. Moreover, during dekulakization, a significant number of middle peasants and the families of Red Army soldiers (sectors of the rural population who should officially have been safe from seizure) were stripped of virtually everything and left standing quite literally in their underclothes.[11]

By 22 February, the villagers of Veriaevo had had enough, and they chased the collectivizers out of the village. The collectivizers ran toward the neighboring village of Gridino. But the peasants of Veriaevo rang the church bells to alert their neighbors, leading to the gathering of a massive crowd in Gridino as well. Part of the crowd in Veriaevo chased after the fleeing collectivizers, while the remaining villagers destroyed the barn in which the confiscated seed grain had been stored. The crowd then broke the windows at the local sel'sovet and smashed whatever they could find in the building. They seized property that had been stripped from peasants labeled as kulaks and dispossessed, returning it to its owners. The crowd

[9] Ibid., ll. 286–286ob.; and l. 398 (OGPU, "Spetssvodka," 24 February 1930). The peasantry was divided by state doctrine into poor (*bedniak*), middle (*serednaik*), and wealthy (kulak) households. Only the wealthy peasants were officially targeted for persecution and "dekulakization." In reality, the labels were used fluidly to punish resistance.

[10] Ibid., ll. 403–4 (OGPU, "Opersvodka," no. 6, 25 February 1930). See Steven L. Hoch, *Serfdom and Social Control in Russia* (Chicago: University of Chicago Press, 1986), p. 175, for a reference to estate workers using the same punishment against women in the days of serfdom.

[11] Tsentral'nyi arkhiv Federal'noi sluzhby bezopasnosti (henceforth, FSB[TSD]), f. 2, op. 8, d. 40, l. 97. (This unpublished document is from the draft manuscript for volume 2 of Danilov, Manning, and Viola, eds., *Tragediia Sovetskoi derevni,* and was shown to me, with the permission of the editors, by Lynne Viola.)

then proceeded to beat the sel'sovet chairman and the wife of a party member for good measure. The disturbance lasted until five or six in the evening.

Meanwhile, in the village of Gridino, the church bells summoned a crowd twice the size of the one gathered in Veriaevo. The crowd beat one brigade member severely and chased the remaining members of the collectivization brigade on to the village of Pavlovka. Veriaevo and Gridino both settled down toward evening. But throughout the night, small groups of local peasants patrolled Veriaevo. In fact, for days the peasants of Veriaevo staffed checkpoints and barricades and refused to allow officials into the village until they had agreed to address the issues of the violations, excesses, and scandalous behavior (*bezobrazie*) of the brigade and sel'sovet members. Whenever officials approached the village, the church bells in Veriaevo rang out and the peasants of Gridino came running.[12] Peasants in the surrounding villages expressed their solidarity with Veriaevo and Gridino. Already on the evening of 22 February, for example, in the village of Andreevka located about five miles from Gridino, a crowd marched through the village holding a black flag.[13]

With rebellion threatening the entire district, an armed detachment to deal with the unrest was formed in the neighboring district of Sasovo, comprising members of the railway security forces and the Sasovo militia. The force was dispatched to Pitelinskii district under the leadership of the secretary of the district party committee, Vasil'chenko, and the chairman of the district soviet executive committee, Subbotin. On the morning of the 23rd, the detachment arrived in Veriaevo, which was calm. Within mo-

[12] GARO, f. 5, op. 2, d. 5, ll. 404, 406 (OGPU, "Opersvodka," 25 February 1930). It is interesting to note the striking similarities as well as some of the differences between this unrest and the postemancipation unrest explored by Daniel Field in the village of Bezdna in 1861. In a telegram to the Ministry of Internal Affairs, the local governor of Kazan wrote: "*Pomeshchiki* and officials are not being touched, but Bezdna is surrounded by peasants on horseback, who don't allow anyone in; yesterday there were already more than two thousand people in Bezdna." In another telegram to the ministry, the Kazan governor reported that "the peasant women have been sent out of the village." Field, *Rebels in the Name of the Tsar* (London: Unwin Hyman, 1989), pp. 38, 40. As we know, women played a crucial role in resisting collectivization. See Lynne Viola, "*Bab'i Bunty* and Peasant Women's Protest during Collectivization," *Russian Review* 45, 1 (1986): 23–42. Pitelino peasants built on the traditions of resistance to serfdom and the resistance of the Civil War period. For remarkably similar accounts of peasant tactics of resistance, see Orlando Figes, *Peasant Russia, Civil War: The Volga Countryside in Revolution, 1917–1921* (Oxford: Clarendon, 1989), pp. 321–53; and D'Ann Rose Penner, "Pride, Power, and Pitchforks: Farmer-Party Interaction on the Don, 1920–1928," Ph.D. dissertation, University of California at Berkeley, 1997, pp. 78–103. In many of their examples, it was the behavior of food procurement brigades that sparked violent unrest.

[13] GARO, f. 5, op. 2, d. 5, l. 407 (OGPU, telegram, 23 February 1930).

ments of the detachment's arrival, however, a crowd of women gathered. When three of the officers decided to look for the local cooperative store to find food, the women blocked their path. The officers responded by firing five shots into the air. With that, the church bells rang out, and a part of the crowd rushed toward the shots. The remaining peasants demanded that the detachment lay down its weapons or leave the village immediately. The secretary of the party committee and the chairman of the district soviet executive committee took fright and quickly retreated to Gridino. In Gridino the bells had already summoned a crowd, which attempted to detain the retreating officials, stopping their horses and throwing sticks at them. The detachment then withdrew to the district center of Pitelino. In response to the bells of the villages of Veriaevo and Gridino, a crowd of *several thousand* peasants coalesced in Veriaevo from at least ten surrounding villages, including Maleevka, Andreevka, Ferm, Mikhailovka, Dmitrievka, Pavlovka, Seniukhino, and Lubonos. According to an OGPU report, Veriaevo's priest had played an active role in the unrest, shouting, "Stand up for the Orthodox faith!" from the church steps.[14] Unfortunately the documents do not detail how this enormous crowd was dispersed, although more troops were dispatched and stationed in Pitelino and the OGPU sent 150 specially trained officers to the area.[15]

On 23 February, at 11 P.M., villagers called a general meeting in Gridino which was attended by more than three hundred people, mainly women. At the meeting, the women demanded that the chairman of the district soviet executive committee, Subbotin, and his assistants, Ol'kin and Kosyrev, be put on trial within the next forty-eight hours.[16] The women threatened to hang these officials on meat hooks if they fell into their hands. They also demanded the return of their recently socialized grain reserves, noting that the grain was simply rotting in its current storage conditions. At the end of the meeting, the villagers resolved to elect a new sel'sovet immediately and to launch an investigation into the excesses of the collectivization drive.[17] It is worth noting that the villagers themselves recognized the pivotal role of the sel'sovet and sought reelections to promote and protect their interests.

For the next few days, the villagers set about undoing collectivization. On the night of 23 February, in the village of Ferm, a group of women

[14] FSB(TSD), f. 2, op. 8, d. 40, l. 97.

[15] Rossiiskii gosudarstvennyi voennyi arkhiv (henceforth, RGVA), f. 33987, op. 3, d. 332, l. 81 (Doklad of the commander of the Moscow okrug military forces to K. E. Voroshilov, 2 March 1930), published in *Tragediia Sovetskoi derevni*, vol. 2, p. 279.

[16] Ol'kin was head of the RAIZO (district land department), and Kosyrev was chairman of the local collective farm.

[17] GARO, f. 5, op. 2, d. 5, l. 426 (OGPU, telegram, 26 February 1930).

warned the former head of the district soviet executive committee that they intended to take back their grain reserves. At midnight, a crowd one hundred strong, including peasants from the neighboring villages of Rusanovka and Sukhusha, arrived to seize the grain reserves. At the same time, in the village of Stanishche, a crowd of women destroyed the communal holding pen for collectivized cattle and beat the local agronomist, while in the village of Obukhova, peasants rallied to prevent the dispossession and dekulakization of one of their neighbors.[18]

On 24 February, in the village of Pet, a crowd of over four hundred peasants repossessed 100 dairy cows, redistributing them to their former owners along with 130 out of 180 confiscated horses.[19] The crowd went to the sel'sovet and asked that the grain reserves be removed from the church, which was being used to store the collectivized grain.[20] In the same village, at 11:00 A.M. on 26 February, there was a meeting of poor peasants. Seventy women gathered from the villages of Veriaevo, Stanishche, Kamenka, and Gogolka and stormed the meeting, demanding that the church be reopened and grain reserves redistributed. The women were persuaded to disperse, but vowed that they would "return in the morning to take the grain reserves by force and settle up with the members of the collectivization brigade."[21]

On the morning of 25 February, the Gridino peasants looted the home of the collective farm chairman Kosyrev, whom they had already demanded be put on trial for his part in the excesses.[22] On the same day, a group of women in the village of Nesterovo took back the cows which had been taken from kulak families, and returned them. To emphasize their point, they broke a window at the home of a sel'sovet member.[23] The women of Znamenko also reclaimed confiscated cattle,[24] while the village schoolchildren tore up posters and portraits of Soviet leaders.[25] According to an OGPU report, on the night of 25 February, a group of "kulaks" from Gridino, Vyskoe, Veriaevo, Pavlovka, Rusalovka, and Nesterovo met secretly to plan an uprising. At this illegal meeting, villagers called for the destruction of the sel'sovet, the redistribution of the seed grain, and the reinstatement of voting rights for all peasants. According to the report,

18 Ibid., l. 425.
19 Ibid., ll. 426, 403–4.
20 Ibid., ll. 425–26.
21 Ibid., l. 429.
22 Ibid., l. 424.
23 Ibid., ll. 426, 428 (OGPU, telegram, 26 February 1930).
24 Ibid., ll. 439–40 (OGPU, "Opersvodka," 3 March 1930).
25 Ibid., l. 429 (OGPU, telegram, 26 February 1930).

the group also called for a slaughter of local and visiting soviet and party workers.[26]

At noon on 26 February in the village of Potap'ev, a group of women gathered near the cooperative store. Armed with fence posts, they headed to the sel'sovet, where they demanded the return of their grain reserves. Brigade workers convinced the crowd to disperse. On 27 February, the unrest turned deadly. OGPU officers arrived in Potap'ev to investigate and root out the "anti-Soviet elements" allegedly behind the unrest. Upon discovering that the OGPU had arrived, villagers sounded the church bell and peasants thronged to the sel'sovet, where the OGPU force was preparing its investigation. The crowd dispersed when the agents fired into the air, but quickly reconvened. At this point, the OGPU agents fired into the crowd, wounding one man and killing a woman.[27] The bells rang out once more, and the crowd then swelled with peasants from the surrounding villages armed with clubs. A platoon arrived and ordered the crowd to disperse, but to no avail. The platoon was ordered to divide the crowd in half. There was a struggle, but when the platoon fired into the air, the crowd dispersed. In the confusion, a second peasant was killed and another wounded. On the same day, OGPU agents were forced out of the villages of Vysokoe and Znamenko.[28]

For days, peasants milled about the village streets in the February cold. In Veriaevo, the crowd called out: "We welcome Soviet power without collective farms, grain collections, and local communists."[29] It was not until March that the regime began to gain the upper hand over events, instituting a repressive clampdown on the district. In all, 333 people were arrested in connection with the Pitelinskii uprising. Of this number, 247 were recorded as middle peasants and 9 as poor peasants, suggesting a significant amount of solidarity across "class lines" in the village.[30] In other words, this was not a "kulak uprising," as the authorities claimed, but a revolt that included large numbers of middle peasants as well as poor peasants. The aftershocks of the uprising continued through March, as the OGPU asked for reinforcements in the area. On 21 March, in Pitelino village, the poor peasants demanded immediate monetary payment for

[26] FSB(TSD), f. 2, op. 8., d. 40, l. 98. The section in italics was underlined by the OGPU.

[27] The report added that she was the wife of a church elder, perhaps as an attempt to justify her murder.

[28] GARO, f. 5, op. 2, d. 5, l. 440 (OGPU, "Opersvodka," 3 March 1930). There is no further mention of this incident in the OGPU reports.

[29] FSB(TSD), f. 2, op. 8., d. 40, l. 97.

[30] GARO, f. 5, op. 2, d. 5, l. 441 (OGPU, "Opersvodka," 3 March 1930); and l. 486 (OGPU, "Opersvodka," 9 March 1930).

work done on the collective farm, a free share of the harvest, the opening of churches, and the return of their local priest, who had been arrested by the OGPU. The report claimed that "in the evenings the whole population gathers to talk about the past and about collective farm life."[31] And in every district, rumors swirled about claiming that on Holy Thursday there would again be an uprising like the February rebellion. March was also marked by repeated attempts on the part of the Pitelinskii peasants to prevent the deportation of kulaks from their district.[32]

The unrest in Pitelinskii contributed to a massive exodus from the collective farms. The exodus was more pronounced in Pitelinskii than in any other district in the county.[33] In a report of 20 February, Pitelinskii district was said to be 100 percent collectivized.[34] Yet by April, the percentage of collectivized farms in Pitelinskii had fallen to six.[35] The OGPU complained incessantly about the negative impact of the Pitelinskii uprising on the surrounding districts, where it had created a "tense" mood among the peasants and empowered the perceived enemies of collectivization, supporting their hope that "soon Soviet power will fall."[36]

Throughout April and May, struggles raged over the designation of collective-farm land. There were bitter clashes between those few peasants who remained on the collective farms and the rest of the peasantry. In Veriaevo on 20 May, the collective-farm member A. P. Klimov was approached by a relative, I. V. Klimov, who said to him, "You took the best land from us, land on which we had already planted millet. You left us without kasha. We will not forget this. It would be better for you to leave the collective farm. Others will follow you."[37]

In June 1930, OGPU reports told of a "grain crisis" in the district.[38] A report of 22 June stated that "a whole host of villages" in Pitelinskii district, among them Veriaevo and Pet, "are experiencing a massive shortage

[31] Ibid., l. 887 (OGPU, "Zapiski," 20 May 1930).

[32] Ibid., ll. 617–617ob. (OGPU, "Informsvodka," March 1930). (Quotation from ibid., l. 887.)

[33] Ibid., ll. 342–44, 528. Peasants poured out of the collective farms not only in Pitelinskii district but in neighboring districts as well (OGPU, "Informsvodka," February 1930).

[34] Ibid., l. 290 (OGPU, "Spetssvodka," 2–3 February 1930).

[35] GARO, f. 2, op. 1, d. 66, l. 124 (Ispolkom, "Statistiki," May 1930).

[36] The OGPU feared the spread and impact of the Pitelinskii rebellion on neighboring districts. See GARO, f. 5, op. 2, d. 5, l. 379 (OGPU, "Spetssvodka," March, 1930). About the mass exodus, see ll. 357–58 (OGPU, "Opersvodka," 9 March 1930). About the impact of unrest in Pitelinskii and Ranenburg as important factors creating a tense mood among peasants in other areas, see l. 329 (OGPU, "Spetssvodka," 27 February 1930).

[37] Ibid., l. 887 (OGPU, "Zapiski," 20 May 1930).

[38] I found this kind of report only for Pitelinskii district, suggesting it was the only district in Riazan to experience such a crisis as early as June.

of grain. Peasants are going to the sel'sovet and begging for bread, even if just to feed their children." On 3 June, the peasants of Stanishche expected that the peasants of Veriaevo would raid the starch factory in Pet. The report went on to predict that peasants would soon begin to take back their grain from the collection points.[39]

Local officials were scapegoated for the events that took place in Pitelinskii district. At a May 1930 trial of those accused of using excessive or illegal force in the course of collectivization, the chairman of the district soviet executive committee, Subbotin, received a sentence of five years in a corrective labor camp; his assistant, Ol'kin, the people's court judge (*narsud*), Rodin, and the head of the district OGPU, Iurkov, received three years; the district party committee secretary, Vasil'chenko, received a sentence of six months hard labor; and the chairman of the Veriaevo sel'sovet, Aleshin, and several other local Veriaevo officials were fired.[40]

The Official Story of the Pitelinskii Uprising

Based on the OGPU reports and telegrams sent from the troubled districts in the heady days of the February rebellion, a portrait emerges of a fairly spontaneous peasant rebellion that spread like a fire from village to village. The reports suggest that the rebellion was caused by the "tactless behavior" of those responsible for collectivizing agriculture in the district and that the rebellion was supported and engaged in by almost all the region's peasants. Support crossed class lines and was rooted in the desire, on the part of the local peasantry, to address the "excesses" of the collectivizers and to protect their political and economic interests.

A slightly different story, one that appeared nowhere in the OGPU reports, surfaced at a late February meeting of Riazan district party secretaries. The secretary of the Pitelinskii district party committee blamed the agitation in Veriaevo on a former deputy to the tsarist State Duma who had a "two-story house" and who in fact, the secretary claimed, was such a large landholder that he was practically the equivalent of a noble landowner (*pomeshchik*). This former deputy supposedly conducted agitation among the peasants after being dekulakized. According to the district party secretary, the trouble began when loyal poor peasants showed local officials that there was grain buried in the forest. When the grain was

[39] GARO, f. 5, op. 2, d. 4, l. 260 (OGPU, "Zapiski," 22 June 1930).

[40] A. N. Ianin, "Vtoroe kulatskoe vosstanie i ego likvidatsiia," *Minuvshee* 4 (1988): 303 n. 5.

brought to the grain collection point, the wealthy peasant who had hidden it demanded that it be returned. When it was not returned, the peasant began to spread rumors that there would be house searches for grain. Spurred on by the rumors, peasants seized the expropriated horses of the dekulakized and returned them to their former owners.[41] By retelling the story in this way the district party secretary downplayed the events in Pitelino, blaming them all on acceptable, traditional enemies—the "pomeshchik" and the "kulak"—when in fact the uprising involved almost all the inhabitants of the unruly villages. What is interesting here is the way that history was being rewritten practically as it happened. In fact, by the time the report on the Pitelinskii uprising reached the center, kulaks were blamed entirely for the unrest.[42]

Another account of the riot was written in 1957 by A. N. Ianin, a former party worker, who witnessed the events in the district. The account was part of an official history of the origins of regional party organizations and collective farms in the Pitelinskii district, and the riot was presented as an example of dangerous kulak opposition to the collective farms. While Ianin wrote of a rebellion that he claimed occurred in early March, his recollection was probably a kind of stylized montage of the February events. His account is an interesting and problematic view of the events. Although it was written twenty-seven years after the uprising, Ianin's account is significant precisely because it captures the essence of the official Stalinist depiction of peasants and peasant rebellion.

Ianin claimed that the trouble began when the secretary of the Pitelinskii district party committee was replaced by one Fediaev "who was considered a talentless worker even in the *volost'* [district]." According to Ianin's recollection, the new chairman of the district soviet executive committee was a "mediocre" member of the local police, one Subbotin, who had been transferred to Pitelino from Shatsk—in other words, both incompetent and an outsider. And the soviet worker Ol'kin, "a man little acquainted with agriculture," was named the chief of the district land department (RAIZO).[43] This "troika" "began to throw its weight around [*khoziainichat'*] in Pitelinskii district. Without any preparatory work among the population, [the troika] began to lead wholesale collectivization there, where they did not permit a common meeting ground, embit-

[41] GARO, f. 2, op. 1, d. 216, ll. 35–36 (protocols of the meeting of the district party committee secretaries of Riazan, 26 February 1930). An editorial note in *Minuvshee* claimed that there was no such member in the First Duma, although there was a Nikita Grigor'evich Osichkin from Tambov in the Second Duma. Ianin, "Vtoroe kulatskoe vosstanie," 298–304.

[42] FSB(TSD), f. 2, op. 8, d. 40, l. 87.

[43] Ianin, "Vtoroe kulatskoe vosstanie," 298.

tered the population, and provoked an open uprising against Soviet power."[44]

Ianin maintained that the dissatisfaction which the troika produced in the population was further exploited by a group of "conspirators" consisting of the "kulak" Os'kin, "who was a former member of the tsarist State Duma";[45] the "kulaks" Papkin and Miagkov; the local priest from Veriaevo; a White Guard officer and former "emissary of Antonov" who was hiding to avoid prosecution; and "some kind of 'woman-kulak' [*zhenshchina-kulachka*] with a criminal past."[46] This list of the guilty implicated in the events at Pitelinskii district offered a virtual catalogue of recognizable and acceptable enemies of the Soviet state. Ianin left no stone unturned as he identified those behind the extraordinary events: political-economic enemies (the kulaks); political-historic enemies (White Guards and emissaries of Antonov, combined into a unique hybrid); former tsarist officials (members of the tsarist Duma); religious enemies (the local priest); wayward women; recidivist criminals; and even Gypsies (Ianin made a point of mentioning that one of the villages was a "Gypsy village").[47] Furthermore, demonstrating a literary flair with just a hint of the supernatural, Ianin added a host of more traditional characters to the mix: "In these villages there appeared mysterious wanderers [*stranniki*], informants [*informatory*], soothsayers [*predskazateli*] spouting the most unimaginable nonsense, spreading wild rumors and gossip that women and children would be socialized."[48] According to Ianin, February was marked by "rabid" agitation among the population against the collective farm and against collectivization in general.

Ianin dated the Pitelinskii riot to the beginning of March. According to Ianin, a crowd of two or three thousand peasants gathered from eleven villages. The crowd was made up "mostly of women," armed with clubs, axes, pitchforks, and firearms and carrying icons and banners. Drawn by the ringing of the church bells of Veriaevo, the women walked to Gridino singing "God Save the Tsar." In Gridino, the size of the crowd grew "at lightning speed" as it prepared to march on Pitelino to demand the "freeing of the arrested priests." Ianin added that the crowd intended to cap-

44 Ibid., 299.

45 Ibid.

46 Ibid., 298.

47 Ibid, 299. For a similar example of blaming outside, traditional enemies for peasant rebellion, see E. J. Hobsbawm and Georges Rudé, *Captain Swing* (London: Lawrence and Wishart, 1969), pp. 239–50.

48 Ianin, "Vtoroe kulatskoe vosstanie," 299.

ture and take over the district center and commit a "pogrom," exterminate communists, and slaughter "all the Soviet workers it despised."[49]

According to Ianin, the procession and the riotous demonstrators were led by a "woman-kulak": "From one pocket of the skirt of this legendary heroine Alena from Pitelino [*Pitelinskaia Alena-bogatyr*] stuck out a pistol; from the other pocket, another pistol; and in her waistband, bullets, like the most authentic bandit-robber."[50] This mythical woman does not appear in any of the OGPU reports. But she is a fascinating character: a relic of the past, the wild woman of the Soviet 1920s who was tamed in both fiction and reality by Ianin's time.[51] There is certainly a mocking tone in Ianin's prose as he recalls the masculine role of this "Alena-bogatyr" of Pitelinskii district, the *bogatyr* being the *male* hero of early Russian folklore.

In Ianin's account, a local police constable and an agronomist from the district went to meet the crowd. They were met with cries of "Beat them!" Furthermore, he noted, "after this, the dense striking of stakes was heard, the crash of craniums, and the constable and the agronomist were no more. They were killed by the mutineers, who continued on their way, sweeping all that they hated out of their path."[52] Ianin writes that the mutineers intended to surround Pitelino and take it by storm, but they were confronted by a detachment of three hundred Red Army soldiers from Sasovo led by the chairman of the county soviet executive committee, Shtrodakh, and the secretary of the county party committee, Gilinskii. According to Ianin, Shtrodakh "rudely" asked the crowd, with his revolver in hand, " 'Why are you rioting [*buntuete*]? You don't like the collective farms?' To which members of the crowd responded, 'And you come here with your gun to terrify us and drag us into the collective?... We won't go!... Down with the collective farm! Down with the *kommuna*!' " In Ianin's account, the Alena-bogatyr then began to taunt Shtrodakh: " 'Here is your collective farm! Have a look!' the woman-kulak-mutineer declared impudently and without shame, lording it over everyone, [and] suddenly raising her skirt, showing Shtrodakh her naked body amid an explosion of laughter and mocking whoops from the crowd of like-minded villagers. Shtrodakh could not control himself in the face of her impudence and shamelessness, and he shot his revolver at the mutineer who was insulting him and killed her."[53] This action inflamed the crowd. Only repeated vol-

[49] Ibid., 299–300.

[50] Ibid., 300.

[51] See Thomas Lahusen, "Socialist Realism Revisited: Or the Reader's Searching Melancholy," *South Atlantic Quarterly* 90, 1 (1991): 102–3.

[52] Ianin, "Vtoroe kulatskoe vosstanie," 300.

[53] Ibid.

leys from the detachment finally dispersed the crowd, which then attacked the collective farm, taking back grain and cattle and destroying account books. "Three collective-farm chairmen and several collective-farm members, communists, and Komsomol members were killed."[54] If Shtrodakh did indeed shoot and kill a peasant woman engaged in a traditionally effective, peaceful, harmless, and age-old tactic of protest, the "moral" violation of the peasant community by outsiders was even further reinforced by his actions.

Ianin's account, written almost thirty years after the Pitelino events, continued the reconstruction of the Pitelinskii rebellion already initiated at the February meeting of the district party secretaries. With graphic gusto, he detailed the acceptable explanations for a (in his eyes) gratuitously violent peasant revolt. He depicted a backward, ignorant peasant mass easily led astray by outside agitators and the archetypal enemies of Soviet power: backward and untamed peasant women; over-zealous and corrupt local officials, the scapegoats—those dizzy with success; kulaks and tsarist remnants. But is there more behind and beyond the official version of events? Do the events at Pitelino contribute something to our understanding of the Soviet countryside at the time of the great break?

Understanding Pitelinskii

From 1928 to the fall of 1929, a crisis situation developed in Riazan. The crisis was rooted in forced grain requisitioning and grain shortages as well as increasingly heated and united peasant opposition to state grain, tax, and rationing policies. In May 1929, the head of the county OGPU, Remizov, conducted an "emergency tour" of Riazan. He reported that there was a reawakening of kulak and religious counterrevolution in the countryside. He noted that peasant protest, ostensibly over the closing of churches and usually involving significant numbers of women and sel'sovet members, inevitably developed into heated criticism of state policy. At these gatherings, peasants complained repeatedly about the shortage of bread, high taxes, and the export of grain. Protest often resulted in demands for the "communists" to leave the village.[55]

The OGPU reports claim that poor peasants feared that state policy would lead to starvation and as a consequence had little faith in the re-

[54] Ibid., 301.

[55] GARO, f. 2, op. 1, d. 15, ll. 53–57 (OGPU, letter, 18 May 1929); and ll. 32–36 (OGPU, "Obzor," 21 May 1929).

gime.[56] The tax policy that was supposed to boost or engender class war in the countryside in the previous two years had not been successful.[57] It would have been more palatable to the center if the OGPU had discovered that opposition in the countryside was coming only from wealthy peasants and especially from the regime's ideological scapegoat, the kulak. Yet the reports quite candidly reflect the degree to which the countryside was still a place of complex and local loyalties and conflicts. One report noted that even though the poor in the village were "barbarically exploited" by the kulak, they continued to support and respect wealthy peasants.[58] The Riazan peasantry was not prepared economically or ideologically for the shift to collectivized agriculture. Although there were clearly tensions and social divisions in the village, these differences were submerged in the face of a greater threat from the outside.[59]

In Riazan, peasants resisted collectivization in a myriad of ways that were similar to those undertaken by peasants elsewhere.[60] Families initiated fictional partitions of land and property.[61] They slaughtered their livestock. In early January in Pitelinskii district, for example, there was a mass slaughter of small livestock such as sheep and young animals. The local peasants were reported to have said: "We'll go to the collective farm but without our livestock. It's all the same. We die of hunger."[62] Fearing they would be labeled kulaks, people also fled their homes and villages.[63] There were 150 such cases recorded by the OGPU by the end of February 1930.[64] A number of Riazan peasants even engaged in a hunger strike to

[56] Ibid., ll. 31–35.
[57] See James Hughes, *Stalinism in a Russian Province* (London: St. Martin's, 1996). Hughes argues that the "social influence" policy, as he dubs it, actually worked to some degree. See esp. pp. 69, 202–9.
[58] GARO, f. 5, op. 2, d. 5, ll. 149, 151 (OGPU, "Zapiski," 16 December 1929). There were still some scattered reports of poor peasant support for dekulakization in February 1930, but they were few and far between. See ibid., l. 288 (OGPU, "Opersvodka," 20 February 1930).
[59] Here I agree with Teodor Shanin, *The Awkward Class* (Oxford: Oxford University Press, 1972), pp. 196–97.
[60] As the first big push for collectivization got underway, Riazan peasants engaged in types of protest that have already been detailed in existing studies of collectivization. Because the catalogue of resistance has been explored elsewhere, I touch on it only briefly here to show the degree to which the behavior of Riazan peasants fits the common patterns of protest to collectivization, before moving on to focus on an aspect of resistance to collectivization which I think has been overlooked in the existing literature. See Lynne Viola, *Peasant Rebels under Stalin: Collectivization and the Culture of Peasant Resistance* (New York: Oxford University Press, 1996); Sheila Fitzpatrick, *Stalin's Peasants: Resistance and Survival in the Russian Village after Collectivization* (New York: Oxford University Press, 1994); and Hughes, *Stalinism.*
[61] GARO, f. 5, op. 2, d. 5, l. 126 (OGPU, "Obzor," 16 December 1929).
[62] Ibid., l. 191 (OGPU, "Spetssvodka," 5 January 1930).
[63] Ibid., ll. 309–10 (OGPU, "Zapiski," 11 February 1930); and l. 411 (OGPU, "Opersvodka," 25 February 1930).
[64] Ibid., l. 411.

protest collectivization.[65] Women refused to let the members of the collectivization brigades talk about the collectivization process.[66] Peasants spoke of the arrival of the collective farm as the coming of the Antichrist, when all would be branded with the mark of the Devil.[67] There were acts of terrorism, arson, and beatings of brigade and collective-farm members.[68] Between 1 February and 14 March, there were twenty-six registered cases of "terrorist acts" in Riazan.[69] Threats and calls to action lamenting the fate of the peasant were glued to fences and walls.[70] These anonymous writings called for a return to the "old life"[71] and threatened those "who drink the blood of the peasant."[72] The OGPU knew of at least thirty-six such postings in February and early March.[73] There was also mass unrest, usually consisting of crowds of one hundred to one thousand peasants which gathered to harass the collectivization brigades and to undo collectivization.[74] There were thirty-four recorded occurrences of such unrest in Riazan in February and the first half of March.[75] Typically, during "mass unrest," women reclaimed collectivized cattle and redistributed them to their original owners. And when, at the end of February, the collective farms were declared "established," women refused to let the collectivized horses plow the fields. By the end of February, peasant households were already signing out of the collective farms en masse. They were further emboldened by Stalin's "Dizzy with Success" speech of 2 March 1930.[76]

The theme of peasant resistance has become prominent in discussions of collectivization.[77] The extent of this resistance and the variety of its

[65] GARO, f. 5, op. 2, d. 4, l. 20 (OGPU, "Spetsdoneseniia," 9 February 1930).

[66] GARO, f. 5, op. 2, d. 5, l. 295 (OGPU, "Spetssvodka," 20 February 1930).

[67] Ibid., l. 189 (OGPU, "Spetssvodka," 5 January 1930); GARO, f. 2, op. 1, d. 213, ll. 74–75 ("Dokladnaia zapiska," not earlier than 11 February 1930); and GARO, f. 5, op. 2, d. 5, ll. 341–42, 348 ("Informsvodka," 14 March, 1930).

[68] GARO, f. 5, op. 2, d. 5, l. 204 (Party *svodka*, January 1930); and l. 279 (OGPU, telegrams, 4–21 February 1930).

[69] Ibid., l. 568 (OGPU, "Spetssvodka," 14 March 1930).

[70] Ibid., ll. 475–76 (Ispolkom, "Informsvodka," February 1930).

[71] Ibid., l. 286ob. (OGPU, telegrams, 22–26 February 1930).

[72] GARO, f. 5, op. 4, d. 4, l. 153 (OGPU, telegram, 13 March 1930); GARO, f. 5, op. 2, d. 5, l. 571 (OGPU, "Spetssvodka," 14 March 1930); and GARO, f. 5, op. 2, d. 5, l. 584 (OGPU, telegram, 22 March 1930).

[73] GARO, f. 5, op. 2, d. 5, l. 568 (OGPU, "Spetssvodka," 14 March 1930).

[74] Ibid., l. 568; and ll. 506–7 (OGPU, "Opersvodka," 13 March 1930).

[75] Ibid., l. 568 (OGPU, "Spetssvodka," 14 March 1930).

[76] Ibid., ll. 562–73 (OGPU, "Spetssvodka," 14 March 1930).

[77] See V. P. Danilov and S. A. Krasil'nikov, eds., *Spetspereselentsy v Zapadnoi Sibirii*, 4 vols. (Novosibirsk, 1992–98); Davies, *The Socialist Offensive;* Fitzpatrick, *Stalin's Peasants;* Hughes, *Stalinism;* Viola, *Best Sons;* Viola, *Peasant Rebels;* and Lynne Viola, Sergei Zhuravlev, Tracy McDonald, and Andrei Mel'nik, eds., *Riazanskaia derevnia v 1929–1930 gg. Khronika golovokruzheniia. Dokumenty i materialy* (Moscow, 1998).

forms are impressive. The most overtly threatening form of resistance was, of course, the violent uprising which involved hundreds, and in some cases thousands, of peasants. Yet not all peasants rebelled, raising the question not of why peasants engaged in mass rebellion but of why in fact so many *did not.*[78] There were more than 6,350 villages in the province of Riazan, yet there were only 34 cases of "mass unrest" involving approximately 175 Riazan villages (or 3 percent), and none were of the scale of the uprising in the Pitelinskii district. How can a rebellion like Pitelinskii be explained, and what light does the explanation shed on the dynamics of peasant-state relations during the first collectivization drive?

Although official transcripts laid the blame on incompetent officials, backward women, kulaks, and other class enemies, the earliest reports of the Pitelinskii unrest, the daily *svodki* from the OGPU, quite accurately described a situation in which *all* villagers, regardless of social and economic conditions, united in their struggles against the collectivization brigade and the sel'sovet. In this regard, the unrest in Pitelinskii mirrored peasant unrest elsewhere in the Soviet Union. This was the case in regard to other features of the rebellion as well.

Rumors, for example, were immensely important in the events in Pitelinskii district. The rumor that allegedly sparked the rebellion was that the plenipotentiaries were "gathering cattle to slaughter and ship to Moscow." The rumor suggests that peasants were aware to some degree of their colonial relationship to Moscow and actively resented it.[79] The rumors about cattle encouraged peasants to come together in protest. Furthermore, the rumors described by Ianin capture and encapsulate the greatest fears of both peasants and state. The peasants feared that women and children would become communal property, and the state feared a "slaughter" of its representatives. Or perhaps both sides claimed that this

[78] One historian who looks at peasant response to collectivization acknowledges the challenge: "The uneven distribution of protest, the reason why riots erupt in one village and not in others, is an intractable problem" (Hughes, *Stalinism*, p. 94). It is curious that one of the most rebellious villages in Hughes's study is called Riazan; in fact it was the headquarters for a revolt that spread to seventeen villages in Siberia in just over two weeks (ibid., pp. 178–79). It would be fascinating to discover whether or not these peasants had resettled from Riazan county.

[79] For more on internal colonization, see Alvin W. Gouldner, "Stalinism: A Study of Internal Colonialism," *Telos* 34 (1977–78): 5–48; and Viola, *Peasant Rebels*, esp. pp. 3, 14–19. Stephen P. Frank's work on the nineteenth-century countryside looks at the problem in a developmental context and suggests that the tsarist regime behaved as a colonizing force as well. See Frank, *Crime, Cultural Conflict, and Justice in Rural Russia, 1856–1914* (Berkeley: University of California Press, 1999). Gouldner sees internal colonization as a Stalinist phenomenon. Viola has a more nuanced approach that pays attention to both the developmental side of colonization and the socialist content.

is what they feared to justify extreme actions. Rumors about the role of accepted and traditional enemies and their role in the unrest began to shape the historical record by the end of February 1930.

Peasant women were at the forefront of protest in Pitelinskii, just as they were across the rest of the Soviet Union during collectivization. Peasant men and women took advantage of the traditional view of women as less threatening and less politically responsible than men. Men were much more likely to be arrested for protest than women and tended to stay on the sidelines unless the women were threatened. Only then could peasant men step in on the grounds that they were defending their womenfolk.[80]

The graphic symbolism of peasant protest must have frightened the authorities, as peasants used and inverted the regime's own tactics and language.[81] Pitelinskii peasants paraded under black or white flags and defiantly challenged the regime by setting up barricades and demanding that all who entered show their documents—a practice that was becoming an everyday part of Soviet life. Pitelinskii peasants demanded the return of the "old ways," of tradition, the church, and the priest, explicitly rejecting the new Soviet order. The children's reaction to the posters of the great leaders further suggests that peasants knew that responsibility ran all the way to the top in the destruction of their communities. Traditional features of Soviet power became the subjects and the objects of peasant protest. The red flag parades of communist festivals were replaced by the black flag of anarchy and the white flag of counterrevolution. The requisite Soviet posters were torn from the walls and shredded by children, who like women, could not be held responsible for their actions.

What the events in Pitelino capture vividly is the high degree of solidarity among the villages of the district. Over and over the villagers worked together, uniting against the outsiders despite any rivalries that may have existed prior to the rebellion. Messengers skied between villages with news of events.[82] Village church bells constantly warned neighboring villages of danger or of collectivizing activity, bringing their inhabitants rushing to confront the collectivizers. Peasants from more than twenty villages called meetings, made plans, and issued demands.

There were a host of common experiences for the peasantry across the Soviet Union during the first collectivization drive. Yet violent uprisings were relatively uncommon. What, exactly, sparked violent unrest? The

[80] See Viola, "*Bab'i Bunty*," 23–42.

[81] GARO, f. 2, op. 1, d., l. 45. The villagers of Zakharevskii district sang to the tune of the "Internationale": "*spasi, gospodi, liudi tvoi*" ("save, lord, your people").

[82] RGVA, f. 33987, op. 3, d. 332, l. 81, published in *Tragediia Sovetskoi derevni*, vol. 2, p. 279.

most obvious explanation would be the most commonly accepted one: the degree of excess engaged in by the collectivizers. And there was certainly much variation in the behavior of collectivization brigades. Even within Riazan itself OGPU reports lamented that the brigade in Mikhailovskii district "cries with the population" and socializes with them.[83] The brigades in Pitelino, however, violated the moral economy of the villages in the district both in a moral and an economic sense. In Pitelino, peasants were pushed beyond the line of subsistence as their last grain was removed from their barns and trunks and even baked bread seized from their homes. But just as important, the peasantry was morally violated. A brigade member raped a local woman in Malye Mochily,[84] and the detachment sent by the state killed at least two Pitelino peasants. The outsiders used unjustified, traditional village punishment against local villagers, such as dragging women around by the braids. The chairman of the county soviet executive committee supposedly shot and killed a woman for lifting her skirt. The final and perhaps most important factor was that local officials, and in particular members of the sel'sovet, cooperated with the brigades and participated in the excesses. It is the active and violent cooperation and participation of sel'sovet members in the excesses in Pitelino that is most important in explaining why violent rebellion occurred here. The organization that was typically *of* the village, the sel'sovet, turned *on* the village.

Sel'sovet officials accompanied the collectivizers as they went door to door taking the peasants' last seeds of grain. Peasants were incensed that it was the sel'sovet which demanded that all grain be turned over within twenty-four hours. When property was destroyed and windows broken, it was the sel'sovet or homes of sel'sovet members that were targeted. Sel'sovet officials were physically attacked. What angered peasants most was that their own local government had betrayed them, when it should have protected them. The first official action recommended by the protesting peasants was the dissolution of the existing sel'sovet and its reconstitution with peasants who would better serve local interests.

The role of the sel'sovet in the Pitelinskii uprising contradicts the prevailing view of the sel'sovet during collectivization. Much of the scholarship on collectivization claims that the sel'sovet was weak and ineffectual.[85] The most repetitive feature of the OGPU reports on collectivization and

[83] GARO, f. 5, op. 2, d. 4, l. 260 (OGPU, "Zapiski," 22 June 1930).

[84] Hughes claims that rape was a common weapon in Siberia (*Stalinism*, p. 191). There are only a few such references in the Riazan materials.

[85] See Moshe Lewin, *Russian Peasants and Soviet Power* (New York: Norton, 1975); D. J. Male, *Russian Peasant Organization before Collectivization* (Cambridge: Cambridge University Press, 1971); and Y. Taniuchi, *The Village Gathering in Russia in the Mid-1920s* (Birmingham: Uni-

peasant resistance nationwide is the complaint that the sel'sovets acted as a "brake" on the collectivization process. This "foot-dragging" of the sel'sovet may well offer a clue as to why more villages across the Soviet Union did not erupt in rebellion during the first wave of collectivization in 1929 and 1930.

In Riazan, there was one sel'sovet for every four villages.[86] Peasants interacted with the sel'sovet and certainly were keenly aware of its existence, if only because it was central in the 1920s to the process of tax assessment and collection, a constant headache for all concerned. Beyond tax issues, as the regime "turned its face to the countryside" in the mid-1920s, there was an increasing realization that the social composition of the sel'sovets did not ensure that they were staffed with the most staunch supporters of the Soviet government. The regime held new elections to the sel'sovets in an attempt to ensure that village government would be made up of more reliable members. Tax and election campaigns brought the regime into closer contact with the village, forcing peasants at least to be aware of the sel'sovet and its theoretical role in the countryside.

The role of the sel'sovet in the 1920s and during the first collectivization drive is pivotal and worthy of further consideration as we attempt to refine our understanding of village and state. Despite the regime's attempts to change the composition of the sel'sovets, the majority of them remained "of the village"—that is, sel'sovet members were villagers themselves, had personal relationships with the peasants of the surrounding villages, and often made decisions based on custom and tradition rather than central ordinance or instruction.

Much of the lower state apparatus, in fact, was "suspect" as belonging more to the village and the region than to the state. Consider the head jailer of the Kasimovskii district, denounced in an OGPU report, who brought vodka for his prisoners, delivered notes among them on the progress of their cases, and took several home to spend nights at his house.[87] This kind of nonstandardized informality of the old order was what the regime faced on the local level and what the regime believed it had to overthrow in the name of modernization, standardization, and progress. This traditional order was not always a benevolent or gentle order, but it was an order that existed and even developed and strengthened in the countryside in the 1920s.

Many sel'sovets were staffed by wealthy peasants with strong patronage

---

versity of Birmingham, 1968). Viola observed that the sel'sovets were unreliable during the collectivization campaign (*Best Sons*, pp. 21–22).

[86] Male, *Russian Peasant Organization*, p. 93.

[87] GARO, f. 5, op. 2, d. 5, l. 168 (OGPU, "Spetssvodka," 1 January 1930).

networks. These individuals used their positions to protect as best they could their family and circles of friends and allies.[88] Before the first collectivization drive, sel'sovet chairmen helped fellow peasants avoid grain requisitioning. In some cases, sel'sovet chairmen issued permission to village members to acquire grain "necessary for their own personal use."[89] In October 1929, a report on the grain requisitioning campaign stated: "Almost all sel'sovets up to this time have made no independent attempts to implement measures decreed by the Central Committee in Moscow and the Council of People's Commissars against the kulak section of the village; they [sel'sovets] do not use the rights granted to them."[90]

The OGPU reports are replete with laments about the "*khvostism*" or "backwardness" (*khvost* means "tail") of the local governmental structure and of the sel'sovets in particular.[91] By December 1929, OGPU reports were complaining that the "*aktiv*," that is those who were in theory active supporters of Soviet power, such as sel'sovet chairmen, local police officers, and local party members, were speaking out against collectivization. Increasingly, members of the sel'sovet refused to turn over their grain.[92] Moreover, according to the OGPU, members of the sel'sovets were sympathetic to the plight of the class enemy. One OGPU report noted that "many of the lower party and soviet organs deal poorly with the crimes of the kulak class. Inventories of property which should be done because of the willful hoarding of grain, in the majority of cases, are never realized, and the property is not sold. Kulaks are given breaks and extensions."[93] In the same report the OGPU complained that sel'sovet members supported their relatives, who were kulaks, accepted bribes in return for assistance, lowered grain requisitioning norms levied on local kulaks, and spread grain procurement obligations out among middle and poor peasants.[94] Members of the sel'sovet in the village of Vysokoe, Shatskii district, were

[88] GARO, f. 4, op. 3, d. 11, ll. 258–62 (OGPU, "Spetssvodka," 28 June 1929); and ll. 114–17 (OGPU, "Spetssvodka," 7 August 1929).

[89] Ibid., l. 108.

[90] GARO, f. 5, op. 2, d. 5, l. 57 (OGPU, "Spetssvodka," 25 October 1929).

[91] GARO, f. 2, op. 1, d. 216, ll. 35–36 (protocols of the meeting of the party district committee secretaries of Riazan, 26–27 February 1930); GARO, f. 5, op. 2, d. 5, ll. 393–94 (OGPU, "Spetssvodka," no. 7/7, 24 February 1930); and GARO, f. 5, op. 2, d. 5, ll. 545–55.

[92] GARO, f. 5, op. 2, d. 5, ll. 80–83 (OGPU, "Spetssvodka," 26 November 1929).

[93] Ibid., l. 10 (OGPU, "Obzor," August–December 1929).

[94] Ibid., l. 10; and ll. 162–68 (OGPU, "Spetssvodka," 1 January 1930). See also the bizarre letter from a worker in Baku in GARO, f. 2, op. 1, d. 306, ll. 301–301ob., about the "unlawful behavior of his family village's sel'sovet chairman, who slaughtered his animals before entering the collective farm and warned his brother to sell his horse quickly because no matter what, they would be dragged into the collective farm."

explicit about their relationship to the countryside: "These are our people and if we apply the control figures [for grain quotas] in their entirety, then the peasants will tear us to pieces."[95] The OGPU presented these examples as evidence of anti-Soviet behavior when in fact most of these cases simply reveal the common workings and existing power structure of the precollectivization village. The examples presented suggest that the sel'sovets were very much part of the village and as a result were in fact a serious brake on collectivization.

As late as February 1930, the OGPU complained that the majority of sel'sovets continued to deter peasants from joining the collectives and that both local party members and sel'sovet members were slaughtering their own livestock.[96] For example, six members of the Berezovskii sel'sovet refused to enter the collective farm. Two of these sel'sovet members, Voronko and Bazanov, spoke out against collectivization at every meeting, calling it "*barshchina*" (a direct reference to labor obligations under serfdom) and violence (*nasilie*).[97] Makarov, a member of the sel'sovet of the village of Velikii Studenets located in the Sasovo district, joined the collective farm but at each meeting spoke out against it, calling it a "whorehouse" (*publichnyi dom*). He urged his fellow villagers not to enter the collective farm, telling them it meant "hunger and ruin." The OGPU agent's conclusion was that "as a result of his activities more than half of the households in the village did not enter the collective farm."[98]

Sel'sovet chairmen represented a voice of reason, complaining over and over that targets for collectivization and requisitioning were too high and impossible to enforce. They continued to assign quotas in customary ways, by "eater," that is by the number of members of a given household, instead of by class.[99] A 1 March report from the Riazan county prosecutor lamented that a whole host of sel'sovets "violate the class line" in this way.[100]

Sel'sovet chairmen were in the most difficult situation imaginable, caught in a vice between the mass of the peasantry on one side and the regime on the other. Their position was precarious and dangerous as they

[95] GARO, f. 5, op. 2, d. 5, l. 162 (OGPU, "Spetssvodka," 1 January 1930).

[96] GARO, f. 5, op. 2, d. 5, ll. 302–6 (OGPU, "Spetssvodka," 16 February 1930).

[97] GARO, f. 5, op. 2, d. 5, ll. 392–93 (OGPU, "Spetssvodka," 24 February 1930).

[98] Ibid.

[99] The Zabelinskii sel'sovet collected oats at ten pounds "per eater" (*po edokam*) and flax at three pounds per eater. The Iarnovskii sel'sovet collected grain of all kinds per eater, the same from the kulaks as from the *bedniaks*. In both cases, the sel'sovet members implicated were tried for violating the class line. GARO, f. 5, op. 2, d. 5, ll. 434–35ob. (report from the Riazan county prosecutor, 1 March 1930).

[100] Ibid.

were often the sole representatives of Soviet power on site, and at best they were torn between regime and village. On 16 March 1930, at 11:00 P.M., a meeting of village activists was called to discuss collectivization in the village of Zabelino, Sarevskii district. Almost the whole village appeared outside the meeting. Cries of "We have no kulaks here. Sign us all out of the collective farm. Or else we will not let you out of the sel'sovet alive," rang out from the crowd of protestors. The wife of the sel'sovet chairman, perhaps taking the side of the crowd or perhaps simply fearing for her husband's life, said to him: "Let's go home, it smells like murder here." But the chairman refused to leave the scene and instead struck her. Villagers in the crowd began to yell, "Down with the collective farm! The brigade members write about us to the OGPU!" The crowd demanded the right to leave the collective farm. Finally, the chairman of the sel'sovet gave the list of those who had signed up for the collective farm to the gathered peasants. They signed out of the collective and woke all the sleeping members of the village so they could sign out too. Among the 126 households signed up for the collective, 110 signed out.[101] Here, the chairman of the sel'sovet attempted to act as a state representative and enforce state policy only so far before he took it upon himself to act in a way he believed would redress the situation. His wife's graphic admonition captures the ugly and tense dangers at the village level during the first collectivization drive.

Like rural party members, the sel'sovet staff believed at this early stage that they had a voice in the general power structure of the state and that they could reason, negotiate, and act in prudent ways with impunity. The sel'sovets were pivotal during the first collectivization drive partly because of the role the regime now expected them to play. As the most basic grassroots element of the state structure, they were expected to be the hubs of collectivizing activity, and in some cases they did facilitate OGPU and brigade work. More often, however, members of the sel'sovet were a very vocal and crucial source of opposition at the village level. Disloyalty within state organs made the regime very nervous, and disloyalty within state organs at the village level empowered the peasantry.

On February 21, in the village of Nekliudovo, Kasimovskii district, a candidate member of the party, Mileshkin, together with a member of the sel'sovet, Ivantsov, asked a villager to write a positive recommendation

[101] GARO, f. 5, op. 2, d. 5, l. 607 (OGPU, "Opersvodka," March 1930). See also Y. Druzhnikov, *Informer 001* (New Brunswick, N.J.: Transaction Publishers, 1997), for an excellent illustration of the precarious position of a sel'sovet chairman in the person of Pavel Morozov's father.

(*otzyv*) for an accused kulak arrested for hostile agitation against the collective farm. Both Mileshkin and Ivantsov signed the letter, and it was circulated around the village. The OGPU reported that, "Seeing the signature of the party member and a member of the sel'sovet, the majority of the peasants signed the recommendation."[102] In the village of Zabelino, the chairman of the sel'sovet signed into the collective farm himself but advised other peasants not to sign up. He told them: "Don't sign up for the collective farm. If we don't have eighty households who want to enter the collective farm, then we will be saved from it." The OGPU claimed that owing to the sel'sovet chairman's actions, collective farms in the area grew very slowly.[103]

Peasants used the state's expectations against the state itself. If party and sel'sovet members were supposed to be examples, then peasants would follow their examples when it suited them. When the brigade members in one village began to insist upon full entry into the collective farm, local villagers said to them: "There you have Sedel'nikov, a party man. He is not entering the collective farm, and there is no way we are entering either."[104]

The regime underestimated the degree to which the sel'sovets were "of the village." There was massive turnover in sel'sovet membership as peasants endeavored to quit their posts or were purged and as the regime scrambled to fill the sel'sovets with loyalists. The sel'sovet was a kind of bridge between peasant and state through the 1920s, a bridge that was largely dismantled during the first collectivization drive.[105]

In Pitelinskii district, however, the sel'sovet was not "of the village" and had likely been staffed by outsiders in a recent, unscheduled election of the kind that was taking place all over the Soviet Union in late 1929 and early 1930. Members of the sel'sovet assisted the collectivization brigade and participated in the excesses. Sel'sovet members smashed locks and confiscated grain, flour, and bread. They participated in dekulakization, which took place at night without the participation of the "masses,"[106] meaning without even a show of democracy. In Pitelinskii, sel'sovet members did not soften the blow of collectivization by dragging their feet or assigning grain quotas according to custom. They allied with the outsiders. This alliance was a key factor in the rebellion.

[102] GARO, f. 5, op. 2, d. 5, ll. 393–96 (OGPU, "Spetssvodka," 24 February 1930). Similar examples were given for other villages and districts.

[103] Ibid.

[104] Ibid.

[105] Male suggests that the sel'sovet may have played this role, but he does not explore the possibility (*Russian Peasant Organization*, p. 114).

[106] GARO, f. 5, op. 2, d. 5, l. 436 (report from the Riazan county prosecutor, 1 March 1930).

Conclusion

Studies of peasant unrest have identified the factors that push peasants to rebel. James Scott has argued that peasants rebel when they are pushed beyond the line of subsistence, when the "moral economy" of the village is violated.[107] Yet many villages were pushed beyond this line in the Soviet Union during the first collectivization drive and relatively few of them rebelled. While pushing peasants beyond the line of subsistence is crucial to explaining the rebellion in Pitelinskii, the complicity of the local sel'sovet as it went to the aid of the detested outsiders sent in to collectivize the villages of Pitelinskii district remains a central factor underlying the rebellion.

In the Pitelinskii district, village officials violated the moral economy and pushed peasants beyond the line of subsistence. If these factors explain why the rebellion occurred, then the irony is that the regime was saved from more rebellions like the one in Pitelinskii by the one feature of the village that the OGPU complained most bitterly about—the way in which sel'sovets acted as a brake on the collectivization process by refusing to cooperate, by allowing peasants to avoid the collectives, by helping wealthy peasants to disguise their wealth, by dividing grain requisitioning demands by "eater" as opposed to class, by providing false documents, and by accepting any kind of excuse to alleviate state policies. These tactics stopped peasants from taking to the street and engaging in open confrontation with armed forces. Such sel'sovet members were weeded out over time as the regime gained a stranglehold on the countryside, but at this crucial juncture they may well have saved the Soviet regime by softening the collectivization onslaught. The resistance of the sel'sovets prevented a total shattering of the moral economy of the peasant. The foot-dragging sel'sovets held their villages together and ironically may have sacrificed them to the state and to the collective farm in the long term.

[107] James Scott, *The Moral Economy of the Peasant* (New Haven, Conn.: Yale University Press, 1976).

CHAPTER FOUR

Subaltern Dialogues

Subversion and Resistance in Soviet Uzbek Family Law

DOUGLAS NORTHROP

> We must address this question very seriously. We can no longer be patient with violations of women's rights. Our country is growing [and] moving ahead; the collective farms are growing; culture is expanding; we are moving forward on all sides with regard to women. We must take care to help them. Among us Uzbeks it is said that only a crazy person gets mixed up in family matters between a husband and wife. This is not so: what about the cases in which signals arose of [bad] relations between husband and wife, [but] based on this sentiment no attention was paid and bad results [followed]? This [advice to leave family affairs alone] is the invention of *boi*s [wealthy people] and the religious clergy and only serves their hostile ends.
>
> —Abdurakhmanov to a conference of Uzbek Stakhanovite collective-farm women, 1940

By 1940, Bolshevik ideology in Uzbekistan had been transformed in important ways by its Central Asian social and cultural context—and in particular by the logic of its *hujum* (assault), a cam-

Drafts of this essay were presented at the University of Toronto, the University of Georgia, and the annual meeting of the American Association for the Advancement of Slavic Studies in Denver, Colorado, in November 2000. For comments and suggestions I am particularly grateful to Lynne Viola, Daniel Segal, and Francine Hirsch; to my colleagues in Athens; and to the editor and anonymous referees for *Slavic Review*, where this article first appeared (vol. 60, no. 1 [2001]: 115–39). Epigraph: Özbekiston respublikasi markaziy davlat arkhivi

paign for European-style women's liberation that had been launched thirteen years earlier, in 1927. This campaign involved a massive and continuing attack on all manifestations of perceived gender inequality and, especially, on the systems of female seclusion practiced in parts of Central Asia and elsewhere. It represented a recasting of the party's message of class revolution into a new lexicon, that of women's liberation, as a way of translating Bolshevism and its state-building project to the Soviet "East." The hujum persisted for decades, both in practice and in rhetoric, and in some ways is still felt today. It became a foundational myth of the Soviet project in Uzbekistan and long served as a crucial legitimation for Soviet power in Central Asia. Shaped by a combination of orientalist, class, public-health, and moral arguments, it reflected a powerful consensus among party workers, many of them Slavs only recently arrived in Central Asia, that such patterns of daily life as were then being practiced in Uzbekistan had to be changed—both for the betterment of Uzbeks themselves and to ensure the success and survival of Soviet power.

Legal reform was one principal strategy employed to make the Soviet vision of an unveiled, fully equal, socially active Uzbek woman a reality and thereby to create a truly "Soviet" Uzbekistan. Party leaders went so far as to announce in 1940 that one could infer the continuing presence of anti-Soviet "class enemies" from the high rate of crimes committed against women.[1] Class enemies and *byt* crimes ("crimes of daily life") went hand in hand, and in a circular logic each was taken to reveal the other. More than twenty years ago, Gregory Massell noted the particular attention paid by Soviet Central Asian officials to law and legal questions, dubbing this approach "revolutionary legalism."[2] This essay explores the ramifications of this legal approach for the wider relationship between Soviet power and Uzbek society, drawing both on local archives and on Uzbek- and Russian-language materials not available to Massell. By focusing simultaneously on questions of gender, nationality, and empire, it also builds on more recent work in Soviet and postcolonial history. Peter Solomon and others have explored the meanings of criminal justice in Stalin's USSR; this essay concentrates on what Wendy Goldman has called

(henceforth, ÖzRMDA), f. 837, op. 32, d. 2066, l. 102 (transcript of conference proceedings).

[1] ÖzRMDA, f. 2454, op. 1, d. 412, l. 137 (draft article by Uzbek Republican Soviet Executive Committee [TsIK] chair Yoldosh Akhunbobaev).

[2] Gregory J. Massell, "Law as an Instrument of Revolutionary Change in a Traditional Milieu," *Law and Society Review* 2, 2 (1968): 195–200, 219–28; and Massell, *The Surrogate Proletariat: Moslem Women and Revolutionary Strategies in Soviet Central Asia, 1919–1929* (Princeton, N.J.: Princeton University Press, 1974), pp. 192–212.

"the collision between law and life," but unlike most prior work it does so with particular reference to the Soviet empire.[3]

This essay also addresses the crucial issue of power—its character and effects—in the Stalinist order.[4] I have found real debates occurring among local and regional cadres about how the Soviet state should best use the family to reshape Uzbek society. The outcomes of these debates were not preordained and were decided only through an ongoing interplay of ideology, argument, and hard-won experience. The very choice of law as a means of social change, too, shows something of an unexpected weakness of Stalinist authority on the ground. Through the laws they passed, Soviet Central Asian leaders did clearly declare their goal of transforming indigenous family life. Yet the questions of power became far more complicated *after* these laws were written, when the problem became one of putting them into practice.

The campaign to liberate Muslim women through law cannot be judged a mere "success" or "failure"; it played out in a manner that was neither simple nor straightforward. Party leaders and women's activists made concerted efforts to emancipate Uzbek women through legal, judicial, and police action, and Uzbek society reacted to, in many ways subverted, and ultimately reshaped these same efforts. As Nicholas Dirks has argued with reference to British law in India, the imposition of legal norms by a colonizing power can create a discursive sphere in which the contradictions of colonial rule both flourish and are laid open for all to see, a situation that certainly existed in Soviet Central Asia.[5] The encounter between Soviet power and Uzbek society—permeable, unstable, and interpenetrated as each side was—resulted in complex processes of interplay and negotiation between the two, not simple dictation by one to the other. This encounter helped to shape *both* sides.

[3] Peter H. Solomon, Jr., *Soviet Criminal Justice under Stalin* (Cambridge: Cambridge University Press, 1996), esp. pp. 447–69. The phrase is adapted from the title of chapter 3 in Wendy Goldman, *Women, the State, and Revolution: Soviet Family Policy and Social Life, 1917–1936* (Cambridge: Cambridge University Press, 1993), p. 101. Recent scholarship has considered wider Soviet campaigns to transform everyday culture and byt, but usually only in Russia proper. See Michelle Fuqua, *The Politics of the Domestic Sphere: The* Zhenotdely, *Women's Liberation, and the Search for a* Novyi Byt *in Early Soviet Russia*, Treadgold Papers, no. 10 (Seattle: University of Washington Press, 1995).

[4] Recent works on this theme include Sheila Fitzpatrick, ed., *Stalinism: New Directions* (London: Routledge, 2000), and the Annals of Communism series published by Yale University Press.

[5] Nicholas B. Dirks, "From Little King to Landlord: Colonial Discourse and Colonial Rule," in *Colonialism and Culture*, ed. Nicholas B. Dirks (Ann Arbor: University of Michigan Press, 1992), pp. 175–208.

Although most Central Asian Bolsheviks during the 1920s were non-Muslim Slavs, and most Uzbeks joined neither the Communist Party nor the Soviet state apparatus, it would be misleading to see the Soviet-Uzbek encounter as a meeting of two discrete, well-defined sides. As I argue elsewhere, in Central Asia these "sides" only emerged out of this interplay over issues like family life and women's status.[6] At the same time, this essay's investigation of law and legal practices shows the two sides interwoven in complicated and lasting ways. Thanks in part to the official New Economic Policy–era stress on *korenizatsiia* (indigenization), by the late 1920s a small but important group of Uzbeks had come to occupy positions of authority in the Central Asian state and party hierarchies. These indigenous men and women helped define Soviet policy, in the hujum and elsewhere, but in many cases they also helped undercut that policy in practice. As a result, it can be difficult to identify particular individuals—such as Abdurakhmanov, quoted in the epigraph—as "Soviet" rather than "Uzbek," or vice versa. Many such individuals spoke both languages (and no doubt others, too): the mixture changed at different times, with different audiences, and when different purposes were pursued. To identify the discursive universe in which an actor was participating, much depends on the context of the utterance—and on the source in which it has been preserved.[7] This essay explores some of the complexities of this Soviet-Uzbek matrix by showing actors playing conflicting and even contradictory roles from within as well as outside the Soviet apparatus.

I first consider how party activists debated and passed a series of new laws designed as templates to regulate personal behavior within the intimate space of the Uzbek family. By using law to define and enforce "proper" behavior, activists hoped to change the terms of debate within Uzbek society, to accumulate what Pierre Bourdieu calls "symbolic capital" by creating "an official version of the social world."[8] These activists made a series of choices to define the new laws, deeming certain customs—and not others—subject to legal action and judicial penalties. The contingent aspects of these choices can be seen in the extensive debates within party ranks on which "crimes" to identify, how to define them, and

[6] See Douglas Taylor Northrop, "Uzbek Women and the Veil: Gender and Power in Stalinist Central Asia," Ph.D. dissertation, Stanford University, 1999.

[7] These notions have been most thoroughly discussed and theorized by linguistic anthropologists. See, for example, Judith T. Irvine, "Shadow Conversations: The Indeterminacy of Participant Roles," in *Natural Histories of Discourse*, ed. Michael Silverstein and Greg Urban (Chicago: University of Chicago Press, 1996), pp. 131–59, esp. p. 135.

[8] The phrase is from Richard Harker et al., eds., *An Introduction to the Work of Pierre Bourdieu: The Practice of Theory* (New York: St. Martin's, 1990), p. 13. On "symbolic capital," see Pierre Bourdieu, *Language and Symbolic Power* (Cambridge, Mass.: Harvard University Press, 1991), pp. 166–67.

how harshly they should be punished. The activists of the party's Zhenotdel, or "Women's Department," in particular, fought to persuade their colleagues and the regional party leadership to carry out a wide-ranging effort to "protect" (in their terms) indigenous Muslim women through law. Once Soviet legislators arrived at a canonical list of what they called "crimes of daily life," though, such tensions and uncertainties were erased wherever possible, and muted wherever not. Soviet police officers, prosecutors, and judges, many from outside Central Asia, then took up the cause, setting out to survey the population, enforce the new rules, and thereby reshape the fabric of Central Asian daily life along "Soviet" lines. Uzbek men and women responded to these new norms in a variety of inventive ways, making their voices heard both inside and outside the Soviet system and ultimately producing a negotiated outcome. The path to Soviet-style women's liberation turned out to be anything but smooth.

Custom Criminalized: Defining a Canon of "Byt Crimes"

Many European colonial regimes of the late nineteenth and early twentieth centuries attempted to govern vast numbers of subjects with a comparative handful of officials and soldiers. Since direct physical force and coercion alone could not guarantee imperial power, these regimes needed other means to control indigenous populations. Laws and legal norms served this purpose, creating codes of behavior against which colonized individuals could be measured and, if all went well (from the standpoint of the colonial authorities), inculcating these norms among their colonial subjects to such an extent that no massive police force would be required. The "protection" of indigenous women from "oppression" was a common justification for such laws, as for instance when British authorities decided in 1829 to ban the practice of *sati* (widow burning) in India. As postcolonial theorist Gayatri Spivak argues, the protection of Indian women from Indian men in this case helped justify colonial British rule. Such a law became, she says, "a signifier for a *good* society which must, at such inaugurative moments, transgress mere legality, or equity of legal policy. In this particular case, the process also allowed the redefinition as a crime of what had been tolerated, known, or adulated as ritual."[9]

By the late 1920s, Soviet Central Asian authorities had also passed a series of laws meant to address the problems posed by such Uzbek "ritu-

[9] Gayatri Chakravorty Spivak, "Can the Subaltern Speak?" in *Marxism and the Interpretation of Culture*, ed. Cary Nelson and Lawrence Grossberg (Urbana: University of Illinois Press, 1988), p. 298, emphasis in the original.

als."[10] These laws established new norms for personal behavior and created legal templates to shape new patterns of family life. Many of these laws took effect piecemeal after 1917, especially between 1924 and 1926. Marriage codes, for instance, underwent radical changes.[11] The practices of polygyny, forced marriage, and bride-price (known as *qalin*, rendered in Russian as *kalym*) were banned. The legal age for marriage was raised from nine, as permitted (nominally) by the Muslim law code of *shariat*, to sixteen. Forcing a woman to marry against her will suddenly carried a potential sentence of five years in jail. Reforms in divorce procedure and property law, too, safeguarded women's rights and ensured women, at least in theory, a degree of economic independence from men.[12] New laws also addressed women's personal safety: it became illegal to mistreat or insult a woman, and in particular to use force or coercion to induce her to wear a veil or remain in seclusion.[13] When violence greeted the hujum during and after 1927—thousands of Uzbek women were attacked, raped, even murdered and mutilated—special laws were passed and confirmed by the Soviet Supreme Court deeming such acts "counterrevolutionary" state crimes, "terrorist acts" meriting the death penalty.[14] The Soviet state thus expressed expansive goals in passing a panoply of laws. State con-

[10] It should be noted that each nationality received its own distinctive set of "crimes"—specific to Kazakhs, Turkmen, Uzbeks, and so on. See ÖzRMDA, f. 86, op. 1, d. 4434, l. 206 (report on Uzbek People's Commissariat of Justice, 1928), and also Northrop, "Uzbek Women and the Veil," chap. 1.

[11] See Partiinyi arkhiv tsentral'nogo soveta narodnoi demokraticheskoi partii Uzbekistana (henceforth, PATsS-NDPUz), f. 60, op. 1, d. 4868, ll. 25–26 (Zhenotdel report on women's work in Turkestan, 1924); and ÖzRMDA, f. 86, op. 1, d. 2772, l. 148 (resolution on qalin, 1926). PATsS-NDPUz, unfortunately, remains closed to scholars. I am grateful to several colleagues for providing typescripts and notes from PATsS-NDPUz holdings. Some wish to remain anonymous; of those I may acknowledge, I thank Shoshana Keller of Hamilton College for kindly sharing her archival notes. References from Keller's notes are recorded as PATsS-NDPUz(K).

[12] Divorce became easier to obtain, and child support and alimony became obligatory on the part of the spouse with the greater degree of financial independence, usually the husband. See Rossiiskii gosudarsvennyi arkhiv sotsial'no-politicheskoi istorii (henceforth, RGASPI), f. 62, op. 2, d. 1224, l. 55 (Zhenotdel investigation of Central Asian judicial system, 1926); ÖzRMDA, f. 86, op. 1, d. 2217, ll. 22–23 (suggested discussion themes, 1926); d. 4434, ll. 208–9. All subsequent citations from RGASPI are also from f. 62, op. 2, and thus specify only *delo* and *list*.

[13] "O predostavlenii osobykh l'got zhenshchinam po okhrane ikh cherez sudebnye uchrezhdeniia ot nasilii i oskorblenii po povodu sniatiia parandzhi," *Sobranie uzakonenii i rasporiazhenii raboche-dekhkanskogo pravitel'stva UzSSR*, part 1, no. 11 (1927), pp. 234–35.

[14] See ÖzRMDA, f. 6, op. 2, d. 462, ll. 28–29 (RKI [Worker-Peasant Inspectorate] report on women's work, 1931); f. 9, op. 1, d. 3417, l. 135 (report of Committee to Improve Women's Labor and Life [KUBT], 1930); f. 86, op. 1, d. 5602, ll. 1–3 (Uzbek Supreme Court reports, 1929); d. 5885, ll. 382–83 (report on the implementation of byt crime legislation, 1929); d. 6574, l. 42 (KUBT report, 1930).

cerns were wide-ranging and quite intrusive; party activists sought no less than to overturn the fundamental character of what they saw as the most intimate and closely guarded spheres of Uzbek social life.

Each of these laws was announced with great fanfare and publicized widely. Soviet officials justified these new legal norms in humanitarian terms, as required by the party's self-proclaimed duty to defend the most defenseless members of Central Asian society. Party leaders painted a horrific picture of Uzbek life and portrayed each of the new laws as self-evidently progressive and humane—as no more than the expressions of modern common sense. The harm caused to young girls' sexual health as a result of underage marriage, for instance, was said to be contributing to the "degeneration of the [Uzbek] nation."[15] In Bolshevik eyes, moreover, the alleged prevalence of pederasty among Uzbek men showed prerevolutionary Uzbek society to be little more than a den of iniquity and perversion.[16] New Soviet laws were needed to protect Uzbek women and children from the patriarchal oppression that dominated their everyday lives.

By 1927, calls could already be heard for standardization across the Soviet state and uniformity within the codes of family law. One party report argued that the current patchwork of "decrees, resolutions, directives, [and] orders" did not constitute a coherent legal framework, and that one was badly needed.[17] The result, it was hoped, would be a unified web of byt law, which would be both consistent internally and easier to explain and enforce. Yet the party's own debates over the process of defining a new category of "byt crimes" reveal internal divisions as well as the contingent aspects of Soviet policy in Central Asia. Even though newspapers and pamphlets trumpeted the inexorable and inescapable logic of Soviet legal liberation, archival records show vividly the constructed nature of this supposedly seamless web. Party activists came to focus on certain Uzbek customs as "oppressive," for instance, while ignoring others that might equally have been included. These choices, while not altogether arbitrary—they certainly drew on orientalist preconceptions of the "East" shared by prerevolutionary Russian scholars, travelers, and administrators—unquestionably reveal at least as much about these party members

[15] See the report from 1929 in RGASPI, d. 2081, l. 16 (socialist competition to eradicate byt crime).

[16] Pederasty was called a common sex crime (along with qalin) in a report of 1928 in ÖzRMDA, f. 86, op. 1, d. 5602, ll. 22–22ob.

[17] RGASPI, d. 1199, l. 21 (Fifth Provincial Conference on Work among Women proceedings, 1927). For the text of existing byt laws before the standardization of 1926–27, see I. A., "Bytovye prestupleniia," *Vestnik iustitsii Uzbekistana*, 1925, nos. 4–5: 27–30. For an exhaustive list of changes considered in the late 1920s, see ÖzRMDA, f. 86, op. 1, d. 5885, ll. 321–62 (Uzbek TsIK resolution, 1929).

Uzbek women, in veils, on the streets of old Bukhara. Courtesy Rossiiskii gosudarstvennyi arkhiv kinofotodokumentov (RGAKFD).

and their views of the world as they do about the problems facing Uzbek women. In the end, an accepted canon of byt crimes did emerge, but neither its shape nor its exact contents were obvious at the outset to all concerned. Throughout 1927, wide-ranging conversations within the party and in discussion circles (*kruzhki*) debated these issues and found few predetermined answers.

Members of the Zhenotdel argued most forcefully for party attention to what they saw as the patriarchal oppression of Central Asian women. The Zhenotdel, of course, had both institutional and ideological interests in promoting such discussions.[18] Composed principally of Russian and other Slavic women activists from outside Central Asia, the Zhenotdel denounced practices such as female seclusion and veiling, polygyny, and the marriage of young girls. Other party organizations—also staffed disproportionately by non-Muslims—generally agreed with the Zhenotdel's bleak portrayal of Uzbek family life. In their view, however, "women's work" should not be the party's top priority when other issues (such as land and water reform, a major focus in 1925–26) were so urgent. The comparatively few indigenous Muslim communists, nearly all male, also generally lobbied for other priorities, often contending (accurately) that an attack on the veil and local forms of family life would backfire against the party. The few Muslim women in the Zhenotdel and other Soviet organizations before 1927, moreover, did not speak with a unified voice. Some of these women favored legal reform to improve the status of Uzbek women, but others supported a focus on economic training, literacy work, and social welfare reform.[19]

These tensions—between Zhenotdel and party leaders, between newly arrived Russians and indigenous Muslims, and between women and men—were expressed in the debates over how (and even *whether*) to proceed with family law reform. Some Bolshevik writers argued that new family and marriage codes should arise from local conditions rather than party dictates. As long as such laws underpinned the party's economic aims, they should be drawn as flexibly as possible—and no laws should be

[18] Its success in making such arguments enabled the Zhenotdel to survive in Central Asia after its official disbanding in Moscow in 1930. Under the name "Zhensektor" (Women's Section), these activists retained an organizational presence in Uzbekistan for several more years, at least through the mid-1930s, due to the special circumstances of women in Central Asia. A Zhensektor report from late 1936 or early 1937, for example, can be found in PATsS-NDPUz, f. 58, op. 13, d. 1169, ll. 7–14. See Dilorom Aghzamovna Alimova, *Zhenskii vopros v Srednei Azii: Istoriia izucheniia i sovremennye problemy* (Tashkent, 1991), pp. 62–64; and Petr Matveevich Chirkov, *Reshenie zhenskogo voprosa v SSSR (1917–1937gg.)* (Moscow, 1978), p. 71.

[19] For more on these issues, see Northrop, "Uzbek Women and the Veil," chaps. 2, 7, 8.

passed without the support of local Central Asian populations.[20] Other party activists, especially in the Zhenotdel, rebuffed this idea, asserting that the widespread existence of byt injustice showed local populations to be *least* qualified to influence Soviet decisions.

Such arguments highlighted the difficulties of creating uniform laws to govern Soviet family and marital relations. Simply adopting the laws used in Russia did not always work. In Russia and elsewhere, for example, "de facto" marriages had been recognized as equal to official marriages—an approach meant to undercut the sanctity of religious weddings. In Central Asia, however, authorities faced different potential problems: in the name of personal freedom, Uzbek men could ignore Soviet beliefs about "underage marriage" and live with a teenage girl—or with several preteenage girls. Since this could not be welcomed by any good Bolshevik, the argument ran, cohabitation without official sanction thus represented a threat, one that could not be permitted in Central Asia as it was in Russia. As an Uzbek government report to Moscow in 1928 explained, "local conditions" had driven Soviet Central Asian authorities to contradict the Russian Republic's legal codes by recognizing only legally registered marriages as a permissible basis for cohabitation.[21]

Difficulties and disagreements created by such "local conditions" cropped up every step of the way, and efforts to define a canon of byt crimes proceeded fitfully. Even if most party and Zhenotdel activists could agree that a particular Uzbek practice oppressed women and therefore had to be changed, they often found themselves tripped up by the details. How should the "crime" in question be defined? Who was responsible for it, and thus who should be deemed the guilty party? How harsh should penalties be, and how strictly should they be applied? Drawing on long-standing orientalist images of the "East" as well as on Marxist ideas of exploitation, for example, most Zhenotdel workers could agree that certain Central Asian marital practices—such as polygyny, qalin, and the marriage of young girls—should be ended. Yet in each case these well-intentioned general beliefs proved difficult to translate in a straightforward manner into specific laws.[22]

20 ÖzRMDA, f. 245, op. 1, d. 222, l. 118 (Peasant union [*Koshchi*] protocols, 1927). On this debate, see also RGASPI, d. 1240, l. 18ob. (Uzbek Central Committee plenary report on hujum, 1927).

21 ÖzRMDA, f. 86, op. 1, d. 4434, l. 208.

22 Due to space limitations, I discuss here only the first of these areas, polygyny, as an illustration of the problems in Soviet lawmaking. Other topics, such as underage marriage and qalin, are discussed in later sections on social responses to the new laws. For more on the complexities of devising legal definitions for this byt canon, see Northrop, "Uzbek Women and the Veil," pp. 344–63.

Few byt issues inspired more unanimity among party leaders and Zhenotdel staffers than polygyny. Nearly all Soviet legislators agreed that the practice was harmful to women and should not be permitted anywhere in the Soviet Union. Such agreement within upper and middle party ranks, however, was not by itself enough to create forceful and effective laws, since loopholes, flaws, and shortcomings quickly appeared in every effort the party made to end the practice. The Uzbek criminal code of 1926 threatened a jail term of up to one year for those marrying concurrently a second (or third or fourth) spouse and declared that all weddings must henceforth be registered at local civil registry offices (Zapis' aktov grazhdanskogo sostoianiia, or ZAGS) to be recognized as legal.[23] Apart from the issue of public compliance, however, the complexities of Uzbek social life soon seeped through this ostensibly unambiguous prescription. How could Soviet authorities require all marriages to be registered at ZAGS? What about existing (religious) marriages, for example? What about the many regions in which it was impossible to find a ZAGS office? After sharp debate within party ranks, such factors helped bring about a decision in 1928 to recognize as legally binding all *pre-existing* religious marriages, and to require ZAGS registration only for new weddings from that point onward.[24]

This apparently reasonable decision, however, only solved the uppermost layer of problems. It did not take long for lower-level staffers to point out its logical flaws. As the party member Kurbanov declared to one closed-door gathering, if *all* religious marriages now had legal force, then what about existing polygynous marriages?[25] Was the Soviet state sanctioning polygyny? Surely not; that would be inconceivable. But if not, how would a monogamous family structure be determined? Only a few possibilities logically existed. Would it be in order of seniority, with a first wife automatically considered "legal" and later spouses shorn of all rights? Would the decision be left to each family (meaning, in practice, the husband) to choose one wife to keep, with the others thrown out onto the street, publicly shamed, and perhaps driven into prostitution? In Kurbanov's blunt depiction, the party faced three equally unpalatable choices: to permit such injustices to cast-off wives, to legalize polygyny, or to permit a married man to live with many women while legally being married to only one of them.

Such problems boggled the mind, and indeed, the party never ad-

[23] ÖzRMDA, f. 86, op. 1, d. 2772, l. 148; d. 3618, ll. 4–11 (family law code, 1926).

[24] See the sharp debate at ÖzRMDA, f. 904, op. 1, d. 200, ll. 8–12 (People's Commissariat of Justice materials on family law code, 1928). See also "Novyi zakon o brake, sem'e, i opeke," *Pravda Vostoka* (henceforth, *PV*), no. 219/1415 (25 September 1927): 3.

[25] ÖzRMDA, f. 904, op. 1, d. 200, ll. 80b.–90b.

dressed the issue of existing polygynous marriages in a forthright manner. Once banned, to be sure, polygyny was never legalized in Soviet Uzbekistan, although it did achieve a kind of de facto recognition. Women in polygynous marriages were encouraged by Zhenotdel workers and local women's clubs to seek a divorce and to pursue the alimony and child-care support to which they were entitled. Yet they were never required to do so, nor were their marriages declared illegal or defunct. The Uzbek criminal code technically only forbade a married person from *entering* into another marriage, not from continuing an existing multiple marriage. "Life itself," as Kurbanov declared ruefully, "forces [us] into this compromise [*Sama zhizn' zastavliaet idti na etu ustupku*]."[26] His words serve as a motto for the overall Soviet effort to transform Uzbekistan through law.

Soviet Law as a Starting Point: Negotiation, Subversion, Creativity

Soviet laws defining "byt crime" thus emerged only after long and sometimes contentious debates within the Central Asian party and government organizations. Obviously, Bolshevik activists and party leaders were not alone in having ideas about how Uzbek social life should be lived, and (despite occasional appearances to the contrary) their debates did not proceed in isolation from Central Asian responses to Soviet power. To the contrary, many party members—even those new to Uzbekistan—believed that Soviet law could advance only with the support of local populations.[27] Perceived or expected social responses often colored Soviet views about how best to proceed and about whether a particular law would work at all. Despite the undeniable and sometimes overwhelming power of the Stalinist state during the late 1930s and early 1940s, the expressed or anticipated views of Uzbek men and women not directly identified with or connected to Soviet power could (and did) produce modifications, extensions, even withdrawals of official legal norms during these years. Such social responses are fundamental to the processes of cultural negotiation that shaped the various, unstable, and changing meanings of Soviet law in Central Asia.

Many Uzbeks outside the party simply ignored the new laws, while others appropriated and subverted Soviet rules and the new judicial system in a wide variety of fascinating and creative ways. In the words of historian William Wagner, who has studied legal reforms and family life in the late tsarist Russian empire, "although the law affects behavior, it is far easier to

[26] ÖzRMDA, f. 904, op. 1, d. 200, l. 9.
[27] ÖzRMDA, f. 245, op. 1, d. 222, l. 118.

change the law than to use it effectively to inculcate specific values, control behavior, or shape social relations in conformity with ideals."[28] His observation is borne out in Stalinist Central Asia. Despite the dramatic show trials to mete out exemplary punishment for such practices as qalin and polygyny, for example, these practices continued largely unabated, albeit in an altered form to avoid the gaze of Soviet police, ZAGS officials, and Zhenotdel activists. Soviet women's workers privately admitted that many early laws governing byt crimes had what they called a merely "declarative" character, given the resolutely non-Soviet sensibility of most Central Asians.[29] The spectrum of social responses to Soviet attempts to define and enforce a legal category of "byt crime" was broad, fascinating, and complex, ranging from vocal support and open hostility at the two extremes to subtle forms of mutual accommodation. In James Scott's phrase, many Uzbek men and women used the "weapons of the weak" against Soviet incursions. From positions both inside and outside the Soviet system they emulated peasants and colonized peoples around the world by generating "hidden transcripts" that spoke back to governmental and judicial structures of power.[30]

Some Uzbek men and women chose openly to resist Soviet efforts through formal protests. They made speeches opposing the creation of "crimes" out of customary practices; they organized large-scale public meetings to show their opposition; they submitted petitions asking for a reconsideration of the new Soviet laws. They appeared to believe their voices mattered: in 1928, for example, one workers' meeting in the New City of Farghona voted publicly, 50–16, against the idea of raising the age of marriage for girls to seventeen.[31] Archival records from the hujum's early days in 1927 show Zhenotdel workers unhappily contemplating organized crowds of several hundred people marching in protest, and the arrest of crowd "ringleaders" failed to dissuade others. By 1929, party reports complained that such anti-hujum "agitation" had taken on a "systematic, organized character" (allegedly led by Muslim clerics), and that verbal assaults against Zhenotdel activists were occurring all across Uzbek-

[28] William G. Wagner, *Marriage, Property, and Law in Late Imperial Russia* (Oxford: Oxford University Press, 1994), p. 383.

[29] RGASPI, d. 1685, l. 85 (theses on Zhenotdel's tenth anniversary, 1928).

[30] The first phrase is drawn from James C. Scott, *Weapons of the Weak: Everyday Forms of Peasant Resistance* (New Haven, Conn.: Yale University Press, 1985). On "hidden transcripts," see his *Domination and the Arts of Resistance: Hidden Transcripts* (New Haven, Conn.: Yale University Press, 1990).

[31] ÖzRMDA, f. 904, op. 1, d. 203, ll. 109–12 (People's Commissariat of Justice materials on the new marriage code, 1928).

istan. Instances of open protest against the unveiling campaign and against Soviet byt legislation continued throughout the 1930s.[32]

Perhaps the most common form of resistance to the new laws was a simple refusal to observe them in practice. It is even possible that in some cases and in some regions violations of Soviet byt norms became *more* flagrant once they had been written into law. While it is difficult to evaluate the extent to which the commission of byt crime represented a form of protest through civil disobedience, clearly the widespread—in some cases virtually universal—infraction of byt laws could not be ignored by any party activist. Local newspapers, indeed, initially showed the hujum's difficulties with remarkable candor. "Yet Another Victim," screamed one headline in November 1927: "Having recently thrown off the *paranji* [veil], Achil'deeva is savagely strangled by her husband."[33] Only when Zhenotdel and party officials complained that such media reports made people reluctant to cooperate with them did the tone of newspaper coverage shift in the 1930s.

Whether discussed in the newspapers or not, rampant violations of Soviet byt laws remained a cause of concern within the party leadership as well as the Zhenotdel, a fact revealed by the confidential archival record. Throughout the 1920s and 1930s, one finds careful attempts to chronicle individual acts of byt crime, to track and analyze broader trends, and to improve police and prosecutorial efforts to stamp out such phenomena once and for all. The codification of such behaviors as crimes, after all—and their placement in a linked pyramid of criminality, with "counterrevolutionary" byt attacks at its pinnacle—had marked *all* byt transgressions, whether violent or nonviolent, as intolerable political acts. The persistence of such acts may not be surprising in the late 1920s, during the turmoil surrounding the hujum, but they continued throughout the 1930s and beyond, and, according to some accounts, increased over time. Rape, murder, and the occasional mutilation of unveiled women and Zhenotdel activists occurred with regularity—by one estimate as many as 2,500 women were murdered during the first three years of the hujum—along

[32] On the 1927 marches, see ÖzRMDA, f. 1714, op. 5, d. 663, ll. 42–43 (criminal proceedings against Mukhamedjon et al. for agitating against women's liberation, 1927–31); ringleaders' arrests in 1928 are described in RGASPI, d. 1688, l. 187 (report on International Women's Day in Tashkent province). "Systematic, organized" resistance in the form of anti-Soviet speeches across Uzbekistan in 1929 is described in ÖzRMDA, f. 86, op. 1, d. 5885, ll. 381–82. For an example from later years, see Shakirkhoja Tagirkhojaev's protests in 1937 about the legality of marriages to unveiled women. ÖzRMDA, f. 837, op. 32, d. 346, l. 2 (investigative brigade materials on the "Red Partisan" *mahalla* [urban neighborhood], Tashkent).

[33] "Eshche odna zhertva," *PV*, no. 1406 (14 September 1927): 5.

with an apparently endless stream of cases involving polygyny, qalin, and forced veiling and seclusion.[34] Even excluding the large number of rapes and "insults" to women, and leaving aside terrorist acts that qualified under Article 64 as "counterrevolutionary" crimes, the remaining categories of byt crime produced almost one out of every ten cases heard in the Uzbek criminal justice system in 1929.[35] Lamentations that the party was losing the war against byt crime continued throughout the pre-1941 period. Prosecutions of qalin and underage marriage increased dramatically in 1938 and 1939, and the rate of byt murder, sexual crimes, and women being beaten appeared to some observers also to be growing.[36] An official list of byt cases from Khorazm province in 1940–41 included murder, attempted murder, rape, underage marriage, and beatings to prevent wives from attending school or training courses. No wonder that at a conference of procurators held in late 1941, well after the war against Hitler had started, these Uzbek officials each reported dozens of byt cases and discussed the unfortunate "shortcomings" (*kamciliklar*) that continued to mar the realm of women's legal rights and to hinder the war effort.[37]

Resistance through noncompliance was not the only Uzbek response to Soviet byt laws. In many cases, Uzbek men and women did not withdraw completely from interactions with Soviet structures but instead creatively negotiated this relationship to produce benefits for themselves—even if doing so ran the risk of conferring implicit legitimacy on Soviet authorities. Soviet cash, for instance, could be used to pay bride-price obligations.

[34] For some of the copious documentation on such crimes during the 1927–29 period, see RGASPI, d. 1214, ll. 12, 26, 43, 47, 54, 59, 74, 79–81, 83, 89–91, 93–94, 96, 132, 140, 154, 156 (OGPU reports on Central Asian women's liberation, 1927); d. 1520, ll. 224–25 (criminal proceedings against communists accused of raping an unveiled woman, 1928); d. 1692, ll. 22, 113–23, 198–99 (Central Asian Party Bureau [Sredazbiuro] correspondence about murdered women's activists, 1928); and PATsS-NDPUz, f. 58, op. 5, d. 815, ll. 175–78 (internal party investigation of members' implementation of hujum, 1929). Numerous published sources include A. Nukhrat, "Na bor'bu s perezhitkami rodovogo byta," *Sudebnaia praktika RSFSR*, 1929, no. 3: 58; and S. Akopov, "Bor'ba s bytovymi prestupleniiami," *Revoliutsiia i natsional'nostei*, 1930, nos. 4–5: 66. The figure of 2,500 murders is from N. Ibragimova and F. Salimova, "Opyt raskreposhcheniia zhenshchin respublik Srednei Azii i Kazakhstana i ego burzhuaznykh falsifikatory," *Kommunist Uzbekistana*, 1985, no. 8: 83–89.

[35] *Materialy k otchetu Tsentral'nogo Komiteta KP (bol.) Uzbekistana V-mu Partiinomu kurultaiu* (Samarkand, 1930), p. 58.

[36] The number of qalin and underage-marriage prosecutions in the Uzbek SSR grew from 152 in the first half of 1938 to 213 during the first four months of 1939. (PATsS-NDPUz, f. 58, op. 15, d. 1383, ll. 39–43 [Uzbek Central Committee report on work with Uzbek girls, 1939].)

[37] ÖzRMDA, f. 904, op. 10, d. 91, ll. 42–46 (Uzbek People's Commissariat of Justice materials on judicial efforts to eradicate crimes against women). Consider the litany of violations in Farghona in ÖzRMDA, f. 2454, op. 1, d. 412, ll. 135–36, or the crime statistics in ll. 144–45.

Despite a widespread reluctance to observe the precise stipulations of the new laws, moreover, it is striking to note that large numbers of Uzbek men and women still traveled to local ZAGS offices to register their marriages legally with Soviet authorities. Frequently, though, indigenous populations took steps both overtly and covertly to make the new system work to their own advantage and often did their best to modify that system's exact provisions. Patterns of creativity were apparent in the Uzbek responses to new Soviet marital laws, such as the regulations meant to prevent qalin, polygyny, and underage marriage.

Soviet attempts to ban qalin quickly ran into trouble as the new laws were bent, broken, and subverted at every turn. According to one report from 1928, qalin in Khorazm province was "almost legal," since it happened in plain sight and was rarely prosecuted. Party investigations turned up continuing evidence of the practice on a massive scale throughout the 1930s and into the 1940s, with bride-price ranging as high as several thousand rubles, forty-five head of cattle, and large quantities of grain.[38] The only real change resulting from the Soviet effort to ban qalin was a shift away from cattle in favor of (more easily concealed) cash payments, on the one hand, and the frequent portrayal of bride-price payments as wedding "gifts" falling outside the scope of the law, on the other.[39] Such "hidden qalin" could easily be concealed from the gaze of Soviet police and prosecutors; in some cases, local authorities assisted in the deception. Local police officers were known to drive away party investigative brigades, for instance, offering their big-city visitors assurances that they had been mistaken, that byt crimes like qalin did not exist in *this* region.[40] Responses on the ground could be creative. One man accused of rape and forced marriage in 1928, for example, tried to turn the tables on his accuser. He argued that she had accompanied him willingly, that they had had sexual relations voluntarily, and that only afterward had she demanded qalin as a form of blackmail. Although his story failed to sway the Soviet court, it is interesting in its attempt to recast him as the victim of qalin rather than as the criminal.[41]

38 The report from Khorazm is in RGASPI, d. 1690, l. 2 (Zhenotdel report, 1928). One partial audit in 1936, for example, found hundreds of cases during the previous year: see PATsS-NDPUz(K), f. 58, op. 12, d. 638, ll. 96, 105 (Uzbek party and OGPU reports). For the persistence of the practice, as well as the magnitude of the prices involved, see PATsS-NDPUz, f. 58, op. 4, d. 1235, ll. 12–13 (OGPU report on the women's movement, 1928); and op. 9, d. 968, ll. 196–97 (report on conference of collective-farm women in Karadaryo, 1933).

39 On the shift to cash, see ÖzRMDA, f. 9, op. 1, d. 3397, l. 88 (Uzbek party reports on byt crime, 1929); on "gifts," see (among many others) ÖzRMDA, f. 86, op. 1, d. 4902, l. 20 (KUBT resolutions, 1928).

40 RGASPI, d. 1224, l. 48.

41 ÖzRMDA, f. 1714, op. 5, d. 322, ll. 83, 98 (criminal case against Iarashev et al., 1929–30).

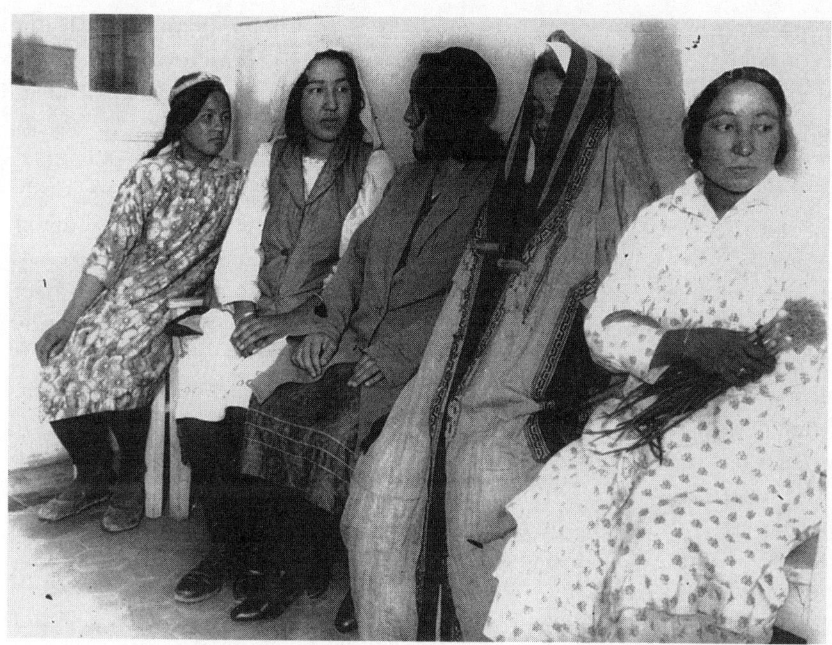

Uzbek women, awaiting examinations to receive certificates of permission to marry. Courtesy Rossiiskii gosudarstvennyi arkhiv kinofotodokumentov (RGAKFD).

Ironically, the very weakness of Soviet efforts to enforce new rules against qalin can be discerned through the records of successful prosecutions. It is quite revealing to consider the cases that actually came before Soviet courts. With thousands of instances of bride-price spread all across Central Asia, criminal accusations generally came to light only if some aspect of the contractual arrangement went awry. Perhaps a man paying qalin in the form of labor decided to seize his bride before working the full agreed-upon term; possibly the young woman refused to participate in an arranged marriage; in some cases, the bride's father reneged on the deal and refused to accept the agreed-upon amount in payment.[42] The wronged party could then threaten to turn to the Soviet courts, but this was a step taken only in extremis, once negotiations had failed, since unlike a *qozi* (Islamic) judge, no Soviet court would enforce the marriage contract. In fact, such an appeal could quite possibly lead to jail time and fines for all the men involved, including those lodging the complaint. For this reason, barring the unlucky few who happened to be visible to Zhenotdel investigators—either because they occupied positions of Soviet

[42] ÖzRMDA, f. 86, op. 1, d. 5885, ll. 387–38.

or party authority or because they had the ill fortune to be present during a spot check or intensive local audit—marriages in which qalin arrangements proceeded smoothly to all parties' satisfaction rarely surfaced in the Soviet courts.

The reported cases thus tend to be exceptional. Each story, of course, no matter what its particulars, served to underscore the self-consciously European horror of Slavic party activists at what they saw as the buying and selling of young girls. But since only in truly extraordinary circumstances would one party to a qalin transaction actually complain to Soviet authorities, these cases also show the boundaries of customary behavior by revealing what acts violated local norms flagrantly enough to trigger such strong social sanctions. Frequently complaints were lodged when one woman was "sold" many times but never actually given in marriage, or when a father or brother tried to squeeze extra money out of a suitor. In 1927, one local official sold his ("very pretty") sister three times for qalin, but he faced trial only when his neighbors complained that he had kept the money and refused to give his sister in marriage to any of the suitors. Another rural Uzbek man was reported in 1936 to have sold his adult daughter to five men over two years; and in 1940, one father was accused of selling his fifteen-year-old daughter for 4,400 rubles and other material goods. After the wedding, though, he seized his daughter—and sent her into hiding in Kazakhstan—threatening to resell her unless her husband paid an additional 10,000 rubles.[43] Clearly, such actions violated accepted codes of behavior among neighbors, not to mention inciting anger among prospective husbands. These cases therefore show Uzbek men using and manipulating the resources of the Soviet legal apparatus to fight a battle antithetically opposed to the one party activists thought they were fighting. Soviet courts were being used to *enforce* rather than overturn the boundaries governing the practice of qalin in Uzbekistan.

Similar patterns characterized Soviet efforts to stamp out polygyny. Although intensive local investigations continued to turn up hundreds of violations during the 1930s, Zhensektor and party activists found it difficult to make headway in enforcing Soviet legislation barring multiple spouses. One delegate to the First All-Uzbek Congress of Female Youth in 1935 complained that men in her region who married second and third wives received paltry prison sentences of only a month or two, after which they returned home and laughed at local Zhensektor workers, taunting them

[43] The case from 1927 is in RGASPI, d. 1250, l. 54 (local party reports on hujum); the one from 1936 in PATsS-NDPUz(K), f. 58, op. 12, d. 638, ll. 96, 105; and the one from 1940 in ÖzRMDA, f. 2454, op. 1, d. 413, l. 72 (articles and speeches of Khursan Mahmudova).

with the question, "What are you going to do [about it]?"[44] Deception, too, played a role: many men obtained false certificates from local *mahalla* (urban neighborhood) commissions stating that they were unmarried, which permitted them to register a new bride at ZAGS. In other cases, they never registered religious weddings at the local ZAGS office.[45] One unhappy party activist, Mostovaia, called such phenomena "hidden bigamy," explaining that if an Uzbek wife did not produce a son she could be taken to ZAGS and divorced in the eyes of the state. Her husband would then marry another wife, but refuse to grant the first wife a divorce according to *shariat*—meaning, given the difficulties experienced by Soviet authorities in making such legal cases stick (not to mention associated claims for child support and alimony), that she could not remarry and had to remain with him.[46] Finally, some men with several wives, including a number of local communists, went so far as to argue that they were serving the Soviet cause by staying married to all their spouses. They were *protecting* these women, they contended, in view of the dangers facing cast-off wives and the current impossibility of an uneducated Uzbek woman's earning an independent, yet honorable, living. If the party had not insisted that he stay married for the sake of social justice, said one such local official, Kadyrov, in 1929, he would of course have divorced all but one of his wives.[47]

Kadyrov's chutzpah may have been unusual, but his playfulness with Bolshevik categories and legal limits was not unique among the reactions to—and reshapings of—Soviet byt law in Uzbek society. Similar patterns of flexibility and creativity were also visible in the last area of marital regulation to be examined here, namely, the rules on underage marriage. The contested and provisional nature of these stipulations were plain to many observers,[48] so it comes as no surprise to find Uzbek men and women will-

[44] ÖzRMDA, f. 86, op. 10, d. 632, l. 209 (transcript of First All-Uzbek Congress of Laboring Female Youth, 1935). Hundreds of cases of polygynous unions were also reported during 1934 in PATsS-NDPUz, f. 58, op. 10, d. 141, l. 32 (Uzbek Central Committee Bureau resolution).

[45] See Emine Mukhitdinova, *Revoliutsionnaia zakonnost' i bytovye prestupleniia na Vostoke* (Moscow-Leningrad, 1929), pp. 29–34. For a case from 1937, see ÖzRMDA, f. 837, op. 32, d. 346, ll. 29, 32.

[46] E. Mostovaia, "Pervoe vsesoiuznoe soveshchanie komissii po uluchsheniiu truda i byta zhenshchin-vostochnits," *Vlast' sovetov*, no. 9 (4 March 1928): 8.

[47] ÖzRMDA, f. 9, op. 1, d. 3397, l. 114. The argument about the contradictions between destroying polygyny and the impossibility of independent economic lives for women was used by "enemies" according to V. Kasparova, "Zadachi 3-go soveshchaniia rabotnikov sredi trudiashchikhsia zhenshchin Vostoka," *Izvestiia TsK RKP(b)*, 1925, no. 9/84: 6.

[48] For a detailed discussion of how these rules were created, see Northrop, "Uzbek Women and the Veil," pp. 356–63.

ing to do whatever was necessary to mitigate the impact of Soviet restrictions, on one hand, and to make the new Soviet system work to their benefit, on the other. Local audits consistently turned up evidence of massive violations of Soviet laws setting a minimum marriage age for girls (and, to a lesser degree, for boys). Again, these cases were likely only the tip of an iceberg, since for the most part only couples who sought to register their marriages with Soviet authorities turned up in such audits. The number of unregistered marriages—such as that of a sixteen-year-old girl discovered in 1939 living with her husband—can only be guessed at, since such cases rarely found their way into Soviet records.[49]

Even among marriages registered at ZAGS, however, underage brides were common. Local audits of civil-registry records turned up hundreds of cases in the late 1920s, and such violations showed no sign of decreasing during the 1930s and early 1940s. They may even have increased when the minimum marriage age for girls was raised to eighteen. One audit in 1935–36 found many marriages of twelve- and thirteen-year-old girls, locating hundreds of cases of underage marriage spread across fifty-four of the sixty-one districts under investigation. The girls involved were mostly between the ages of eleven and fifteen, although some were as young as eight or nine. Another report from 1940 listed a series of cases in which thirteen- to sixteen-year-old girls had been withdrawn from school, veiled, and married to older men.[50]

Uzbek parents—both mothers and fathers, it is important to note—and matchmakers (*sovchilar*) employed various strategies to marry their daughters off before they attained the requisite age. Subterfuge served as a principal tactic. Since ZAGS offices required official certificates (*spravki*) to prove a girl's age, for example, the production of false spravki became a cottage industry. Occasionally a bribe was required—one woman was prosecuted in 1939 for offering 200 rubles to a mahalla commission worker to obtain a false spravka for her seventeen-year-old daughter—but often local Soviet workers and mahalla commission members were only too happy to oblige.[51] Even doctors, whose scientific expertise served as a

[49] This case is described in PATsS-NDPUz, f. 58, op. 14, d. 1092, ll. 1–2 (report on women's work in the October and Kirov districts of Tashkent, 1939).

[50] For a party investigation of Bukhara in 1928, see ÖzRMDA, f. 86, op. 1, d. 5718, l. 208. The audit of 1935–36 is reported in PATsS-NDPUz(K), f. 58, op. 12, d. 638, ll. 95, 105. The 1940 report is in ÖzRMDA, f. 2454, op. 1, d. 412, ll. 130, 139.

[51] The case from 1939 is in PATsS-NDPUz, f. 58, op. 14, d. 1092, ll. 1–2. Other cases of girls as young as twelve being given spravki attesting to their legal age for marriage—often with the connivance or support of local officials—are in ÖzRMDA, f. 86, op. 1, d. 3031, l. 11 (transcript of First Uzbek Congress of Female Soviet Members, 1927); d. 3626, l. 103 (Qashqadaryo KUBT materials, 1927).

court of last resort in certifying the age of girls who appeared too young to marry, could be malleable. Substantial numbers of inflated age certificates were discovered as late as 1941, despite the existence of criminal sanctions against medical fraud.[52] If a ZAGS official appeared reluctant to register a marriage, the applicant's family could assure him or her not to worry, that the family would take the responsibility of dealing with any troublesome Soviet investigators who took an interest in the case—and given the sympathy of local police and Soviet officials, such investigators were unlikely to look very hard.[53] Substitution also proved a simple but effective way to deceive ZAGS officials. One eight-year-old girl in Jizzakh was able to marry a twenty-eight-year-old man in 1929, for example, thanks to her older sister's willingness to appear at the ZAGS office in her name to pass the medical examination. Similar cases occurred throughout the 1930s.[54] In some circumstances, men tried substitution as well. One Uzbek man, for example, was denied a health certificate to marry in 1929 after being diagnosed as syphilitic. Seeking to evade this restriction, he sent a healthy man to the doctor in his place. Unfortunately for him, the plan was discovered (apparently by chance), and he was arrested.[55] Many similar cases, however, must certainly have gone undetected.

These patterns of deception—and the culpability and dubious loyalty of many in the Soviet judicial, police, and civil-registry apparatus—emerge with particular clarity in a case recounted by one Sarymsakova, a delegate from Andijon, to an Uzbek Party Congress in 1929. According to her, local authorities were complicit in dodging the requirements of Soviet byt law, and local mahalla commissions often committed "criminal mistakes" in cases of underage marriage. The corrosive influence of such behavior on Soviet authority could be seen in the story of an unnamed twelve-year-old girl who was to be married in Andijon in 1929. As Sarymsakova told it, the local mahalla commission had provided this girl with a spravka attesting falsely that she was of legal age to marry. The commission then sent her to the ZAGS office, first dressing her in a heavy *khalat* to make her appear more solidly built and placing cotton wadding on her chest to make

[52] ÖzRMDA, f. 904, op. 10, d. 91, ll. 5–6. For criminal sanctions since the early 1930s, see f. 86, op. 1, d. 6556, l. 162 (party resolutions and reports on cultural work among Uzbek women, 1930).

[53] ÖzRMDA, f. 86, op. 1, d. 5594, ll. 234ob.–235 (transcript of Second Congress of Andijon Soviets, 1929).

[54] RGASPI, d. 2080, l. 1 (Zhenotdel discussions of attacks on activist women, 1929). For a similar case in 1935, see ÖzRMDA, f. 86, d. 10, l. 634, l. 225 (First All-Uzbek Congress of Laboring Female Youth proceedings).

[55] ÖzRMDA, f. 86, op. 1, d. 5594, l. 236.

her appear more fully developed. Sarymsakova, a ZAGS employee, became suspicious and, surmising that the girl was younger and slighter than she appeared, sent her to a doctor for examination. When the doctor fixed the girl's age at not more than eleven, her marriage application was denied. But the story did not end there. After this application had been denied, Sarymsakova herself endured repeated harassment from a local police officer, Sabirjon, who insisted that she had been wrong to request the doctor's exam.[56]

Reworking Bolshevism from Within: The Uzbek Soviet Apparatus

This episode shows the potential for an important subversive response by Uzbek men and women to Soviet byt law, namely, to work within Soviet institutions to transform them. Many Uzbeks who gained Soviet or party positions used their newfound authority to block the hujum. This approach amounted to a "nativization" of the Soviet apparatus—a principal goal of the party's *korenizatsiia* policy during the 1920s and 1930s—but did so in ways that were neither expected nor wanted by party leaders. Obviously, not all Uzbeks responded in the same way, and some served in Bolshevik posts with great distinction and loyalty; Sarymsakova, for one, presented herself to the congress in this light, and no evidence exists to the contrary. Uzbek Central Executive Committee chair Yoldosh Akhunbobaev, party first secretary Akmal Ikramov, and Council of People's Commissars chair Faizulla Khojaev, among others, helped to define party policy in the region, and thus played a role in starting and shaping the hujum. Yet many Uzbek professions of support appear strategic: either situational or designed to further other, sometimes hidden, cross-cutting personal and ideological agendas. In any event, not all Uzbeks reacted with support. More often than not, Uzbek personnel within the Soviet and party apparats hindered the hujum, sometimes consciously and sometimes not.

It is not always possible to determine whether such obstruction was a product of conscious action (or inaction) or whether it resulted from bureaucratic inertia, a lack of training, or some other cause. Clearly, some of the difficulties that marred the unveiling and legal campaigns were not intentional products of conscious resistance. Recent scholarship has shown the chaos, disorganization, and disagreement in many Soviet institutions, in Russia and elsewhere. In Central Asia, the massive effort to recruit Uzbek cadres during the early decades of Soviet power—seen with such high hopes by Bolshevik leaders in both Moscow and Tashkent as crucial

[56] Ibid., l. 232.

in providing the Central Asian populace with indigenous models of socialist behavior—worked simultaneously against the efficiency of socialist rule. It required party and government agencies first to rely on ill-trained, semi-skilled, and sometimes completely illiterate local personnel.

This situation had unhappy consequences for the effectiveness of Soviet justice no less than for the efficiency of Soviet administration. Some Central Asian staff workers were unable to understand the "formal juridical language" used in laws and were at a particular disadvantage when these laws had not yet been translated from Russian into indigenous languages.[57] Others refashioned Soviet institutions and authority to work in a way consonant with their own expectations and experiences: one customs officer arrested a woman in 1929, for example, when she appeared before him without a veil. *Pravda Vostoka,* the main Soviet regional newspaper, complained that Soviet courts in Uzbekistan had, under the direction of indigenous judges, taken on a tinge of *shariat* norms. Men had been convicted of entering a house with unveiled women inside and had been found guilty of drinking alcohol, although neither action was a crime under the new Soviet code.[58]

Similar problems cropped up in the courts, where judges and procurators faced manifold difficulties in carrying out the judicial effort to punish Uzbek "crimes of daily life." Many byt cases collapsed, as a result of neglect, incompetence, or sabotage, before ever reaching trial. According to one internal report, for example, the proportion of such failed cases in Uzbekistan reached nearly 50 percent by 1930. Even when problems appear to have resulted from ineptitude as much as from conscious obstruction, higher party leaders and investigators, conditioned by the framework of the hujum, frequently portrayed them as evidence of political deviance and oppositionism. The same report, for example, argued that the high rate of byt cases failing to reach trial showed the prevalence of "Right-opportunist practices" in the Central Asian judicial system. "This shows," it concluded, "how in many places the courts do not serve us, nor [do they serve] the proletarian state, nor the proletariat, nor the party, nor the la-

[57] See the discussions of Turkmen staff members and delays in the early 1930s, for instance, in ÖzRMDA, f. 6, op. 2, d. 462, ll. 10–11, 94–134; f. 9, op. 1, d. 3397, ll. 96–107. A similar report on the Uzbek campaign is in f. 736, op. 3, d. 77, ll. 5–11ob. (Zhenotdel reports on local women's work, 1928). Sometimes the ethnically Russian staff proved unable to address indigenous populations at all: see, for example, the case of a speech to Tajik women in 1927 that was delivered in Uzbek. RGASPI, d. 1694, l. 20 (OGPU reports on hujum, 1928).

[58] The *Pravda Vostoka* complaint is in M. Grek, "*Shariat* v sovetskom sude," *PV,* no. 287/1781 (13 December 1928): 5. For the customs officer in 1929, see Iu. Larin, *Evrei i antisemitizm v SSSR* (Moscow/Leningrad, 1929), p. 13.

boring masses, but rather the kulak, either openly or in a roundabout manner."[59]

Although such accusations may appear overblown—and certainly the use here of the politically loaded tag "kulak" reveals more about party leadership priorities than about Uzbek society—much evidence suggests that many Uzbek staff workers during the 1920s and 1930s *did* consciously use their positions to hinder the Soviet byt campaign. From the perspective of party leaders, such subversion from within the Soviet apparatus could be maddeningly hard to trace and eradicate. Foot-dragging and purposeful obfuscation, after all, could easily be masked as genuine confusion, all the more so because high illiteracy rates and poor communications made confusion a more-or-less normal state of affairs. Police and court paperwork could be lost intentionally as well as accidentally. In some cases, local officials actually hid the murder of women activists from their superiors in Tashkent.[60] All these problems flowed from the perceived need to involve Uzbek men and women in the campaign to stamp out byt crime, both as part of the broader *korenizatsiia* effort and to give credibility to the ostensibly universal norms of personal behavior enshrined in the hujum and the new byt codes. The unintended possibilities opened by this reliance on Uzbek personnel, however, soon became apparent.

The failure (in Soviet eyes) of local police officers, prosecutors, and judges to recognize the political nature of byt crimes lay at the heart of these problems. As a result, women's activists contended, local officials were reluctant to punish byt criminals with the requisite severity. Men arrested for "insulting" unveiled women could sometimes gain release in as little as two hours.[61] The need for a different kind of rapidity—for Soviet justice to be swift as well as sure—remained a continuing theme of party discussions, suggesting that delaying tactics were common among local authorities. Many indigenous officials, after all, were not particularly concerned about eradicating such "crimes" as underage marriage, polygyny, and qalin; and unannounced local audits and confidential investigations found a persistent pattern of failure among local courts and police districts to press for the rapid resolution of such cases. In 1929, for example, byt cases in Khorazm province could take several years to resolve.[62] Similar lamentations about judicial foot-dragging were heard throughout the

[59] RGASPI, d. 2691, ll. 30–31 (transcript of First Central Asian Congress of Zhensektor Workers, 1931).

[60] Anna Louise Strong, *Red Star in Samarkand* (New York: McCann, 1929), p. 257.

[61] PATsS-NDPUz, f. 58, op. 3, d. 1598, l. 35 (OGPU report on hujum, 1927).

[62] *Rezoliutsii Uzbekskogo soveshchaniia rabotnikov sredi rabotnits i dekhkanok* (Tashkent, 1929), p. 16.

1930s and 1940s, as local procurators came under fire for permitting lags in the speed with which women's complaints earned their day in court.[63]

Only a small percentage of cases, moreover, worked their way through the system to a conviction and punishment. An audit in 1928 found 120 cases of underage marriage at one local ZAGS office, in the Old City of Bukhara, but noted that only 10 cases were prosecuted that year in the entire province. During the same year, courts in Andijon province heard only 5 such cases.[64] Even violent crimes appeared to fall between the cracks of prosecutors' workloads. Officials in Khorazm, for instance, reported 20 prosecutions for the murder of activist women in 1928, a figure included in the official total of 203 such murders for the year in Uzbekistan. Yet an independent investigation later discovered that at least 68 such murders had occurred in Khorazm province during 1928, most going unreported and unpunished.[65] Indeed, many local officials appeared eager to reclassify the most serious crimes downward (although doing so was deemed a "Right deviation")[66] by, for example, declaring that a woman's murder or attempted murder had been a "simple" crime (that is, a crime of passion or jealousy) rather than a "counterrevolutionary" crime subject to the death penalty.

All these problems in the Soviet judicial apparatus continued throughout the 1930s and into the 1940s. An internal evaluation of the court system in Namangan province in 1941 is fairly typical. It harshly criticized judicial personnel for failing to classify crimes properly and to apply maximum penalties for byt crimes, for dismissing byt cases without cause, and for obtaining "illegal" verdicts of "not guilty" in what was deemed a clear contravention of the facts.[67] In the angry words of an Uzbek Central Committee Bureau resolution from late 1939, "The organs of the procuracy and courts, which are obliged to lead a decisive struggle against violations of women's rights, [have instead], through the taciturn and indifferent attitude of some party organizations, in most cases not attached the necessary political meaning to the [continuing] fact of brutal violence against activist women, [instead] regarding [this violence] as byt trifles

[63] See ÖzRMDA, f. 904, op. 10, d. 91, ll. 7–10, and Iuldash Saidov, "V Surkhạn-Dar'e oslablena rabota sredi zhenshchin," *PV*, no. 204/5068 (5 September 1939): 2.

[64] ÖzRMDA, f. 86, op. 1, d. 5885, l. 386.

[65] Ibid., ll. 381–83. See also ÖzRMDA, f. 86, op. 10, d. 1091, l. 6 (party reports on women's work, 1936–37).

[66] ÖzRMDA, f. 6, op. 2, d. 462, l. 29.

[67] This report is in ÖzRMDA, f. 904, op. 10, d. 91, ll. 47–55. Similar reports from 1941 describing the provinces of Samarkand and Bukhara are in ll. 58–69 and 72–97, respectively. All such regional courts came under severe scrutiny in a resolution of the Uzbek Commissariat of Justice Collegium (ll. 70–71ob.).

(*bytovye melochi*) and in some cases indulging a mocking attitude toward women."[68] But in Soviet Central Asia by 1939, there could by definition be no such thing as "byt trifles": that had been the point of criminalizing patterns of intimate and social behavior in the hujum. Such patterns could no longer be portrayed as a concern only of the (now defunct) Zhenotdel. The investment of huge amounts of political capital in the Soviet vision of liberation for Muslim women made such continuing transgressions a matter of grave concern for all true Bolsheviks in Central Asia. As a result, any "indulgence" of improper byt behaviors among Uzbek officials represented a grave danger to the Soviet project and to Soviet authority as a whole.

Languages of Power: Uzbeks outside the Party

If Uzbek members of the Soviet judicial and police apparatus found ways to slow or reverse the campaign to define certain patterns of family life as "criminal," Uzbek men and women outside the Soviet system also entered the fray. A fierce battle, both discursive and physical, ensued over the definitions of proper forms of everyday life in southern Central Asia; and efforts to use law and the courts to shape these definitions represented an important front in that struggle. Soviet activists, as already discussed, mobilized a mix of medicine, morality, and Marxism to make the case that so-called traditional byt norms were oppressive, unhealthy, and evil. But their Uzbek opponents subverted Soviet activists' legal and moral spaces and constructed languages to challenge Soviet claims. Polygyny, qalin, and underage marriage, for example, could be portrayed as markers of propriety and devoutness—and by the late 1920s, of national and cultural authenticity—rather than "crimes." By drawing on supposedly timeless conceptions of Uzbek social customs and Muslim religious norms, threats of punishment could be made against those who transgressed pre-existing (if newly constructed) codes of "proper" behavior, such as women who unveiled or Soviet officials who threw men in jail for paying qalin.[69] When a Soviet women's activist ventured into a village outside Tashkent in 1929, to take one extreme example, her body was returned the next day to the city center in a cart, cut into pieces. Her mutilated corpse was thus sent into the public space in Central Asia most identified with Soviet and Russian power with a note attached that read, "Here is your women's free-

[68] PATsS-NDPUz, f. 58, op. 15, d. 81, ll. 10–11 (resolution of the Uzbek Central Committee Bureau, 1939).

[69] See, for example, the letter to Soviet officials threatening such retribution in RGASPI, d. 1694, l. 50.

dom!"[70] Notions of "justice," punishment, and retribution, not to mention the dramatic use of public space, were not uniquely the property of Soviet officials, prosecutors, judges, and activists.

Those Uzbeks, Tajiks, Turkmen, and others who opposed the formulation of new norms of "byt crime" for religious, national, political, and cultural reasons found it comparatively easy to resist the new rules by ridiculing and manipulating the Soviet judicial system. Since from the Muslim perspective ultimate judgments about truth and falsity did not properly fall within the jurisdiction of a Soviet court, witnesses could be produced who would impede a trial by corroborating false alibis, disparaging the victims of byt attacks, or discrediting Soviet officials. In 1929, for example, when the activist Tagirova was murdered by her husband and other male relatives, the guilty parties dragged her corpse to the edge of the village and concocted a story to explain her death. When Soviet investigators nevertheless found sufficient evidence to convene a trial, many witnesses appeared to attest to this story—although happily for the courts (and the only reason that the case later appeared in published accounts), the truth about the murder was "unmasked" in the end.[71] Again it is important to note, though, that such cases appear in official records only on the margins, coming to light only if and when these schemes to mislead the court failed. Many other invented stories or planted witnesses must certainly have succeeded in avoiding detection, and such subversions of the judicial process may have been widespread.

In other, even more interesting cases, Soviet courts and procedures were manipulated to become an instrument working against stated Soviet goals. It has already been shown, for instance, how Soviet courts unwittingly helped police the boundaries of "proper" qalin payments. Such subversions also operated to undercut party personnel. Some anti-Soviet Uzbeks, for example, showing a sense of ironic humor, went so far as to accuse Bolshevik allies of having transgressed—of all things—Soviet byt law and arguing that they needed to be disciplined and punished. In one such case in 1928, a group of Uzbek men brought charges in Soviet court against members of their local mahalla commission. Having mobilized (and apparently coached) supporting witnesses, they accused the commission of running women's liberation meetings while drunk and of forcing women to attend—in short, of violating the code of byt conduct expected of Soviet officials. The Soviet court declared that these accusations were manufactured and convicted the accusers of perjury. The prominent cov-

[70] Strong, *Red Star in Samarkand*, p. 256.

[71] T. T. Inoiatov, "Sudy sovetskogo Uzbekistana v bor'be s feodal'no-baiskimi perezhitkami," *Trudy SAGU* (Novaia seriia, iuridicheskie nauki) kn. 4, 1958, no. 124: 26–27.

erage given to these perjury sentences reveals the deep concern felt by Soviet authorities about the dangers of such a provocative technique, which threatened to subvert the entire system of justice through show trials and educational theater by turning it against its makers.[72]

The very terms of authority in the formulation of Soviet laws were contested and unstable. Once it became clear, for example, that the party treated scientific and public-health arguments as "objective" and thus beyond attack, indigenous opponents of the new byt laws attempted to appropriate the medical and scientific terms of debate. To take one example, consider the debate in the late 1920s over raising the marriage age for girls. In 1928, a meeting of ninety-five union workers in Surkhondaryo (one of the most "backward" regions of Uzbekistan according to party leaders) argued that the marriage age of Uzbek girls should be *reduced,* from sixteen to fifteen. Their argument was clever: "Considering the slower physiological development of Europeans," the resolution declared, "[we] consider it desirable to raise the marriage age for European women to seventeen and for [European] men to nineteen."[73] If Russians wanted higher marriage ages, these Uzbeks had no objection—as long as Russian rules applied to Russians only! The problem in their eyes arose only when colonial political structures and Western medical science imposed externally derived norms on a culture and society that had no need or desire for them. Uzbek union members here announced their willingness to attack the Bolshevik transformation of cultural norms into legal distinctions by subverting their principal tactic—constructing biomedical distinctions through each culture's allegedly distinctive, racially differentiated rate of child development. Unfortunately, the party leaders' response to this resolution is not recorded, but they could not have welcomed such attempts to appropriate their own banner of "objectivity" and scientific certainty.

Finally, Uzbek women themselves occupied a unique position in this struggle over law. Both as agents and as the ostensible beneficiaries of Soviet byt liberation, they had the potential to point out with a comparative degree of freedom the colonialist assumptions and internal contradictions of the new Soviet byt laws. On one hand, these women enjoyed far greater latitude than Uzbek men to protest any aspect of the hujum.[74] Women had many more possibilities for voicing their fears, anxieties, and

[72] N., "Druz'ia chachvana i ichkari," *PV,* no. 1595 (7 May 1928): 4.

[73] ÖzRMDA, f. 904, op. 1, d. 203, l. 106. See also l. 128.

[74] This argument, of course, parallels that of Lynne Viola, who has shown how Russian and Ukrainian women used preconceptions about female weakness and customary roles to lead protests against collectivization. Soviet authorities likewise tended to perceive them as manipulated, not free, actors insofar as they opposed Soviet efforts. See Viola, "*Bab'i Bunty* and Peasant Women's Protest during Collectivization," *Russian Review* 45, 1 (1986): 189–205.

opposition to new laws. Given the party's analysis of Central Asian society as fundamentally patriarchal, after all, in Soviet eyes any Uzbek woman who opposed "liberation" could not be "criminal" in the same manner as her husband, brothers, and father. A young girl by definition could not give her consent to a marriage for qalin, for instance, and only the payer and recipient of bride-price were subject to penalties under Soviet law.[75] Any opposition voiced by a local woman to these new rules was taken by party analysts to show either ignorance (which could be rectified through education) or manipulation and control by male relatives (which would be overcome through the hujum itself). In either case, it was almost inconceivable that she would be subject to lasting criminal sanctions. Even when women led openly defiant protest marches to their local soviet, arrests were made only in exceptional cases.[76]

This interpretation of women's latent sympathy for the Soviet program, which underpinned the hujum itself, thus created spaces for women that did not exist for men. But women as well as men had been socialized into local norms of propriety and decorum, and these beliefs cannot be understood merely as a form of false consciousness or as an act of complicity in their own oppression. Women who observed the principles of strict seclusion, after all, could enjoy great influence and moral authority within their households and communities.[77] Given this fact, it is not surprising to discover some women taking advantage of the resulting opportunities. Mothers as well as fathers had arranged marriages for their thirteen-, fourteen-, and fifteen-year-old daughters, for example, and while seeking good matches they also paid attention to the issue of how much qalin could be obtained. By the early 1930s, some party activists wrote confidentially to their superiors to complain that indigenous women helped hide evidence of byt crimes and thus represented a noteworthy part of the byt problem.[78] Even so, *female* criminals in Central Asia were amnestied en

[75] ÖzRMDA, f. 86, op. 1, d. 2772, l. 148; d. 3933, ll. 88–89.

[76] Such women were usually described as the wives of *bois* or Muslim clerics, and generally only a few "ringleaders" were arrested for a short time. See ÖzRMDA, f. 86, op. 2, d. 27, l. 41 (report by Zhukova and Shadieva on women's work, 1928); RGASPI, d. 1419, l. 40ob. (Sredazbiuro information on International Women's Day, 1928); d. 1689, l. 55 (Sredazbiuro discussions of Central Asian holidays, 1928); d. 2064, l. 48ob. (OGPU reports on hujum, 1929).

[77] Some women, for instance, became *otins*, a uniquely Central Asian institution in which women served as religious teachers with full oversight responsibility for other female believers. *Otins* enjoyed positions of very high status and honor, equivalent in many ways to that of (male) mullahs and with a similar charge to uphold and spread the faith. See Habiba Fathi, "Otines: The Unknown Women Clerics of Central Asian Islam," *Central Asian Survey* 16, 1 (1997): 27–43.

[78] ÖzRMDA, f. 9, op. 1, d. 3385, l. 54 (report on byt crimes in Turkmenistan, 1929–30).

masse in 1928, a step meant as a celebratory commemoration of the Zhenotdel's tenth anniversary.[79] The adoption of gender liberation as shorthand for Soviet revolution helped bring about such an approach, despite the foreseeable consequences: the release of female byt offenders further undercut efforts to enforce the new laws.

To be sure, most Uzbek women did not declare open opposition to the new byt laws. A small minority actively welcomed the Soviet attack on indigenous forms of patriarchy and worked hard to help eradicate female seclusion and subordination.[80] Some local women took advantage of Soviet courts when it was in their interest to do so, while most simply ignored them. At the same time, female opposition, where it existed, represented a much deeper threat in principle to the hujum as a whole, and thereby to Soviet power in Central Asia, than is shown by the small number of women willing to stand up and speak out against such foreign forms of "liberation." Zhenotdel and party activists remained hamstrung by the ideological necessity of treating *all* indigenous women as potential revolutionary allies and by their consequent inability to take action against recalcitrant women. The resulting threat these women presented is plain. Their actions, along with those of their male counterparts, suggests something of the scope for resistance remaining in—indeed, in some ways created by—the strictures of the Stalinist state in prewar Uzbekistan. Clearly, that state held enormous power, in many obvious and crucially important ways. Nevertheless, the many creative patterns of popular response and subaltern resistance to Soviet laws show how Uzbek women and men simultaneously found ways to shape the world in which they lived. The final outcome—as measured in the character of Uzbek daily life as it was lived in the intimate and social spaces of family, neighborhood, and town—resulted from an ongoing interplay between these two always interwoven and mutually shaping sides, not through dictation by one to the other.

[79] For more on this amnesty, see ÖzRMDA, f. 86, op. 1, d. 5885, ll. 476 and 489–92.

[80] This group of indigenous female activists is the focus of many Soviet (and some Western) publications. Apart from a small number of female relatives of top party leaders and those inspired by pre-Soviet *jadid* reformers, the footsoldiers of this cohort were drawn disproportionately from socially marginal groups like widows and orphans. As such, they occupied positions largely outside local kin networks, which meant they were not subject to the same control by male relatives and benefited from new Soviet social, educational, and welfare institutions. See, for example, *Pervyi s''ezd trudiashcheisia zhenskoi molodezhi Uzbekistana* (Tashkent, 1936), pp. 63–66; *Probuzhdennye velikim Oktiabrem: Sbornik ocherkov i vospominanii* (Tashkent, 1961); and V. P. Pal'vanova, *Emansipatsiia musul'manki: Opyt raskreposhcheniia zhenshchiny sovetskogo Vostoka* (Moscow, 1982), pp. 163–201. A good recent study of this group is Marianne Ruth Kamp, "Unveiling Uzbek Women: Liberation, Representation and Discourse, 1906–1929," Ph.D. dissertation, University of Chicago, 1998.

CHAPTER FIVE

Sexual and Gender Dissent

Homosexuality as Resistance in Stalin's Russia

DAN HEALEY

The collapse of communism and the opportunities to examine new sources have encouraged students of Soviet society to explore evidence of popular discontent in Stalin's Russia. Scholars may disagree about whether foot-dragging or absenteeism constitute genuine resistance to the regime or its economic program. They may question the extent to which feigned compliance on the collective farm or drunkenness on the shop floor reveal resistance. Yet by and large, historians—even those unsympathetic to the concept of resistance as deployed in this volume—agree that discontent was real, and that this unhappiness was reflected in a range of deviant, destructive, or simply stubborn behaviors that did not conform to the evolving Stalinist ethos.

Many, perhaps most, students of Soviet society and politics would, however, find it difficult to recognize the place of homosexuality anywhere on the spectrum of resistant behaviors. How, they might ask, could deviant sexuality constitute a form of resistance? Presumably, homosexuals were simply following the dictates of their hormones (or their psychosexual development or, more fashionably, their genes), and then getting caught by the police. Weren't homosexuals in Stalin's Russia just one more group among the many tragic victims of the times? Like certain social groups, national minorities, and *byvshie liudi* ("former people," or elites from the prerevolutionary era), didn't homosexuals simply suffer the fate of a suspect group status, subject to "social engineering" and repression? Moreover, except for

The author gratefully acknowledges the support of the Social Sciences and Humanities Research Council of Canada, the Stalin-Era Research and Archives Project of the University of Toronto, and the Wellcome Trust (grant no. 488142).

the occasional talented artist or poet, wasn't Russia a comparatively innocent (that is, elemental and pure) agrarian nation? Were there enough homosexuals in the Soviet Union to constitute resistance in the first place?

These questions surely exaggerate the state of current attitudes on this topic and do not reflect the most imaginative thinking being done in the historical profession. Yet our general failure to consider the diverse histories of Soviet sexualities serves to replicate not only Stalinist silences but the gender conservatism of cold-war historiography. Historians of Russia have enriched our understandings of society by revising traditional Marxist and totalitarian models and applying insights from peasant studies, labor and gender history, and other areas in comparative, cross-cultural contexts. In an analogous fashion, the insights available from queer theory and from associated currents in the histories of sexualities can be productive devices for revising our ideas about Soviet sexualities, allowing us to transcend the reductionist and sexist habits of mind we have inherited from both right and left.

Building on feminist sociology and the new historiography of sexualities, queer theory proposes that "heterosexuality" and "homosexuality" are not eternal, natural, or universal aspects of the human condition, but rather historically rooted and culturally specific constructs for organizing the way we love.[1] Anthropologists and historians who evaluate their subjects through these constructs often risk cultural imperialism and anachronism. Nineteenth- and twentieth-century Western and Central European sexologists invented our hetero/homo divide, prescribing moral norms veiled as scientific knowledge. Sexologists transformed what had been ill-defined vices supposedly the province of any wayward rake or virago ("sodomy," "pederasty," "tribadism") into an essentialized condition, "homosexuality," determined by a biological substrate. (The root cause usually mooted was at first degeneration, but claims would later be made for psychosexual, hormonal, and genetic explanations.) Modern states, through medical and legal regulation, processed individuals according to these norms: some deviants were identified, arrested, and imprisoned, while others (often at first from affluent social groups) received psychiatric treatment. The trajectory of these interventions in the inter-

[1] Some principal texts include Michel Foucault, *The History of Sexuality*, vol. 1: *An Introduction*, trans. R. Hurley (London: Penguin, 1978); Guy Hocquenghem, *Homosexual Desire* (Durham, N.C.: Duke University Press, 1993); Judith Butler, *Gender Trouble: Feminism and the Subversion of Identity* (London: Routledge, 1990); Eve K. Sedgwick, *Epistemology of the Closet* (Berkeley: University of California Press, 1990); Gilbert Herdt, ed., *Third Sex, Third Gender: Beyond Sexual Dimorphism in Culture and History* (New York: Zone, 1993); Jonathan Ned Katz, *The Invention of Heterosexuality* (New York: Dutton, 1995).

ests of "biopower" (the management of populations in its widest sense) varied by country. But the outcome was to produce an abiding and stigmatized identity as "homosexual" within individuals who experienced desire for their own sex.

Significantly for our discussion of resistance, these individuals were not passive vessels: they responded by appropriating "a host of definitions and meanings which could be played with, challenged, negated, and used."[2] "Homosexuals" engaged in a dialogue with sexologists and, one might add, the state, exploiting and extending the possibilities available in their identification as a "species" supposedly endowed by nature (and confirmed by modern science) with a specific sexuality.[3] Queer historians propose the concept of "identity as resistance" for same-sex-loving people living within dominant sex/gender systems.[4] By recognizing and manipulating the new definitions of homosexuality as a biomedical anomaly, men and women who loved their own sex claimed a right to that love because it was "just the same in nature as the normal man's attraction to a woman."[5] The doctors' diagnosis became, in the hands of patients, a birthright, a claim with social and political ramifications.

The first wave of homosexual emancipation, a primarily German movement founded in 1897 and extinguished almost immediately after the Nazis' rise to power, was led by socialist physician, sexologist, and homosexual Magnus Hirschfeld. This movement based its claims for justice on a rationalist faith in learning and science. Seeking possible explanations for the origins of sexual variation, Hirschfeld corresponded with researchers and wrote avidly about the latest developments in degeneration theory, psychoanalysis, and, especially during the 1910s and 1920s, the new science of the hormones, endocrinology. Across Europe, intellectuals who experienced same-sex desire produced a range of arguments in defense of it. Many relied on the biomedical explanation; some also chose to emphasize the transhistorical persistence of homosexual desire, and in

[2] Jeffrey Weeks, *Against Nature: Essays on History, Sexuality, and Identity* (London: Rivers Oram, 1991), p. 77.

[3] Foucault, *History of Sexuality*, vol. 1, p. 43; on the complicitous dialogue of homosexuals and sexologists, see Harry Oosterhuis, "Richard von Krafft-Ebing's 'Step-Children of Nature': Psychiatry and the Making of Homosexual Identity," in *Science and Homosexualities*, ed. Vernon A. Rosario (London: Routledge, 1997); and Oosterhuis, "Medical Science and the Modernization of Sexuality," in *Sexual Cultures in Europe: National Histories*, ed. F. X. Eder, L. Hall, and G. Hekma (Manchester: Manchester University Press, 1999).

[4] Weeks, *Against Nature*, pp. 74–79.

[5] From an autobiographical sketch, "History of My Illness," written by "female homosexual" and "transvestite" Evgeniia Fedorovna M., in A. O. Edel'shtein, "K klinike transvestitizma," *Prestupnik i prestupnost': Sbornik II* (1927), pp. 273–82.

particular, the noble emotions invested in this desire in ancient Greece and Rome.[6] In the first three decades of the twentieth century, Russia was not untouched by this Europe-wide response to the medical redefinition of same-sex love.[7]

Of equal importance for understanding "identity as resistance" is the argument that identification with a subculture enabled large numbers of men to express same-sex desire in the teeth of oppression by the dominant sexual system. Comparatively small numbers participated in the intellectual flowering of the first wave of homosexual emancipation, but large cohorts of youths and men took part in the concealed world of the male homosexual subculture. Young men growing up in the city or arriving there for the first time encountered that subculture's rituals, argot, habits of gesture, and traditions of sexualized territories. These mechanisms, many of them concealed or bearing ambivalent "innocent" and subcultural meanings, enabled men to hail each other across social boundaries that otherwise separated them. Prostitution, friendship, mentoring, romantic love, and other forms of affinity characterized sexual contacts in this world. The subculture offered individuals who experienced same-sex love opportunities for self-expression despite society's prohibition of such relations. To be sure, not all those who felt same-sex desire chose to pursue it. But all individuals facing this dilemma confronted a series of conscious choices about how they might go about their daily lives. The men inhabiting and maintaining the homosexual subculture were historically significant actors who used the tactics of the weak to construct "a gay world."[8]

[6] On Hirschfeld's scientific activities and political movement, see James Steakley, "*Per scientiam ad justitiam*: Magnus Hirschfeld and the Sexual Politics of Innate Homosexuality," in *Science and Homosexualities*, ed. Rosario.

[7] Evgenii Bershtein, " 'Psychopathia sexualis' v Rossii nachala veka: Politika i zhanr," in *Eros i pornografiia v russkoi kul'ture/Eros and Pornography in Russian Culture*, ed. M. Levitt and A. Toporkov (Moscow: Ladomir, 1999); Dan Healey, *Homosexual Desire in Revolutionary Russia: The Regulation of Sexual and Gender Dissent* (Chicago: University of Chicago Press, 2001), chap. 4.

[8] George Chauncey, writing about the emergence of a gay subculture in New York City in the early twentieth century, argues that "[t]he history of gay resistance must be understood to extend beyond formal political organizing to include the strategies of everyday resistance that men devised in order to claim space for themselves in the midst of a hostile society. . . . The full panoply of tactics gay men devised for communicating, claiming space, and affirming themselves—the kind of resistant social practices that the political theorist James Scott has called the tactics of the weak—proved to be remarkably successful in the generations before a more formal gay political movement developed." Chauncey, *Gay New York: Gender, Urban Culture, and the Making of the Gay Male World, 1890–1940* (New York: Basic, 1994), p. 5, citing James C. Scott, *Weapons of the Weak: Everyday Forms of Peasant Resistance* (New Haven, Conn.: Yale University Press, 1985); and Scott, *Domination and the Arts of Resistance: Hidden Transcripts* (New Haven, Conn: Yale University Press, 1990). Chauncey argues that for New

Queer theorists and practitioners of the new histories of sexualities are not merely interested in how queer sexualities are constructed but also ask how hegemonic heterosexuality has been produced as a modern medical-moral artifact.[9] Studying heterosexuality means analyzing its constituent elements. We are invited to dismantle and question the linkages and distinctions between sex (as an apparently dimorphic, biological given), gender (a social matrix mapped onto bodies and personalities), and sexualities (eros channeled according to a sex/gender system). This analytical work continues to launch a range of projects globally in the histories of sexualities, sexology, and culture; it suggests rich potential for research in our field, going far beyond a revisiting of the persecution of homosexuals in Stalin's Russia.

Whatever the intriguing possibilities for future research, scholars interested in applying these theoretical frames must undoubtedly start with fundamental questions about the regulation of sexualities. This essay examines key issues in the history of Soviet sodomy (*muzhelozhstvo*) laws: their formation, and resistance to them during the Stalin years. It is a history for which the presumed core source base remains untapped. To the best of my knowledge, no researchers, foreign or Russian, have approached the FSB (Federal'naia sluzhba bezopasnosti, or Russia's current secret police) or Presidential Archives with a request for materials on the proposal, debate, decree, and enforcement of the 1933–34 sodomy law. The disincentives inherent in such a request need no elaboration. Yet they remind us that research in postcommunist conditions is still subject to significant limitations. We should remember too that similar lines of research find barriers to access in our own countries, including a source base fragmented by jurisdictional complexities, sequestered by privacy and access restrictions, and censored by systematic homophobia. Despite these obstacles, it is still possible to exploit various sources now available.

York's gay men, tactics of both display and concealment were crucial to the construction of a subculture. Display within the subculture in the form of the use of sexualized territories, slang, styles of dress, and gesture attracted other participants. Concealment tactics "should also be considered a form of resistance," since they enabled the gay world to develop and survive alongside the dominant heterosexual order; Chauncey, *Gay New York*, p. 374 n. 5.

[9] "Queer" is usually understood to describe stigmatized sexualities that transgress the modern heterosexual norm. Some familiar sexological terms for the kinds of sexualities it comprehends include homosexuality, bisexuality, transsexualism, transvestism, and hermaphroditism; but the analytical attraction of "queer" lies in its postmodernist refusal to acquiesce to the fusing of biological sex, gender, and sexuality that sexological labels inflict. See Annamarie Jagose, *Queer Theory: An Introduction* (New York: New York University Press, 1996); and Pat Califia, *Sex Changes: The Politics of Transgenderism* (San Francisco: Cleis, 1997). To avoid the impression of anachronism that use of "queer" creates in an historical setting, I refer instead to "sexual and gender dissent."

A publication in the bulletin of the Archive of the President of the Russian Federation (APRF), released to justify the decriminalization of sodomy in 1993, partially lifted the veil on the origins of the 1930s decree. Details can be further corroborated by documents from Russian state archives. Evidence for the enforcement of the antisodomy law, for example, can be found in sentencing and criminal case file documents for some thirty-six defendants tried before the Moscow city courts between 1935 and 1941. An additional, important range of sources, suggested by queer theory and histories of sexualities and previously ignored by most historians, comes from published forensic medical and psychiatric literature. Using this source base, Soviet constructions of homosexuality as both medical phenomenon and *byt* (custom or everyday life) crime can be established and their evolution traced. The varied authorship of these sources poses questions about the origins, levels, and types of resistance at play and leads to an assessment of the conceptual value of resistance when considering sexual and gender dissent under Stalin.

Bolsheviks, Byt, and Homosexualities

Bolshevik ideas about same-sex love are poorly documented and little understood. The early revolutionary regime inherited a set of legal traditions, policing practices, and medical developments that influenced Soviet approaches. Although this inheritance can only be summarized here,[10] its chief characteristic was a focus on anal intercourse between males, whether it was consenting, forced, or abused a trust. The Nicholaevan civilian sodomy ban of 1835 and the Petrine military ban before it were concerned with preserving male hierarchies. The perceived submission of one man to another in anal intercourse (expressed in so-called active/passive terms) violated structures of authority. Women's same-sex love did not attract similar concern and, along with forms of gender dissent, rarely came to the attention of officials.[11] In contrast to other European powers, Russia enforced its sodomy ban only sporadically. By 1905, prosecutors in St. Petersburg and Moscow were ignoring consensual sodomy and trying cases only when the use of force was in evidence (in Moscow's court records, "rapes" or *iznasilovaniia*) or when boys under

[10] For a fuller account, see Healey, *Homosexual Desire in Revolutionary Russia.*

[11] On tsarist sodomy legislation, see Laura Engelstein, *The Keys to Happiness: Sex and the Search for Modernity in Fin-de-Siècle Russia* (Ithaca, N.Y.: Cornell University Press, 1992), pp. 57–71; for an example of comparative disinterest in women's same-sex relations, see Dr. Zuk, "O protivozakonnom udovletvorenii polovago pobuzhdeniia i o sudebno-meditsinskoi zadache pri prestupleniiakh etoi kategorii," *Arkhiv sudebnoi meditsiny i obshchestvennoi gigieny* no. 2, sec. 5 (1870), pp. 8–13.

fourteen were involved. Even after 1905, with the recorded increase in crime, only eight such cases were prosecuted in the two capitals.[12]

This era also saw a dramatic increase in public discussion about same-sex relations and their regulation. Laura Engelstein has documented the debate among jurists on the sodomy ban, pointing to a conservative wing that sought to retain it and a liberal wing, led by V. D. Nabokov, which opposed it on privacy grounds.[13] The flood of French, German, and Austrian sexological literature proffering the medicalized view of the homosexual, which found a cooler reception among doctors in Russia, did acquire more authority in the last decade of the *ancien régime*. A wide readership beyond the medical profession was exposed to the sexological turn, especially after 1905 when censorship relaxed and entrepreneurs rushed to satisfy demand for popular scientific genres.[14] In 1906, Mikhail Kuzmin published the world's first homosexual coming-out narrative with a happy ending, *Wings* (*Kryl'ia*), and the novel became a "catechism" for a generation.[15] While Social Democrats inside Russia deplored Kuzmin and, perhaps by extension, a politics of homosexual emancipation, their counterparts in exile were exposed to the long-standing commitment of Europe's leading Social Democratic Party to repeal antihomosexual legislation in Germany. This commitment had been secured by the socialist Magnus Hirschfeld of Berlin, who argued that homosexuals constituted a biological "third sex" entitled to civic dignity and respect.[16]

Socialist thinking about sexuality gravitated toward two potentially contradictory poles: forces intent on dismantling the old order and those concerned with constructing a new one along rational lines. Dismantlers of bourgeois philistinism like Aleksandra Kollontai devoted their efforts to the elimination of the influence of church and state over the private

[12] Late Imperial Russia, however, saw a sharp increase in sodomy convictions in the Caucasus and a jump in the proportion of non-Slavic inhabitants among those convicted in this region. On enforcement in the capitals, see B. I. Piatnitskii, *Polovye izvrashcheniia i ugolovnoe pravo* (Mogilev, 1910), p. 33; I. B. Fuks, *Gomoseksualizm kak prestuplenie. Iuridich. i ugol.-politich. ocherk* (St. Petersburg, 1914), p. 83. Data for 1905 through 1913 come from annual editions of the Ministry of Justice's *Svody statisticheskikh svedenii po delam ugolovnym* (St. Petersburg, 1905–1913).

[13] Engelstein, *Keys to Happiness*, pp. 63–71.

[14] Healey, *Homosexual Desire in Revolutionary Russia*, chap. 4.

[15] On the novel and its influence, see Simon Karlinsky, "Death and Resurrection of Mikhail Kuzmin," *Slavic Review* 38, 1 (1979): 92–96. On Kuzmin, see John E. Malmstad and Nikolay Bogomolov, *Mikhail Kuzmin: A Life in Art* (Cambridge, Mass.: Harvard University Press, 1999).

[16] On SPD support of Hirschfeld's campaign, see Gert Hekma, Harry Oosterhuis, and James Steakley, "Leftist Sexual Politics and Homosexuality: A Historical Overview," in *Gay Men and the Sexual History of the Political Left*, ed. G. Hekma, H. Oosterhuis, and J. Steakley (Binghamton, N.Y.: Harrington Park Press, 1995).

sexual lives of citizens. Authentic relationships, "based on the unfamiliar ideas of complete freedom, equality, and genuine friendship,"[17] were expected to flourish after private property and the state that supported it had been abolished. Experimentation in love relationships was a healthy consequence of revolution. During the 1920s, Kollontai became the Soviet Union's leading representative on the international committee of the World League for Sexual Reform (WLSR), the main forum for Hirschfeld's coalition-building sexual politics.[18] The WLSR hailed Soviet intentions to dismantle the old sexual order, expressed in the radical sexual legislation of the new Soviet republic. But the potentially clashing aspiration to channel sexual energies into "healthy" grooves would exercise greater ideological appeal among ascetic Soviet radicals. Vladimir Lenin's few pronouncements on sexual matters were entirely devoted to quashing ill-defined leftist talk about freedom "from the serious in love . . . from childbirth . . . [and] freedom for adultery".[19] While Lenin said nothing about homosexual emancipation as such, Clara Zetkin represented him as having little regard for particularist sexual politics. In Zetkin's 1925 account of Civil War–era conversations with Lenin, the leader articulated an impatience with sex talk in the party's youth wing and among women, and a desire to confine the troublesome question to the custody of science and the counsel of older, experienced (and mostly male) communists.[20]

These representations of Lenin-as-sex-rationalizer come to us heavily mediated, published five years after they were supposedly voiced, and often reproduced because they suited the sexual politics of Stalinism. In contrast, when the Bolsheviks came to power in October 1917, they drew on a spectrum of liberal and radical attitudes toward sexuality. Bolsheviks had no single line on homosexuality, but reacted to questions of same-sex love according to context. The criminal code for the Russian Republic included the elimination of the tsarist antisodomy statute.[21] Although

[17] Alexandra Kollontai, "Sexual Relations and the Class Struggle," in *Selected Writings of Alexandra Kollontai*, trans. Alix Holt (London: Allison and Busby, 1977), p. 241.

[18] For Kollontai's appointment to the WLSR international committee, see Rossiiskii gosudarstvennyi arkhiv sotsial'no-politicheskoi istorii (henceforth, RGASPI), f. 134, op. 1, d. 448, ll. 1–3; on the WLSR, see Ralf Dose, "The World League for Sexual Reform: Some Possible Approaches," in *Sexual Cultures in Europe*, ed. Eder et al.

[19] See correspondence between Lenin and I. F. Armand, 1915, in V. I. Lenin, *Polnoe sobranie sochinenii*, 5th ed. (Moscow, 1960), vol. 49, pp. 51–52, 54–57.

[20] Klara Tsetkin, *O Lenine. Vospominaniia i vstrechi* (Moscow, 1925); for an English translation of the chapter on marriage, sex, and family, see Clara Zetkin, *Lenin on the Woman Question* (New York: International Publishers, 1934), pp. 7, 10–11.

[21] The Bolsheviks' coalition partners, the Left Socialist Revolutionaries (LSRs), drafted a proposed criminal code in January 1918 that explicitly decriminalized consensual adult sodomy. See Gosudarstvennyi arkhiv Rossiiskoi Federatsii (henceforth, GARF), f. A353, op.

archival sources reveal little about their reasons for doing so, the Bolsheviks involved in codification expressed a determination to secularize crime legislation. The precedent of the French Revolution (when offenses with religious resonance such as sodomy were purged from French penal law) significantly influenced their thinking.[22] The code they finally approved in 1922 dramatically secularized the old tsarist definitions of sex crime, invoking instead terminologies derived from forensic medicine and even the police blotter. The six relevant articles in the new code also employed largely gender-neutral formulas, a distinct break with the past. The 1922 Russian Republic criminal code, and the revised code that followed in 1926, contained no mention of "sodomy."[23] Soviet Russia was the most significant power since revolutionary France to decriminalize male same-sex love; sentences for the same acts ranged from five years (for "unnatural vice") in Germany to life (for "buggery") in England.[24]

Modernizing sexual regulation left the political status of same-sex love in Soviet Russia ambiguous. The only senior figure to speak about the law and its positive meaning for homosexuals, Health Commissar Nikolai Semashko, did so in early 1923, while visiting Hirschfeld's Institute for Sexual Research in Berlin, and his words were not reported on at home.[25] Some Soviet psychiatrists linked their interest in homosexuality to cutting-edge currents in hormone research, many of them following leads pro-

---

2, d. 164, ll. 115–16. The Bolsheviks only began to codify criminal law from 1920, but their early drafts also decriminalized sodomy. GARF, f. A353, op. 4, d. 301, l. 11ob.

[22] For a chief drafter's commentary, see GARF, f. A353, op. 4, d. 301, ll. 25–26ob.

[23] The tsarist terminology included *liubostrastnye deistviia* (nonpenetrative sexual assault), *liubodeianie* (heterosexual rape), *muzhelozhstvo* (sodomy), and *krovosmeshenie* (incest): GARF, f. A353, op. 4, d. 301, ll. 11ob.–12. For example, *Ugolovnyi kodeks RSFSR (1922). Sobranie uzakonenii i rasporiazhenii rabochego i krest'ianskogo pravitel'stva* no. 15 (1922), item 153; see Special section, Chapter V(4), "Crimes in the Field of Sexual Relations," articles 166–71, later revised as *Ugolovnyi kodeks RSFSR (1926). Sobranie zakonov i rasporiazhenii raboche-krest'ianskogo pravitel'stva SSSR* no. 80 (1926), item 600; Special section, Chapter VI, (no subtitle), articles 150–55.

[24] Only in Italy did a similarly progressive outcome occur. Unification imposed the French-influenced law of the North on the entire kingdom by 1900. In Germany, however, Prussia's ban on male same-sex acts was forced on principalities that had decriminalized sodomy under French influence. In Austria-Hungary, male and female same-sex relations had been prohibited, and successor states inherited the ban; Czechoslovakia considered decriminalization but did not implement it (until 1961), while Poland decriminalized sodomy in 1932. See Flora Leroy-Forgeot, *Histoire juridique de l'homosexualité en Europe* (Paris: Presses Universitaires de France, 1997), pp. 66–67; and David F. Greenberg, *The Construction of Homosexuality* (Chicago: University of Chicago Press, 1988), p. 352.

[25] Semashko had asked to see a film on homosexual emancipation, and then "stated how pleased he was that in the new Russia, the former penalty against homosexuals has been completely abolished." *Jahrbuch für sexuelle Zwischenstufen*, no. 23 (1923), pp. 211–12. See also Grigorii Batkis, *Die Sexualrevolution in Russland* (Berlin: Syndikalist, 1925), p. 22.

posed by Hirschfeld himself.[26] The medical view of homosexuality adopted by these men of science, misinterpreted as "morbidizing" and hostile to "gays" by Simon Karlinsky, was enlightened and sympathetic within the European context.[27]

Soviet jurists, too, believed the new legislation was part of the sexual revolution. As one legal authority wrote, "science, and much legislation following from it . . . had taken the view that the commission of sodomy with adults infringed no rights whatsoever . . . and that the intrusion of the law into this field is a holdover of church teachings and the ideology of sinfulness."[28] An obscure lawyer in the Commissariat of Justice argued that the law should continue to punish public displays of homosexuality (as "hooliganism") and that "clubs" of "pederasts" should be treated just like "dens" of female prostitution.[29] Following a police raid in 1921 on a private party of cross-dressing sailors, soldiers, and workers in Petrograd and a conflicting series of articles on this unusual gathering in legal and medical literature, however, debate on the issue stalled.[30] There is no evidence that laws on hooliganism and dens of vice were applied against homosexuals during the New Economic Policy (NEP) of the 1920s.

The male homosexual subculture that had evolved since the late nineteenth century reconstituted itself in Russian cities during NEP.[31] Sexo-

[26] These psychiatrists included E. K. Krasnushkin, M. Ia. Sereiskii, and V. P. Protopopov. Hirschfeld corresponded with hormone researchers, suggesting to them lines of inquiry involving sexual orientation, and promoted their work in scientific and popular publications defending homosexuals. See Chandak Sengoopta, "Glandular Politics: Experimental Biology, Clinical Medicine, and Homosexual Emancipation in Fin-de-Siècle Central Europe," *Isis* 89 (1998): 445–73.

[27] Simon Karlinsky, "Russia's Gay Literature and Culture: The Impact of the October Revolution," in *Hidden from History: Reclaiming the Gay and Lesbian Past*, ed. M. Duberman, M. Vicinus, and G. Chauncey (New York: New American Library, 1989). For a full account of Soviet medicine's enlightened as well as hostile views on same-sex love, see Healey, *Homosexual Desire in Revolutionary Russia.*

[28] Quotation, E. P. Frenkel', *Polovye prestupleniia* (Odessa, 1927), p. 12; see also P. I. Liublinskii, *Prestupleniia v oblasti polovykh otnoshenii* (Moscow/Leningrad, 1925), pp. 117–27; S. V. Poznyshev, *Ocherk osnovnykh nachal nauki ugolovnogo prava,* 2: *Osobennaia chast'.* (Moscow, 1923), p. 60.

[29] G. R., "Protsessy gomoseksualistov," *Ezhenedel'nik sovetskoi iustitsii,* no. 33 (1922), pp. 16–17.

[30] Ibid.; V. P. Protopopov, "Sovremennoe sostoianie voprosa o sushchnosti i proiskhozhdenii gomoseksualizma," *Nauchnaia meditsina,* 1922, no. 10: 49–62; V. M. Bekhterev, "O polovom izvrashchenii, kak osoboi ustanovke polovykh refleksov," in *Polovoi vopros v shkole i v zhizni,* ed. I. S. Simonov (Leningrad, 1927).

[31] See Healey, *Homosexual Desire in Revolutionary Russia.* On the subculture's evolution in one city, see Healey, "Moscow," in *Queer Sites: Gay Urban Histories since 1600,* ed. David Higgs (London: Routledge, 1999).

logical, emancipationist, and self-fashioned currents of self-awareness circulated in this milieu much as they had before 1914, although Soviet publishing restrictions did not permit the dissemination of flagrant apologetics for homosexuality.[32] Individuals continued to read both tsarist and Soviet popular-medical literature on sexuality for clues to their identity. In their interviews with psychiatrists it is evident that many continued to think of their sexual identities and to represent them to doctors in the terms set by medical literature, often claiming that their sexuality must be a natural biological phenomenon.[33] The denizens of the male homosexual subculture also consciously and discreetly forged and maintained links based on sexual affinity. The subculture used public space and male homosociability to conceal relations that cut across hierarchies of class, age, ethnicity, and occupation. Male prostitution and less systematic sexual barter were significant features of the subculture's public face. In the late tsarist city the "little homosexual world" (as one jaundiced critic dubbed it in 1908) had flourished with the availability of commodified privacy (bathhouse private cabinets, hotel and restaurant rooms, bars and dance-

[32] For a prerevolutionary bricolage of European sexology and homosexual apologetics, see P. V. Ushakovskii [pseud.], *Liudi srednego pola* (St. Petersburg, 1908). For psychiatric case histories that indicate that subjects understood the biomedical model of homosexuality, see V. M. Bekhterev, "O polovykh izvrashcheniiakh, kak patologicheskikh sochetatel'nykh refleksakh," *Obozrenie psikhiatrii,* 1915, nos. 7–9: 1–26; V. A. Belousov, "Sluchai gomoseksuala-muzhskoi prostitutki," *Prestupnik i prestupnost'. Sbornik II* (1927), pp. 309–17; and Edel'shtein, "K klinike transvestitizma." Personal constructions of the consciously homosexual self during the 1920s and early 1930s can be found in Riurik Ivnev, "Selections from Ivnev's Diaries," in *Out of the Blue: Russia's Hidden Gay Literature,* ed. Kevin Moss (San Francisco: Gay Sunshine, 1997); and for the period from 1905 through 1934 in the diaries of Kuzmin, described in Malmstad and Bogomolov, *Mikhail Kuzmin.* For further discussion of the patterns of NEP-era self-awareness in the male homosexual subculture, see Healey, *Homosexual Desire in Revolutionary Russia,* pp. 41, 46–48.

[33] Evgeniia Fedorovna M.'s "History of My Illness," written in 1926 or 1927 by "female homosexual" and "transvestite" Evgeniia Fedorovna M., reproduced in Edel'shtein, "K klinike transvestitizma," demonstrates a self-taught individual's understandings of the biomedical model of homosexuality and the emancipatory claims that flowed from it. In addition to her own enthusiastic arguments, Evgeniia's text incorporated a brief passage found in Ushakovskii, *Liudi srednego pola,* on Sigmund Freud (citing correctly his contention that homosexuals were not degenerates) and listing famous members of the "intermediate sex" (Wilde, Michelangelo, Tchaikovsky), a favorite justification of emancipationists. On this text, see Healey, *Homosexual Desire in Revolutionary Russia,* pp. 69–72. For similar examples, see Belousov, "Sluchai gomoseksuala-muzhskoi prostitutki," p. 315 (a male prostitute familiar with sexological texts by Moll, Forel, and possibly Krafft-Ebing); Protopopov, "Sovremennoe sostoianie voprosa o sushchnosti i proiskhozhdenii gomoseksualizma," p. 52 (a soldier's self-acceptance results from reading medical literature); A. K. Sudomir, "K kazuistike i sushchnosti gomoseksual'nosti," *Sovremennaia psikhonevrologiia* 5, 11 (1927): 371–77 (a twenty-six-year-old Kiev woman argues that "her inversion . . . is a completely normal phenomenon").

halls).[34] The municipalization of many of these suspicious sites, and the surveillance of those leased to NEP entrepreneurs, revived and perhaps strengthened the subculture's exploitation of marginal space: public toilets, boulevards, courtyards, and parks. Experts paid little attention to this subculture.

The comparatively progressive legal disposition, with its suggestion that homosexuality was a problem for medicine and not the police, was in a sense confined to "politically loyal groups" within the Soviet Union's most "advanced" republics. Bolshevik attitudes toward male same-sex love beyond this revolutionary heartland were very different. Activists developed an analysis of "pederasty" and other patterns of same-sex relations that focused on ways of life (*byt*) as the crucible of undesirable sexualities for elements viewed as hostile to the revolution or, in non-Slavic union republics, regarded as "backward." In these contexts, medical explanations of sexual anomaly as a hormonal variation and emancipatory claims of homosexuality as a transhistorical constant were ignored by Bolsheviks with political axes to grind. "Pederasty" among Orthodox clergy or between clergy and novices, for example, was exposed and condemned as a feature of religious "culture" in show trials staged by antireligious campaigners. Here prosecutors sought to whip up popular fury at the recruitment of healthy teenage boys into the sexual excesses and depravities of monastic and ecclesiastical life.[35] Whether the prosecutors succeeded in generating proletarian antihomosexual feeling is impossible to judge from the brief accounts of these trials in the atheist press, but a political discourse was articulated that tied some men's same-sex relations to religious byt.[36]

[34] For a satirical Baedeker to this world in the capital, see V. P. Ruadze, *K sudu! Gomoseksual'nyi Peterburg* (St. Petersburg, 1908).

[35] See, for example, GARF, f. A353, op. 3, d. 745 (Dokumenty o kontrrevoliutsionnoi agitatsii monakhov Novoirusalimskogo monastyria i po obvineniiu episkopa Palladiia v rastlenii mal'chika, 1919 g.); N.P., "Monakhi pred sudom v roli razvratitelei maloletnikh i nesovershennoletnikh," *Ezhenedel'nik sovetskoi iustitsii* no. 42 (1922), pp. 13–15; N. P., "Sviatoi otets. K predstoiashchemu protsessu ieromonakha Vissariona," *Bezbozhnik* no. 6 (209), 6 February 1927: 6; K. Petrova, "Protsess d'iakona Tkachenko. (Gor. Vladikavkaz)," *Bezbozhnik* no. 42 (244) 16 October 1927: 5; M. Sheinman, *Religioznost' i prestupnost'* (Moscow, 1927), pp. 55–56; F. U—v, "Ikh 'kul'tura,' " *Bezbozhnik* no. 70 (428), 20 December 1930: 8.

[36] A debate in *Bezbozhnik* over the Sodom story showed that a comparatively thoughtful antireligious leader like E. Iaroslavskii was alive to the tensions between enlightened understandings of "pederasty" in history and the issue's power as a polemic device. In a 1923 essay, "Sodom's Sinners and Sodom's Righteous Men," he proposed that church emphasis on "pederasty" in the tale imposed "the morality of remote biblical times" on "workers" today; a clearer danger was the incest of the story's final scenes, when Lot's daughters bear him sons following Sodom's destruction: "Sodomitskie greshniki i sodomitskie pravedniki," reprinted in E. Iaroslavskii, *Protiv religii i tserkvi*, vol. 5 (Moscow, 1932–33), pp. 114–18. In reply to a party activist criticizing him for failing to condemn pederasty, Iaroslavskii lambasted the visceral approach to pederasty and the refusal to notice the other sin (incest): "V zashchitu bib-

As Soviet power expanded southward and eastward, "sodomy" was outlawed in the new republics of Soviet Azerbaijan (1923), Uzbekistan (1926), and Turkmenistan (1927), again as a result of Bolshevik assessments of local byt. In the two Central Asian republics, criminal code articles "against survivals of primitive custom" further described same-sex practices in ethnographic detail characteristic of this branch of revolutionary lawmaking. Numerous articles explained and prohibited the keeping of *bachi* (feminized boy dancers, singers, and prostitutes, who worked in itinerant troupes) and the trade in contracts for bachi. Those who organized schools of bachi were criminalized like procurers who kept female prostitutes in other union republics. In Soviet Uzbekistan, the sexual harassment of *men* was made a crime, a gender inversion of the Russian Republic's pathbreaking legislation protecting women from the same offense.[37] The reason for this unusual law protecting men was the same as for women: it was feared that men or youths in dependent circumstances were at risk of prostitution. Historians have remained silent about these striking measures, despite an awareness of the significance of Soviet gender regulation imposed on these regions.[38]

The Bolsheviks' socialist project encompassed both up-to-the-minute emancipatory sentiments and rationalizers' social engineering to ensure that young men turned out "normal." This twin tug of impulses can be constructively compared to Soviet policies on (female) "prostitution" (for male clients). (The patriarchal heterosexual sex/gender system made the qualifiers unnecessary to contemporaries.) Soviet law eschewed the for-

---

lii protiv sodomlian," *Bezbozhnik* no. 20 (9 May 1923): 3; cf. correspondence with the activist, RGASPI, f. 89, op. 4, d. 6, ll. 119–21.

[37] For early Soviet sodomy penalties, see M. S. Khalafov et al., eds., *Istoriia gosudarstva i prava Azerbaidzhanskoi SSR (1920–1934 gg.)* (Baku, 1973), p. 373; D. S. Karev, *Ugolovnoe zakonodatel'stvo SSSR i soiuznykh respublik. Sbornik* (Moscow, 1957), pp. 215, 433. For analysis of local forms of "sodomy," see N. D. Durmanov, *Ugolovnoe pravo. Osobennaia chast'. Prestupleniia, sostavliaiushchie perezhitki rodogo byta* (Moscow, 1938), p. 68. For the most comprehensive scholarly view of the *bachi*, see I. Baldauf, *Die Knabenliebe in Mittelasien: Bačabozlik* (Berlin: Freie Universität, 1988). For Soviet Uzbekistan's laws prohibiting "the compulsion of a woman to enter into a sexual liaison or to satisfy sexual passion in any form by a person in relation to whom the woman is materially or professionally dependent," and prohibiting "the compulsion of a man to sodomy by a person in relation to whom the victim is materially or professionally dependent, or is in the guardianship of," see Karev, *Ugolovnoe zakonodatel'stvo*, p. 208 (article 215 on women), p. 217 (article 278 on men).

[38] See, for example, Gregory J. Massell, *The Surrogate Proletariat: Moslem Women and Revolutionary Strategies in Soviet Central Asia: 1919–1929* (Princeton, N.J.: Princeton University Press, 1974). In both contexts where Bolsheviks attacked male same-sex relations as anti-Soviet, Orthodox clergy and those who profited from the *bachi* already constituted class-alien elements, because of either their worldview or their economic activities. Their alien status stimulated the attention paid to their sexual irregularities.

mal criminalization of the prostitute. Despite police interest in applying penal sanctions, health and welfare officials (led, incidentally, by Semashko) dominated a discourse focused on the emancipation of women and the redemption of the prostitute through education, training, and labor. The state tried to reconcile contradictory approaches to the female prostitute by establishing an interdepartmental commission "on the struggle with prostitution." Women in the NEP-era sex trade were counted, observed, and interviewed by police, social workers, and psychiatrists; some were "treated" in "labor prophylactoria," where industrial training was combined with venereal-disease therapy. As the most visible manifestation of public sex, female prostitution and its subculture of the city boulevards were subjected to a thorough analysis during NEP. The features of modern byt that encouraged women to sell their bodies were closely dissected by experts and monitored by the police.[39]

During the first two five-year plans, the female prostitute was shunted from the custody of medicine first to social welfare officials and then swiftly into police hands. These moves were part of a wider drive to cleanse the Soviet city of street subcultures deemed incompatible with socialism. The Commissariat of Internal Affairs had successfully proposed a special program of measures that became the First Five-Year Plan's "struggle with social anomalies" (female prostitutes, "professional" beggars, the homeless, and alcoholics).[40] The "social anomalies" (*sotsanomaliki*) were to be placed in workshops and camps run by the Welfare Commissariat. Protests from the commission on prostitution (still led by Semashko as health commissar) had little effect. During the First Five-Year Plan, welfare officials managed a mixture of "social patronage" measures (designed to get prostitutes into factory work, or—less plausibly—to send those among them who were migrants back to the village) and increasingly coercive forms of compulsory labor. By 1931, the Welfare Commis-

[39] See Elizabeth Waters, "Victim or Villain: Prostitution in Post-Revolutionary Russia," in *Women and Society in Russia and the Soviet Union*, ed. Linda Edmondson (Cambridge: Cambridge University Press, 1992); N. B. Lebina and M. B. Shkarovskii, *Prostitutsiia v Peterburge* (Moscow, 1994); and Frances L. Bernstein, "Envisioning Health in Revolutionary Russia: The Politics of Gender in Sexual-Enlightenment Posters of the 1920s," *The Russian Review* 57 (1998): 191–217.

[40] See "Sotsial'nye problemy raspredeleniia. Trud i kul'tura" in *Piatiletnii plan narodnokhoziaistvennogo stroitel'stva SSSR*, vol. 2 (Moscow, 1929), p. 242, cited in G. A. Bordiugov, "Sotsial'nyi parazitizm ili sotsial'nye anomalii? (Iz istorii bor'by s alkogolizmom, nishchestvom, prostitutsiei i brodiazhestvom v 20–30-e gody)," *Istoriia SSSR*, 1989, no. 1: 60–73. A plan to set up labor colonies for "3,000 inveterate professional women prostitutes" was announced in November 1926 by the Commissariat of Internal Affairs' representatives to the Central Council for the Struggle with Prostitution (as the interdepartmental commission was then named). See Gosudarstvennyi arkhiv Saratovskoi oblasti (henceforth, GASO), f. R229, op. 1, d. 1132, l. 39 (minutes of the Central Council's meeting of 9 November 1926 in Moscow).

sariat had established "special regime" colonies for prostitutes and professional beggars outside Moscow and Leningrad; ten camps to isolate "inveterate" (*zlostnye*) prostitutes were secretly planned. Recidivists were handed over to police and sent to labor camps. In early 1933, a Leningrad conference on the "socially anomalous" expressed satisfaction that hardened female prostitutes were now routinely sent to labor colonies; with full employment, there was no justification for antisocial behavior.[41] Similar sentiments accompanied crackdowns on the "professional" beggar, the homeless, and "criminal elements," while the 1932 passport legislation furnished the means to identify the socially anomalous by highlighting their flawed work, housing, or personal situations.[42]

Male homosexuals or "pederasts" were not named among the *sotsanomaliki* to be eradicated. There were no interdepartmental commissions to study male homosexuality—for the question had not been conceived as a unified phenomenon—and no turf wars for custody of the homosexual. But the most public aspect of male same-sex love in the Soviet Union—its reliance on urban streetscapes and public sex—was particularly vulnerable in the crisis atmosphere of the First Five-Year Plan. This was especially so since many of the same boulevards and haunts used by men seeking sex together were also the centers of the heterosexual sex trade. As a result of this awareness about the public face of the male homosexual subculture, the secret police proposed to recriminalize sodomy.

In September 1933, OGPU Deputy Chief G. G. Iagoda wrote to Stalin suggesting that a law against "pederasty" was needed for all Soviet republics. Secret police raids in Moscow and Leningrad had recently led to the arrest of 130 men observed in "salons, centers, dens, groups, and other organized formations of pederasts." Although Iagoda also caught Stalin's attention with suggestions of an espionage threat, no later correspondence, nor the draft decree he produced in December 1933, mentioned spying. The lack of a strong emphasis on espionage seems curious, considering how the new law was eventually presented to and by foreign communists.[43] Instead, Iagoda referred to groups of "pederasts" who op-

[41] Evidence for these measures and plans from Leningrad archives is presented in Lebina and Shkarovskii, *Prostitutsiia v Peterburge*, pp. 152–58.

[42] For urban social cleansing as a factor in Stalinist terror, see David Shearer, "Crime and Social Disorder in Stalin's Russia: A Reassessment of the Great Retreat and the Origins of Mass Repression," *Cahiers du monde russe* 39, 1–2 (1998): 119–49; and Paul Hagenloh, " 'Socially Harmful Elements' and the Great Terror," in *Stalinism: New Directions*, ed. Sheila Fitzpatrick (London: Routledge, 1999).

[43] Our accounts about this law mention fear of espionage among homosexual circles, understood to be in the service of Nazi Germany, as the prime motive for the sodomy ban. Influential texts on this point have been the "Letter of an Old Bolshevik," in Boris I. Nicolaevsky, *Power and the Soviet Elite: "Letter of an Old Bolshevik" and Other Essays* (London: Pall

erated "salons" for "orgies" and engaged in the "recruitment and corruption of totally healthy young people, Red Army soldiers, sailors, and students." Revealingly, Iagoda proposed in his draft statute that sodomy "for payment, as a profession, or in public" should incur heightened penalties.[44] This descriptive phrase remained in the draft for five months and was approved by the Politburo (December 1933) and other important central organs, only to be excised a week before official publication on 7 March 1934, probably on the advice of government jurists.[45] The law as published contained no references to professional, paid, or public sodomy. A late decision was evidently taken to sanitize the new statute to limit foreign and domestic speculation about public sex between men and male prostitution in the socialist state.[46] The secret police were plainly aware of homosexual use of urban space and viewed it as analogous to the undesirable presence of female prostitution.

"He Showed Me the Places Where Pederasts Meet": Identity as Resistance

Unlike other aspects of the so-called Stalinist great retreat of the second half of the 1930s, such as the 1935 toughening of juvenile criminal law and the 1936 restrictions on abortion and divorce, the antisodomy statute received almost no publicity. It did not stimulate a flood of internal circulars for prosecutors or court officials, nor did it generate a paper trail as

Mall, 1966), p. 31; Wilhelm Reich, *The Sexual Revolution* (New York: Pocket, 1969 [1936]), p. 254; and Sidney Webb and Beatrice Webb, *Soviet Communism—A New Civilisation*, 2d ed. (London: Victor Gollancz, 1937), p. 1060. For a fuller account, see Dan Healey, *Homosexual Desire in Revolutionary Russia*, chap. 7.

[44] See "Iz istorii ugolovnogo kodeksa: 'Primerno NAKAZAT' etikh Merzavtsev,' " *Istochnik*, 1993, nos. 5–6: 164–65, citing Arkhiv Prezidenta Rossiiskoi Federatsii (henceforth, APRF), f. 3, op. 57, d. 37, ll. 25–26.

[45] GARF, f. 1235, op. 141, d. 1591, ll. 1, 5–6. (My thanks to David Shearer for this reference.) As late as 28 February 1934, the Iagoda draft mentioning prostitution and public sex was approved by the Russian Republic Central Soviet Executive Committee and the Council of People's Commissars; on this date the draft was distributed to the Russian Republic Commissariat of Justice and the USSR and Russian Supreme Courts. It seems likely that one of these bodies suggested the simplified final version dropping these elements. Legal officials probably argued that male prostitution and public homosexual acts could be punished without an ethnographic description of the subculture. They also would have pointed to the inconsistency of criminalizing male homosexual prostitutes but not female heterosexual prostitutes.

[46] Ukraine and the Tajik SSR unaccountably adopted the Iagoda draft statute before 7 March 1934, and sodomy "for payment, as a profession, or in public" was explicitly criminal in these republics. Karev, *Ugolovnoe zakonodatel'stvo*, pp. 114, 345.

bureaucrats monitored enforcement. Undoubtedly, materials exist in the files of the Presidential Archive and the FSB.[47] The early victims of this law (like the 130 "pederasts" arrested in Moscow and Leningrad in 1933) were processed by the secret police, and therefore their documents are likely to remain inaccessible in the archives of the FSB. Nevertheless, available evidence from memoirs, the published APRF documents, and literary sources offers documentation of a range of responses to the antisodomy law.

Fragmentary evidence hints at responses imbued with a homosexual self-awareness that implied, more often than it explicitly expressed, an emancipatory sexual politics. That Russians should have been reluctant to defend these politics openly under circumstances of extraordinary oppression is in the comparative context unexceptional. Nowhere except in Germany up to 1933 did a homosexual rights movement exist; and nowhere else did organized, self-acknowledged homosexuals intervene publicly in the national political culture.[48] Perhaps the most common response to the Soviet antisodomy law among educated homosexuals was eloquent circumspection.

Mikhail Kuzmin's diary and published correspondence for late 1934 (he had been ill through the winter and resumed writing in May 1934) maintain the relaxed tone of previous notebooks,[49] even though his earlier notebooks, which he had sold that winter to the State Literary Museum, were now in the hands of the secret police (despite State Literary Museum chief V. Bonch-Bruevich's defense of what was dubbed a "trashy" acquisition).[50] In these circumstances, Kuzmin's diary of May–December 1934 acquires a defiant subtext. Brief essays on the aging writer's past dominate, including some oblique hints about his sexual liaisons, homosexual friends, and "effeminate" antics. Discussions about politics are con-

[47] The 1993 *Istochnik* publications show that APRF, f. 3, op. 57, d. 37, a file evidently devoted to the antisodomy law, contains at least forty-five pages, of which only nineteen were cited.

[48] Hirschfeld's Scientific-Humanitarian Committee, which promoted the decriminalization of male homosexuality in Germany, had contacts with interested individuals in several European nations, and a functioning branch in the Netherlands. During the 1920s, small groups of homosexuals briefly organized in Prague and Chicago, but it appears that authorities in both cities moved to disband them quickly; see John Lauritsen and David Thorstad, *The Early Homosexual Rights Movement (1864–1935)* (New York: Times Change, 1974), pp. 31–33.

[49] M. A. Kuzmin, *Dnevnik 1934 goda* (St. Petersburg, 1998).

[50] S. V. Shumikhin, "Dnevnik Mikhaila Kuzmina: Arkhivnaia predystoriia," in *Mikhail Kuzmin i russkaia kul'tura XX veka: Tezisy i materialy konferentsii 15–17 maia 1990 g.*, ed. G. A. Morev (Leningrad, 1990). Bonch-Bruevich continued to defend the purchase of the Kuzmin diaries until early June 1934; a party commission investigated the deal and on 20 June censured him for it. RGASPI, f. 17, op. 120, d. 111, l. 2.

fined to the local and literary. Yet Gleb Morev's exhaustive commentary to these writings notes a "dark phrase" in a letter of October 1934 that betrays Kuzmin's awareness of the dangerous new landscape. Obliquely referring to the arrest of a mutual acquaintance under the sodomy law, the poet wrote, "In that regard (probably because of my advanced years), it has turned out all right." Kuzmin sensed his particular exposure as the Soviet Union's most notoriously open homosexual, yet he did not curb the decades-long project of self-exploration in his diaries.[51]

Another openly homosexual poet, Nikolai Kliuev, refused to stop writing verses in praise of young men, according to a 1959 report given by a onetime patron, literary functionary Ivan Gronskii. Gronskii said he had arranged an academic ration for Kliuev in 1932. Then, in 1934, he confronted Kliuev about his homoerotic poems. When Kliuev refused to "write normal verses," Gronskii telephoned Iagoda to have the poet deported from Moscow. Kliuev was arrested on 2 February 1934, interrogated in the Liubianka, and exiled to Siberia on 5 March. He was charged with anti-Soviet agitation, not sodomy—perhaps because of his passionate poetry denouncing collectivization. Rearrested in exile, he was shot as a counterrevolutionary in 1937.[52] Until a less homophobic reading of Kliuev's secret police file is available, the circumstances of his repression will remain murky.[53] Yet it seems clear that Kliuev's defiant stance on his sexuality was at least partially instrumental in triggering his exile, an element of his fate worthy of further exploration.[54]

The most defiant and articulate reaction to the new antisodomy statute that has yet emerged came from a foreigner involved in a same-sex relationship with a Russian. Stalin received a letter in May 1934 from British communist and Moscow resident Harry Whyte.[55] An editorial employee at

[51] Kuzmin's advancing illness resulted in his death in 1936. For Morev's commentary on this letter, see Kuzmin, *Dnevnik 1934 goda*, pp. 329–31.

[52] See I. M. Gronskii, "O krest'ianskikh pisateliakh (Vystuplenie v TsGALI 30 sentiabria 1959 g.). Publikatsiia M. Nike," in *Minuvshee: Istoricheskii al'manakh 8*, ed. Vladimir Alloi (Moscow, 1992), pp. 148–51; and Vitalii Shentalinskii, *Raby svobody: V literaturnykh arkhivakh KGB* (Moscow, 1995), pp. 265–74. See also N. M. Solntseva, *Strannyi eros: Intimnye motivy poezii Nikolaia Kliueva* (Moscow: Ellis Lak, 2000), pp. 105–7.

[53] Shentalinskii's retelling of Gronskii's story purges it of the homosexual element to make Kliuev a more sympathetic anticommunist victim; we cannot know what references to the poet's sexuality he has omitted from his account of the NKVD documents.

[54] A pseudonymous chronicler of homosexual St. Petersburg characteristically shrugs that further enquiry "is not worth the effort." See Konstantin K. Rotikov, *Drugoi Peterburg* (St. Petersburg, 1998), p. 180. On Rotikov's camp extravaganza, see Brian James Baer, "The Other Russia: Re-Presenting the Gay Experience," *Kritika* 1, 1 (2000): 183–94.

[55] Garri Uait [Harry Whyte], " 'Mozhet li gomoseksualist sostoiat' chlenom kommunisticheskoi partii?': Iumor iz spetskhrana," *Istochnik*, 1993, nos. 5–6: 185–91. The subtitle of this publication—"Humor from the special collection"—is indicative of the confused political in-

the *Moscow Daily News,* Whyte asked Stalin to justify the new law. His long missive opened with a question for Stalin: "Can a homosexual be considered fit to become a member of the Communist Party?" The journalist laid out Marxist arguments against the blanket prohibition of sodomy which, he claimed, introduced contradictions in Soviet social life by imposing "sexual leveling" on a harmless minority and by ignoring scientific evidence. The new law undermined the achievement of previous Soviet laws protecting sexual liberty and inviolability.

Whyte likened the social position of homosexuals to that of other groups in society suffering from arbitrary discrimination, naming women, "colored races," and national minorities. Science, he argued, had demonstrated the biological origin of the small minority of congenital homosexuals. Whyte drew a fine distinction between a communist's personal life (to which private sphere his sexual proclivity ought to be consigned) and cases in which homosexuality became a public, political issue in bourgeois societies. It was thus appropriate for Marxists to attack the right's abuse of homosexuals and sexual hypocrisy. The letter cited Marx and Engels on political aspects of homosexuality and praised the Comintern's current attacks on homosexuals among the leadership of Germany's Nazi Party. Whyte reminded Stalin of his criticism at the Seventeenth Party Congress in 1934 of "leveling" (*uravnilovka*) in wages, living standards, and "tastes and personal byt" as a form of "primitive asceticism" unworthy of Marxism. These comments against leveling "have a direct connection to the question" of homosexuality, the journalist argued, since the new law forced a biologically distinct minority to comply with "sexual leveling."[56] Whyte also chronicled his efforts to learn the whereabouts of his lover, arrested in secret police raids on Moscow homosexuals between the announcement of the Politburo decree of December 1933 and its formal enactment in March 1934. The fate of this Russian, and of Whyte himself, is unknown. Stalin read this letter, writing on it "an idiot and a degenerate," and sent it to the archives. It acquainted him with an unfamiliar current in

---

terpretations of the 1993 sodomy decriminalization decree emanating from the presidential administration. Whyte's letter is attributed to APRF, f. 3, op. 57, d. 37, ll. 29–45—that is, from the same file as the Iagoda–Stalin correspondence on the sodomy law of 1933–34, published in the same issue of *Istochnik,* pp. 164–65. Whyte called himself "head of the editorial staff" (*zaveduiushchii redaktsiei*) and a top shockworker, but his name does not appear on the masthead of the *Moscow Daily News.* It published one book review by Whyte: H. O. Whyte, "Koltzov—the Journalistic Artist," *Moscow Daily News* no. 77 (278) (3 April 1933): 2.

[56] Uait, "Mozhet li gomoseksualist," 185, 188–91. Whyte cited Kaganovich on population growth in the USSR to deny that there was any harm to national vigor; and he pointed to the prestige of homosexual André Gide as an "ardent friend of the USSR." Whyte's awareness of the history of Marxist views of homosexuality was not exceptional. See Hekma et al., eds., *Gay Men and the Sexual History of the Political Left.*

European left sexual politics, and because of its use of Marxist discourse, it undoubtedly influenced the few Soviet attempts to defend the legislation publicly.[57] In this respect, Whyte's letter to Stalin was the most direct and explicit act of resistance to the antisodomy law. Significantly, it was the voice of an outsider, mistakenly appealing to a sexual politics of liberation, when voices for the rational ordering of sexuality had long been dominant.

Reactions to the new law were not confined to isolated efforts to speak to power about its injustice. Individuals continued to experience same-sex desire and to express it. They defied the ban at great potential cost. The minimum sentence for voluntary sodomy was three years; for sodomy involving the use of force or the abuse of a dependent relationship, five to eight years were prescribed. Trial records (mostly sentencing and appeal documents) from the Moscow city court contain descriptions of the male homosexual subculture that the new law was supposed to destroy. Paradoxically, it is the survival of the subculture and not its demise that is documented in these summaries. The trials reveal the continuing existence of sociability, street cruising, and public sex, especially in the vicinity of Moscow's Boulevard Ring, a focal point since the late tsarist decades.[58] Men seeking sex together continued to rely on the techniques of concealment and outwardly innocent sociability that had long disguised their purpose from the dominant sex/gender system. Like-minded men recognized and met each other across the divisions of class, age, and occupation that otherwise would have separated them. This blend of innocent public presence and concealed invitations to sex was evidently difficult to police.

Meeting places included private flats, public toilets, and the capital's boulevards. In November 1934, two friends in their forties—Bezborodov, a cook, and Gribov, a clerk (and a gregarious "ringleader" whose address-book fell into police hands)—met in central Moscow. "Wishing to drink alcohol," they visited the flat of one Petr—"by nickname 'The Baroness'—who kept an entire den of homosexuals." The court labeled this flat one of the significant "meeting places of pederasts," although the fate of the Baroness and his "den" is unclear.[59]

57 Most notably, Maksim Gor'kii, "Proletarskii gumanizm," *Pravda*, (23 May 1934): 3; and Gor'kii, "Proletarskii gumanizm," *Izvestiia*, (23 May 1934): 2. On the international context of the legal change and Soviet defenses of it, see Healey, *Homosexual Desire in Revolutionary Russia.*

58 Healey, "Moscow," pp. 49–50.

59 Tsentral'nyi munitsipal'nyi arkhiv Moskvy (henceforth, TsMAM), f. 819, op. 2, d. 11, l. 241 (sentence of Bezborodov and eleven others, 1935). All names from these cases have been altered to preserve anonymity. Bezborodov was the first man arrested, perhaps as a result of his sexual relationship from June to September 1934 with Venediktov, a party member.

Another gathering place was Hermitage Park. The Boulevard Ring linked this small green space to nearby Trubnaia Square, where one of the capital's busiest "meeting places"—a public toilet—was located. This facility was underground, circular in shape, with cubicles against the perimeter facing inward. There were no doors on the stalls, which had simple holes in the floor.[60] All users could see each other, and this perverse panopticism enabled meetings as well as preventing them. Investigated for sodomy in 1941, a man named Levin described his discovery of this facility: "Once in the autumn of 1940 I left a restaurant on Tsvetnoi Boulevard and was walking toward my apartment on Neglinnaia Street. On the way I stopped in the toilet on Trubnaia Square and there, against my will, an act of sodomy was committed with me. A man came up to me and began to masturbate, touching my penis. I did not particularly object. A month and a half after this I once again went to the toilet on Trubnaia Square, but this time with the deliberate intention of committing an act of sodomy. In this manner I committed acts of sodomy about five or six times."[61] Levin invited some partners home to sleep overnight with him; others he had sex with on the spot.

The availability of sexual partners in a notorious "meeting place" well after 1934 suggests that a continuous and concealed sociability among homosexuals persisted. Similarly, Sretenskii and Chistoprudnyi Boulevards, mentioned in a psychiatrist's study of a "male prostitute" in 1927, continued to figure as meeting spots in the mid-1930s.[62] In 1935, Anisimov (a thirty-five-year-old party member and engineer) and Brodskii (a twenty-seven-year-old tram driver) "met by chance on Sretenskii and other boulevards of the city of Moscow with men-pederasts [*muzhshchiny-pederasty*], and entered into sexual intercourse with them in toilets, in apartments, and on the boulevards."[63]

Nikitskie Gates Square had a men's toilet fulfilling the same role from the 1920s onward. In 1937, the highly sociable Tereshkov and a friend were "caught red handed during mutual masturbation" in a police raid there.[64] This vicinity figured in other confessions as well. One defendant explained to interrogators: "In 1936, in the apartment where I lived,

[60] Personal communication, Viktor Oboin of the Russian Library of Lesbians and Gays (GenderDok), 4 November 1995. The gregarious Tereshkov had met the same sex partner near here two summers running (1936 and 1937). TsMAM, f. 819, op. 2, d. 30, l. 43 (sentence of Tereshkov and nine others, 1938).

[61] TsMAM, f. 819, op. 2, d. 51, l. 83 (case file of Andreevskii and two others, 1941). "Sodomy" in these terse court documents might mean any manual, oral, or anal sexual contact between males.

[62] Belousov, "Sluchai gomoseksuala-muzhskoi prostitutki."

[63] TsMAM, f. 819, op. 2, d. 10, l. 297 (sentence of Anisimov and Brodskii, 1935).

[64] TsMAM, f. 819, op. 2, d. 30, l. 42 (sentence of Tereshkov and nine others, 1938).

Afanas'ev, an artist of the ballet, moved in. . . . He showed me the places where pederasts meet: Nikitskii Boulevard and Trubnaia Square." Another defendant said that in the early 1930s, a friend "told me that the chief places for pederasts were Nikitskii Boulevard, Trubnaia [Square], a bar on Arbat, and the Central Baths." By this time, the bar and baths were municipalized. (These were rare references to formerly commercial spaces frequented by the subculture in this era.)[65] These two confessions taken from the same 1941 case file illustrate the tantalizing difficulties associated with such sources. The similarities in content perhaps reflect coaching from interrogators and standard phrases employed by clerks; but Nikitskii Boulevard and Trubnaia Square appear in other sentencing documents as "meeting places" for men seeking sex with men—notably the raid on the Nikitskie toilets that netted Tereshkov. Another similarity, also reflected in other trials, is the suggestion that friends shared information about these sexualized territories of the subculture. The subculture would not have existed and reproduced itself if successive cohorts of homosexuals had not been aware of its crucial feature, the use of marginal public spaces for discreet encounters.

Men shared information not only because police attention could curtail activity at a particular site but also because the construction projects of the first five-year plans drastically altered much of central Moscow. The Boulevard Ring remained relatively untouched and was a refuge from disruptions prevailing elsewhere in the center. But construction brought with it new attractions and opportunities. The remarkable catalogue of the activities of film executive Ivan Siniakov, tried in 1937 for aggravated sodomy, suggests that the transformation of Moscow into a model socialist city was paradoxically responsible for the emergence of new homosexual territories in the heart of the capital.

The court heard how Siniakov found large numbers of sex partners among the sailors, soldiers, and civilian men he met on embankments and boulevards in Leningrad, Sevastopol, Moscow, and even Penza and Kursk during the 1930s. Most of these relations involved sexual barter, an exchange of small gifts, or benefits for sexual favors. In 1936, Siniakov struck up acquaintances with sexually available soldiers and sailors in Sverdlov Square, located in front of the Bolshoi Theater; later the next year, he met more sex partners in uniform, in nearby Manezh Square.[66] These are the earliest references in the trial records to homosexual contacts made in these squares, located near the Okhotnyi Riad Metro sta-

65 TsMAM, f. 819, op. 2, d. 51, ll. 57, 106ob. (case file of Andreevskii and two others, 1941).
66 TsMAM, f. 819, op. 2., d. 25, ll. 129–30 (sentence of Siniakov, 1937).

tion. The opening of the Metro in 1935 and the reconfiguration of central streets leading to the massive Hotel Moskva (where Mokhovaia Street and Okhotnyi Riad became Prospekt Marksa in the 1930s) lured the curious. Servicemen on leave and civilians visiting the capital in the late 1930s flocked to the Metro and especially the cluster of stations in this district.[67] By the 1950s, probably thanks to these new transportation links, Sverdlov Square, with its patch of greenery in front of the Bolshoi Theater, had become the focal point of new cruising patterns, surpassing the older haunts associated with the Boulevard Ring.[68]

If a crucial element of the regime's motives for the antisodomy law was the elimination of this homosexual street culture, a particular form of byt, then the evidence suggests that the law failed; men seeking sex with other men continued to use the tools of the homosexual subculture to meet. They exploited notorious sites, and they do not appear to have abandoned the practice even in the face of what presumably was increased police surveillance. They established relations that crossed the solidarities of party membership, education, occupation, social status, and age.[69] Sexual barter and sex in public places between men did not cease but were consciously pursued in the midst of greatly increased danger. Men who might have quite sensibly chosen to stay at home and remain safe, celibate, and isolated, instead deliberately made choices to maintain a subculture of male-male sexual affinity. In the context, these acts constituted a remarkable form of social disobedience.

The record also speaks about others whose obstructive responses to the

[67] On the reconstruction, see Evan Mawdsley, *Blue Guide: Moscow and Leningrad* (London: A. and C. Black, 1991), pp. 120–22; and Timothy Colton, *Moscow: Governing the Socialist Metropolis* (Cambridge, Mass.: Harvard University Press, 1995), pp. 326–28.

[68] The square in front of the Bolshoi Theater acquired subcultural designations in the 1950s–70s, but the history of this folklore is obscure. See, for example, the entries under "Shtrikh," "Pleshka," "Direktor pleshki" (a reference to the adjacent Marx monument), "Goluboi zal," "Gomodrom," and "Shliapki" (recalling a milliner's shop nearby) in Vladimir Kozlovskii, *Argo russkoi gomoseksual'noi subkul'tury: Materialy k izucheniiu* (Benson, Vt.: Chalidze, 1986), pp. 45, 73. The square as cruising spot survived into the 1990s. See David Tuller, *Cracks in the Iron Closet: Travels in Gay and Lesbian Russia* (Boston: Faber and Faber, 1996), pp. 22, 98; Laurie Essig, *Queer in Russia: A Story of Sex, Self, and the Other* (Durham, N.C.: Duke University Press, 1999), pp. 88–89. In the late 1990s, the city administration drastically remodeled the square's street furniture and removed foliage to expose it to easier surveillance, ending its subcultural career.

[69] Defendants in the case of Tereshkov and nine others, in 1938, included two party members (an engineer and a student); nonparty defendants were a physician, a teacher, a bookkeeper, the "technical secretary" in a factory, an artist and a ticket collector from the Bolshoi Theater, a cook, and a salesman from "shop number 23"; a teenage youth was also implicated but not charged. He was the youngest person named in the case; most of the accused were in their thirties, and the oldest was forty-eight.

antisodomy law deserve attention. Legal and medical experts are a category of actors in this drama who did not always play according to their assigned scripts. In contrast to the illegal and violent methods that we can presume were used without remorse on "homosexuals" by the secret police, ordinary courts and the Russian Republic Supreme Court often appeared to resist their role in enforcing the law of 7 March 1934. To a lesser extent, medical professionals used in the identification of "pederasts" for the police were also sometimes reluctant to assume these functions.

Sentencing and appeal patterns suggest that judges upheld the new law with vigor for a brief time and then treated men accused of sodomy with some leniency except where additional factors were involved. Only one case, the trial in 1935 of Bezborodov and eleven others, included in its sentence any politicized statement of the rationale behind the legislation: its purpose was to punish "sodomy as an antisocial system [*pravlenie*] of sexual liaisons between men." No other sodomy trial records available for viewing in the Central Municipal Archive of Moscow (TsMAM) contain such justifications, suggesting that any initial zeal may have been replaced by routine.[70] A comparison of the sentences handed down in the Bezborodov case with those dispensed in the very similar Tereshkov case of ten men tried for sodomy in the midst of the terror in 1938 produces unanticipated results. In the 1935 case, eight out of twelve accused received the maximum penalty of five years, and none received any reduction on appeal.[71] (Appeals for reduced sentences and acquittals went directly to the Russian Republic Supreme Court, were heard quickly, and were not unusual.) By contrast, on 1 August 1938, eight of the ten men in the Tereshkov case received minimum three-year terms, and only the "ringleader" merited the maximum five years. The city court immediately suspended one of the three-year sentences; five other recipients of the minimum sentence appealed to the Supreme Court and received suspensions. Five weeks after the trial, only three of the original ten convicted were still in custody.[72] In the other cases in this sample, sentences above the minimum three years were exceptional, handed out only to "ringleaders" and those found guilty of additional offenses.[73]

[70] TsMAM, f. 819, op. 2, d. 11, l. 245 (sentence of Bezborodov and eleven others, 1935). On the full range of available sodomy trials open to view at TsMAM, see the bibliography in Healey, *Homosexual Desire in Revolutionary Russia.*

[71] TsMAM, f. 819, op. 2, d. 11, l. 245 (sentence of Bezborodov and eleven others, 1935).

[72] TsMAM, f. 819, op. 2, d. 30, ll. 46–47 (sentence of Tereshkov and nine others, 1938).

[73] Sodomy sentences were moderate in comparison with other forms of sexual crime (rape, sexual abuse of children and minors). Group rapes (of women) were the most severely penalized and politicized sexual crime. See Healey, *Homosexual Desire in Revolutionary Russia,* chap. 8.

Men convicted of sodomy who appealed their sentences to the Supreme Court were more successful in getting reduced penalties than rapists, but less successful than individuals charged with (usually nonviolent) sex crimes involving young persons.[74] Evidentiary factors probably influenced the higher court: violent sexual assaults against adult women were easier to document with forensic medical evidence and police testimony, while child abuse and sex with teenagers could be more difficult to demonstrate and might be successfully challenged by the defendant's advocate. Successful appeals on sodomy convictions were generally the result of skillful pleading by defense lawyers.

The advocates' trump card was the "personality, lack of previous convictions, and family situation" of their clients.[75] After the initial period of stringency, the Supreme Court seemed eager to be persuaded by these claims. Evidence also suggests that advocates, judges, and investigators found the fig leaf of a marriage, family ties, or a sexual life with women sufficient to dispense with a law that was perhaps regarded as distasteful. Sometimes testimony was altered in court: in one case, an episode of mutual masturbation, when the peripatetic Tereshkov shared a bed with a married schoolteacher (facts established in interrogation), mysteriously became "a wet dream [*polliutsiia*]" while they slept, and charges against the teacher were dropped.[76] The 1941 acquittal of a twice-married man followed similar behind-the-scenes revisions of the evidence, and courtroom testimonials from friends and neighbors demonstrating that the accused had "been friendly" with women and "not so friendly with the guys."[77]

Like jurists, forensic medical specialists also appeared at times reluctant to accept responsibility for this legislation. Their role was to identify "pederasts" for the police and courts. In reality, the courts of the 1930s rarely resorted to medical expertise to secure convictions, relying instead on denunciations and confessions. But experts had long believed that receptive anal intercourse left detectable traces, and police and procurators ensured that this lore was included, however awkwardly, in new rules on "forensic medical obstetric-gynecological examination" in criminal investigations.[78] These instructions, devised in early 1934 by a committee of po-

[74] Twenty-five percent of those convicted under article 154a (sodomy) got reductions on appeal, as compared with 17.5 percent of convicts under both sections of article 153 (rape), 33 percent of convicts under article 151 (sex with "sexually immature" persons, defloration), and 31 percent of convicts under article 152 (depraved acts with children/minors). See ibid.

[75] TsMAM, f. 819, op. 2, d. 30, l. 47 (sentence of Tereshkov and nine others, 1938).

[76] Ibid., l. 45.

[77] TsMAM, f. 819, op. 2, d. 51, esp. ll. 68, 99ob., and 110 (case file of Andreevskii and two others, 1941).

[78] GARF, f. A-482, op. 25, d. 879, ll. 22–29 (Pravila ambulatornogo sudebno-meditsinskogo akusher.-ginekologicheskogo issledovaniia, June 1934). These rules were the first attempt to

lice, procuracy, and health commissariat officials, spelled out anatomical signs of "pederasty" (in men, boys, and women, in that order) at the conclusion of a section on heterosexual rape. The use of the term "pederasty" and not "sodomy" in this code perhaps signals the involvement of party or secret police officials in its composition. In a 1935 textbook on "forensic gynecology" written by some of the same medical experts who contributed to these instructions, the role of the doctor in identifying "pederasts" for the police was evaded. The authors made the conceptual leap from "pederasty" to "homosexuality" and "lesbian love," arguing that the phenomena were better understood by hormone experts or psychiatrists, were especially prevalent in Germany "among the 'big shots' of the fascist movement," and were not the province of forensic gynecologists at all.[79] Despite these objections, in the postwar Stalin years, the detection of "pederasty" would become routine for forensic doctors, and investigators would invoke their expertise more frequently.[80]

The gendered context for this lore reflected discomfort with imagining men as "passive" objects of male desire. Courts and police often recorded whether men accused of sodomy adopted "active" or "passive" roles in anal intercourse, often expressed in bluntly gendered terms.[81] This was an eloquent redundancy, since in law insertive and receptive partners were equally guilty. Because, in fact, the authorities infrequently resorted to medical expertise in the 1930s, the question of "who did what to whom" lacked any scientific pretense. The obsession was an expression of anxiety about masculine vulnerability, a reflection of the values of the dominant sex/gender system that all actors in this drama inhabited.

Even with the fragmented records available, it is evident that there were different social responses to the Stalinist antisodomy statute. Intellectuals who developed openly homosexual personas in the prerevolu-

---

standardize expertise in sex crime cases, an area fraught with conflict between doctors and police.

79 E. E. Rozenblium, M. G. Serdiukov, and V. M. Smol'ianinov, *Sudebno-meditsinskaia akushersko-ginekologicheskaia ekspertiza* (Moscow, 1935), pp. 45–46.

80 See M. I. Avdeev, *Sudebnaia meditsina*, 3d ed. (Moscow, 1951), pp. 375–76; on forensic medicine's role after 1953, see Healey, *Homosexual Desire in Revolutionary Russia*, pp. 239–40.

81 "I gave in to him and we committed a sexual act. First I took the role of a woman, then he did." TsMAM, f. 819, op. 2, d. 51, l. 16 (case file of Andreevskii and two others, 1941). "We became close and then committed acts of sodomy. . . . First he used me, and then I him." Ibid., ll. 57–58. "Pavlov, for whom the active role was physically impossible [because of a war wound], was the object of Shelgunov, but nevertheless his active strivings he expressed in his emotional ties with Shelgunov, who on this level played the role of a woman [*igral rol' zhenshchiny*]." TsMAM, f. 819, op. 2, d. 11, ll. 241–42 (sentence of Bezborodov and eleven others, 1935).

tionary era (Kuzmin and Kliuev) reacted with degrees of defiance. A foreign communist, exploiting the privileges of a loyal outsider, dared to contest Marxist ideology with Stalin. Uncountable numbers of men, from professional engineers to cooks and tram drivers, continued to express same-sex desire in the urban territories they maintained and reproduced in the face of police persecution. Local judges and justices of the Supreme Court sought to reduce the impact of a harsh law with soft and suspended sentences. They colluded with police and criminal investigators to exculpate some defendants, by rewriting courtroom scripts to manufacture heterosexual credentials. Some medical professionals evaded their new responsibilities before the antisodomy law. This range of reactions reflected the diverse motives and interests of those involved.

Sexual and Gender Dissent as Resistance

Considering the case of homosexuality through the prism of resistance affords us a nuanced, nonessentializing view of the players in this social drama. The impression that there was a single group of "unconscious" victims crushed by a monolithic party-state machine cannot be sustained. Instead, a disaggregated set of actors appears both among those we call "homosexuals" and those we think of as in authority. None of this challenges the fact that the party and secret police determination to eliminate the urban subculture of the "pederast" defined the terms of engagement. Nevertheless, the picture is more complex. Some men who felt same-sex desire refused to abandon a self-constructed homosexual identity; others expressed their desire by sustaining a subculture that preserved attributes of mutuality (but not community, impossible to construct in this context).[82] If the resulting "culture of the toilet" seems a paltry achievement of this resistance, one should set it in its international context.[83] The Nazi onslaught in Germany extinguished the first wave of modern homosexual emancipation, destroying the chief repositories and promoters of its memory.[84] German men continued to meet for sexual and romantic li-

[82] The subculture based on concealed sex between men enabled emotional bonds to develop, but the culture was weakened by surveillance and arrests. A shared sense of oppression did not develop into the network of relations understood by Americans as "gay community." See Daniel Schluter, "Fraternity without Community: Social Institutions in the Soviet Gay World," Ph.D. dissertation, Columbia University, 1998.

[83] For a negative evaluation of this "culture," see M. Anikeev [pseud.], " 'Liudi byli zagnany v tualety, i ot etogo ikh kul'tura—tualetnaia,' " *Uranus*, 1995, no. 1: pp. 46–47.

[84] Hirschfeld died in exile in 1935. On the end of the German emancipationist movement, see James Steakley, *The Homosexual Emancipation Movement in Germany* (New York: Arno, 1975).

aisons despite the greatly increased surveillance and violence turned against them.[85] In Britain, France, and the United States, war preparation and fear produced a conservative turn in social policy, characterized by the repression of public discourse about same-sex love and the stepped-up arrest and imprisonment of male homosexuals in particular. Businesses catering to homosexuals were often suppressed, and those allowed to survive endured new levels of harassment and coercion. Sex reform organizations crumbled. The "culture of the toilet" was an experience shared across national boundaries until tiny homophile groups made a cautious appearance in the 1940s and 1950s.[86]

Homosexuals were not the only resisters. Soviet legal officials staffing the ordinary organs of justice were in a peculiar position, subordinate to the party and the police. The degree of direct influence from more powerful institutions (e.g., the secret police) over the conduct of sodomy trials in the ordinary courts cannot be gauged. Procurators, judges, and advocates were endowed with substantial powers over the subjects at their disposal, given that the notional minimum sentence of three years for consensual sodomy entailed deportation to the camps. Against our expectations of a monolithic and draconian authority, Soviet judges frequently mitigated the penalties for sodomy. These acts paralleled the softening in enforcement and sentencing policies adopted by judiciary officials in the case of other harsh laws. Peter Solomon suggests that the "paradox" of Stalin-era judges refusing to hand down the severe sentences for which many of the period's laws were famous was the result of the

[85] An estimated 100,000 men were arrested for homosexual crimes during the Third Reich, and of this number 50,000 were sentenced. Most served their time in ordinary prisons, but some 5,000 to 15,000 homosexuals were sent to concentration camps where it is estimated that they suffered a 60 percent mortality rate, much higher than political prisoners (41 percent) or Jehovah's Witnesses (35 percent). Convicted homosexuals liberated from concentration camps in 1945 were often not released by the occupying powers but were treated as criminals and forced to serve out their sentences. The few survivors were not recognized as victims of Nazi persecution until the 1990s. See, for example, Günter Grau, ed., *Hidden Holocaust? Gay and Lesbian Persecution in Germany 1933–45* (London: Cassell, 1995), p. 6; and Richard Plant, *The Pink Triangle: The Nazi War against Homosexuals* (New York: Henry Holt, 1986), pp. 180–81, 234–35. For the evidence of the survival of homosexual subcultures in Nazi Germany, see Frank Sparing, "*. . . wegen Vergehen nach §175 verhaftet": Die Verfolgung der Düsseldorfer Homosexuellen während des Nationalsozialismus* (Düsseldorf: Grupello, 1997).

[86] On these issues, see Barry D. Adam, Jan Willem Duyvendak, and André Krouwel, eds., *The Global Emergence of Gay and Lesbian Politics: National Imprints of a Worldwide Movement* (Philadelphia: Temple University Press, 1999); Jeffrey Weeks, *Coming Out: Homosexual Politics in Britain from the Nineteenth Century to the Present* (London: Quartet, 1990); Chauncey, *Gay New York;* and Jeffrey Merrick and Bryant T. Ragan Jr., eds., *Homosexuality in Modern France* (Oxford: Oxford University Press, 1996).

state's lack of control over the judiciary. Judges had been selected for their ideological credentials, and most lacked more than a few years' schooling; furthermore, they were subject to the authority of local party officials, not central agencies of control. The result was (from the perspective of the party leadership in Moscow) an erratic and unreliable judiciary that used the wide discretion at its disposal to satisfy its own notions of "revolutionary justice." These conditions changed only during the final years of the Stalin era when centralized control, more conventional career structures, and improved general and legal education transformed the outlook of Soviet legal cadres and produced a more conformist judiciary.[87]

The element of resistance in justice workers' actions with regard to the sodomy law needs to be balanced against their role in fixing the male homosexual as a resistant identity. These trials made the subculture acutely aware of its new status. The legal organs conducted most of these cases in camera, so they cannot be interpreted as displays for mass edification, but should be understood as opportunities to reforge the individuals in the dock. They were micropolitical rituals in which a new discourse of heterosexual masculinity was scripted and rehearsed in opposition to the "antisocial system of sexual liaisons between men."[88] Like Soviet tropes about the female prostitute, this was a redemptive discourse, and it seems to have been used only with those whose occupation and class credentials were judged sound.[89] In this arena, gestures of mercy were represented as votes of confidence in the "normalized" character of those men who were acquitted or discharged on suspended sentences. Merciful justice may also have satisfied a sense among judges that a harsh law, albeit one against a deviant practice, was being applied with restraint. These approaches, if representative, contrast markedly with the Nazi persecution of male homosexuals, which followed a trend of intensifying violence during the Third Reich.[90]

[87] Peter H. Solomon, Jr., *Soviet Criminal Justice under Stalin* (Cambridge: Cambridge University Press, 1996), pp. 451–53, 464–65.

[88] Healey, *Homosexual Desire in Revolutionary Russia*, pp. 227–28.

[89] Of the thirty-six named defendants in the Moscow sodomy trials sample, only three were from declassed elements (clergy or ex-clergy); seven were workers and twenty-six were white-collar clerical or professional-managerial employees.

[90] Acquittals in Third Reich trials of male homosexuals declined after 1933, and fines and sentences imposed became harsher. After 1937, homosexuals who had served prison sentences could legally be sent on to concentration camps for "reeducation." The Reich Office for Combating Homosexuality and Abortion, established in 1936, coordinated surveillance and card files on male homosexuals; by 1940 it had details on over 41,000 men. Grau, *Hidden Holocaust?* pp. 103–6, 131–32. Without access to FSB and APRF records, comparisons of Stalinist and Nazi surveillance and persecution of homosexuals remain incomplete. No evidence

Resistance was only one response to the antisodomy law. There were those who sought to accommodate it by marrying, with varying degrees of deliberation, and with or without the collusion of wives in hiding a husband's homosexual inclinations.[91] Celibacy was an option about which little is known. Self-destruction through suicide, alcohol abuse, and perhaps other forms of inward-directed hostility was probably frequent.[92] In late Soviet society the KGB reportedly recruited informants among homosexuals, and similar forms of coerced cooperation with the secret police cannot be ruled out for the Stalin era.[93] These reactions, by their very nature secretive, are impossible to quantify and difficult to document, but we should acknowledge that they were present to some degree. In other societies where legislation persecuted men seeking sex with men, similar responses were commonplace, and there is little in these coping mechanisms that can be entirely and solely attributed to Stalinist terror.

What value does knowledge of resistance to the Stalinist antisodomy law have? I make no apology for exploring this material as a contribution to the "usable past" of a vulnerable group in postcommunist Russia. The repeal of the antisodomy law in 1993 appears to have occurred as a result of commitments to abstract principles, the human rights standards set by the Council of Europe. There is scant evidence that the Russian state under Yeltsin had an appreciation of the humanity of the people the law persecuted.[94] President Putin's commitment to human rights and his administration's support for social pluralism remain to be demonstrated. Sexual minorities, meanwhile, need fresh narratives to nourish activism and community building.

Historians of Soviet society need these narratives, too, in order to refresh our thinking about sexualities and gender in this era. Homosexuals

---

of any Soviet bureau corresponding to the Reich Office for Combating Homosexuality has emerged in any accessible state or party archival collections, including archives of the RSFSR Justice Commissariat, the USSR Procuracy, the USSR Supreme Court, or the Central Committee of the Communist Party.

[91] On the marriages of Eisenstein, Richter, and others, see Karlinsky, "Russia's Gay Literature and Culture," p. 362.

[92] A professor of Marxism-Leninism, arrested in Moscow on sodomy charges after his wife denounced him in 1950, had been receiving psychiatric treatment for chronic alcoholism since "a friend" had died two years before. TsMAM, f. 901, op. 1, d. 1352. On this case, see Healey, "Moscow," p. 54.

[93] Kozlovskii, *Argo russkoi gomoseksual'noi subkul'tury,* pp. 155–56; and Masha Gessen, *The Rights of Lesbians and Gay Men in the Russian Federation* (San Francisco: International Gay and Lesbian Human Rights Commission, 1994), p. 18.

[94] On the circumstances in which repeal occurred, and the failure to amnesty those imprisoned under it, see Gessen, *Rights of Lesbians and Gay Men,* pp. 24–33.

were not insignificant and "unconscious" victims, but diverse individuals who expressed same-sex desire in a variety of ways. The state's attention to "pederasts" and homosexuals focused on a subculture, a form of byt, and apparently served to reproduce and even institutionalize the "culture of the toilet." This subculture was not new in the 1930s; indeed, in this crisis era it drew on traditions developed in Russian cities from (at least) the 1870s. What was novel was the increased surveillance the Soviet state now devoted to it, attention that in nineteenth-century Paris and Berlin had done much to determine the identity of the homosexual. By reducing men's same-sex love to a physiological urge furtively satisfied in public space, we view the homosexual subculture through the policemen's lens. Historians of Soviet society need to examine the experience of same-sex love with more empathy and theoretical sophistication to appreciate the resistance inherent in the homosexual identity. In Stalin's Soviet Union, this identity, shaped decades earlier by resistance to the predominant sex/gender system, acquired an ideological significance that paradoxically ensured its proliferation.

CHAPTER SIX

Economic Disobedience under Stalin

ELENA A. OSOKINA

Soviet society under Stalin was anything but passive economically. It participated not only in the sphere of the planned centralized economy, but—and this subject has not yet found a proper place either in Russian or in Western historiography—in an illegal underground economy known as the "shadow economy" or the "black market." In its black-market activity, Soviet society reveals itself to have been relatively independent and disobedient to official economic policies. The goal of this essay is to explore illegal economic activities in the 1930s, the ways and forms in which they developed, their scope and limits, and the role they played in the everyday life of the Soviet people. One of the most important questions that needs to be addressed is the precise nature of the black market: did it constitute a form of popular resistance under Stalin?[1]

Nineteen twenty-seven was the final year of the relatively prosperous New Economic Policy (NEP).[2] The forced industrialization of the late

I would like to thank the participants of the panel "Subalterns and Resistance in the Stalinist 1930s" at the conference "Rethinking the Stalin Era: The Impact of Archival Research" (Toronto, 30 September–3 October 1999) who took part in discussions of an earlier version of this paper. I would also like to acknowledge my husband, Richard Mark Lang, for carrying out the primary editing of this text, and Lynne Viola for the final editing.

[1] Analysis of black-market activity in this essay is limited to the sphere of consumer products, with a focus on trade and other forms of distribution of food and manufactured goods. Consequently, the sphere of production is analyzed only as it relates to food and manufactured goods for domestic consumption. Chronologically, the essay covers the period from the end of the New Economic Policy in 1927–28 to the German invasion of the USSR in 1941.

[2] When I say that the New Economic Policy brought prosperity, I have in mind most of all its achievements in supply and consumption. Research conducted by the Central Statistical Bureau (Tsentral'noe statisticheskoe upravlenie, TsSU) recorded yearly improvements in the food supply, which reached its highest point in 1926. See *Trudy TsSU,* vol. 30: *Sostoianie pi-*

1920s required (according to the Stalinist leadership) a concentration of resources (finances, food and goods reserves, raw materials, human resources, and so on) in the hands of the government to be invested directly into heavy industry and military production. To obtain a monopoly and to stop competition over resources, the Politburo launched a massive campaign of repression against the private sector of the economy. Consequently, it proclaimed for the socialist sector a monopoly in the production and a near monopoly in the supply of food and manufactured goods for the population.

As a result of arrests and confiscation of properties in the towns and the countryside, the sphere of private production and trade narrowed drastically.[3] Not only was there a quantitative decrease in the number of private entrepreneurs and their products, but there were also important qualitative changes in this sphere in that some forms of private production and trade were prohibited completely. From this point on, the Soviet leadership permitted private activity to be no more than an appendage of state production and trade. Earnings from private trade and production, more-

---

taniia gorodskogo naseleniia SSSR, 1919–1924 (Moscow, 1926), no. 1; *Sostoianie pitaniia sel'skogo naseleniia SSSR, 1920–1924* (Moscow, 1928), no. 2; *Sostoianie pitaniia gorodskogo naseleniia SSSR v 1924–1925 sel'skokhoziaistvennom godu* (Moscow, 1926), no. 3; *Sostoianie pitaniia gorodskogo naseleniia SSSR v 1925–1926 sel'skokhoziaistvennom godu* (Moscow, 1927), no. 5. Carr and Davies assert that in 1926 workers and peasants had better diets than before the revolution. See E. H. Carr and R. W. Davies, *Foundations of a Planned Economy, 1926–1929* (New York: Macmillan, 1971), p. 697. During NEP, famine did not threaten the country. However, one should not idealize NEP; it was not a time of abundance, and the standard of living for most of the population remained low. The prosperity of NEP was *relative*, compared to the preceding period of the Civil War and the First Five-Year Plan that followed.

The improvement of material well-being under NEP does not necessarily imply popular support for the regime. There was a lot of dissatisfaction during NEP, which gave rise to popular support of regime policies during the First Five-Year Plan. On the social unease and dissatisfaction NEP engendered in society, see Alan Ball, *Russia's Last Capitalists: The Nepmen, 1921–1929* (Berkeley: University of California Press, 1987); Katerina Clark, *Petersburg, Crucible of Cultural Revolution* (Cambridge, Mass.: Harvard University Press, 1995); and Eric Naiman, *Sex in Public: The Incarnation of Early Soviet Ideology* (Princeton, N.J.: Princeton University Press, 1997).

[3] On private industry and trade under NEP and the liquidation of the private sector of the economy at the end of the 1920s and the beginning of the 1930s, see V. A. Arkhipov and L. F. Morozov, *Bor'ba protiv kapitalisticheskikh elementov v promyshlennosti i torgovle, 20-e–nachalo 30-kh godov* (Moscow, 1978); Ball, *Russia's Last Capitalists;* A. Banerji, *Merchants and Markets in Revolutionary Russia, 1917–30* (New York: St. Martin's, 1997); R. W. Davies, *The Industrialization of Soviet Russia*, vol. 3: *The Soviet Economy in Turmoil, 1929–1930* (Cambridge, Mass.: Harvard University Press, 1989); V. P. Dmitrenko, *Torgovaia politika sovetskogo gosudarstva posle perekhoda k nepu, 1921–1924* (Moscow, 1971); Sheila Fitzpatrick, "After NEP: The Fate of NEP Entrepreneurs, Small Traders, and Artisans in the 'Socialist Russia' of the 1930s," *Russian History/Histoire Russe* 13, 2–3 (1986): 187–233; and Elena A. Osokina, *Our Daily Bread: Socialist Distribution and the Art of Survival in Stalin's Russia, 1927–1941* (Armonk, N.Y.: Sharpe, 2001).

over, were not to exceed the basic income needs of the entrepreneurs; profits were strictly forbidden. The state also prohibited the employment of permanent hired workers for production or sales.[4] The main means of production and distribution remained under state ownership. Thus, the leadership declared only small-scale individual private activity to be lawful.

Legal Forms of Private Activity in the Sphere of Production

During the 1930s, the legal sphere of private production and trade became substantially smaller than it had been in the years of the New Economic Policy, not to mention the capitalist economy of prerevolutionary Russia. Nonetheless, a legal private sector continued to exist.[5]

Legal forms of private agricultural production were limited to the individual plots and gardens of collective farmers (*kolkhozniki*), the households of those peasants who refused to enter the collective farms and survived dekulakization (the so-called *edinolichniki*), the small plots of land (*ogorody*) cultivated by city dwellers and government employees living in the countryside, and the subsidiary economies of enterprises and organizations. Artisans (*kustari* and *remeslenniki*), whether members of cooperatives or working individually, represented the only legal form of private production of manufactured goods during the 1930s.

The individual plots and gardens of collective farmers made up a major sector of private production in agriculture. Even so, it took a considerable amount of time for the leadership to define its policy in this sphere. The 1930 statute on collective farms granted collective farmers permission in principle to have individual plots, without providing any specifics on the size or nature of the plots. It was only in 1935, after long discussions in a special Politburo commission, that a new collective-farm statute appeared,

[4] Artisans' cooperatives were allowed to have hired labor as a temporary expedient or as would-be members for trial periods of up to one month. See Julie Hessler, "A Postwar Perestroika? Toward a History of Private Enterprise in the USSR," *Slavic Review* 57, 3 (1998): 520.

[5] For many decades Russian and Western historiography presented the Soviet economy of the 1930s as almost completely "market-less." At best, historians wrote about *legal* market activity but limited that activity to the peasant market—the so-called *kolkhoznyi rynok.* More recently, the study of legal market activity has increased. On the legal market in the 1930s, see Davies, *Soviet Economy in Turmoil,* pp. 87–88, 289–303; G. A. Dikhtiar, *Sovetskaia torgovlia v period sotsializma i razvernutogo stroitel'stva kommunizma* (Moscow, 1965), pp. 120–22; Hessler, "A Postwar Perestroika?" 516; Basile H. Kerblay, *Les marchés paysans en U.R.S.S.* (Paris: Mouton, 1968); Stephen Kotkin, *Magnetic Mountain: Stalinism as a Civilization* (Berkeley: University of California Press, 1995), pp. 242–56; Elena A. Osokina, *Ierarkhiia potrebleniia: O zhizni liudei v usloviakh stalinskogo snabzheniia, 1928–1935 gg.* (Moscow, 1993), pp. 117–21; and Osokina, *Our Daily Bread,* pp. 110–14, 178–80.

clarifying the acceptable size of individual plots. According to this statute, collective farmers could have in their individual use no more than 0.5 to 1 hectare of land and one to three cows, depending on the region where they lived. (During Politburo discussions, Stalin proposed a limit of one cow per family; he considered two cows to be too many for a peasant household.) The produce from these individual plots was intended to be the main source of peasant subsistence; however, it would also make up a very important part of sales in the so-called collective-farm market (*kolkhoznyi rynok*). By 1937, peasants' individual plots and gardens provided more than half of the country's total production of potatoes and other vegetables and more than 70 percent of all dairy products and meat.[6]

The households of edinolichniki represented another legal form of private agricultural enterprise in the 1930s. By the mid-1930s, edinolichniki constituted about 10 percent of all peasant households and had in their use about 6 percent of all cultivated land. Despite their small numbers, edinolichniki played an important role in providing produce for the collective-farm market. New research has demonstrated that these independent peasant households proved to be more economically effective than the collective farms.[7]

Under the conditions of the growing supply crisis in the early 1930s, the state allowed city dwellers and rural inhabitants employed in the government sector of the economy (e.g., workers and employees at state farms, rural doctors, and teachers) to have small plots of land on which to cultivate vegetables. These plots made up another sector of private agricultural production in the 1930s. People either received land for their use through the organizations where they worked or simply made use of it spontaneously without permission. In addition to individuals, enterprises and government organizations also received legal permission to create farms to supply food for their workers and employees. With the approach of mass famine in the early 1930s, the state actively stimulated this small-plot policy in the mass media. Newspapers and radio called on people to organize "Dneprostrois of cabbage production" and "Magnitkas of chicken incubators."[8] Every city or town had a belt of gardens around it; every available piece of land was used, whether within town or nearby. Food grown on these individual plots and factory farms usually did not go

[6] I. E. Zelenin, "Byl li kolkhoznyi neonep?" *Otechestvennaia istoriia*, 1994, no. 2: 118.

[7] See Zelenin, "Byl li kolkhoznyi neonep?" 105–21; Zelenin, "Kollektivizatsiia i edinolichnik (1933–pervaia polovina 1935 g.)," *Otechestvennaia istoriia*, 1993, no. 3: 35–55.

[8] Dneprostroi and Magnitka (short for Magnitogorsk) were two of the massive construction projects of the First Five-Year Plan.

to the market. Instead, it supplied the family's table or the factory dining rooms of workers and employees.[9]

The legal private production of manufactured goods in the 1930s was limited to artisans. By the early 1930s, most of them had become members of cooperatives—the result of the state's policy of forced cooperation.[10] Artisans had to buy a license from the government to engage in private activity, and they paid a tax. Raw materials to produce goods legally were only available through the cooperatives at fixed prices. According to law, artisans had to produce goods by themselves—hiring workers to increase production was prohibited. Artisans could sell their products only through their cooperatives or in the market at fixed prices. In the mid-1930s, the government further limited the size of artisanal production. A 1935 decree by the Central Soviet Executive Committee (Tsentral'nyi ispolnitel'nyi komitet)–Council of People's Commissars (Sovnarkom, short for Sovet narodnykh komissarov) limited production to work only on the customer's order and only with the customer's materials. Those who worked with their own raw materials to produce goods for sale (even at the fixed prices) would be denied licenses. Artisans could privately produce goods only during their free time (if they were employed in the state sector of the economy) and only with their employer's permission. Those who were not members of the cooperatives were barred from manufacturing clothes, linens, hats, leather shoes, notions, leather saddles and harnesses, and any goods made out of nonferrous metals. The sale of raw materials to independent artisans was also prohibited. In March 1936, some trades were re-legalized (e.g., shoe repairing, carpentry, dressmaking, upholstery, hairdressing, laundering, locksmith work, photography, and plumbing); however, almost all activities that involved the processing of food or other agricultural products for sale remained prohibited to individuals. Violators of these rules were now subject to criminal prosecution.[11]

[9] At the end of the 1930s, the government restricted its policy on small plots. According to the Council of People's Commissars–Central Committee resolution of 28 July 1939, individual plots of nonpeasant rural residents could not exceed 0.15 hectare of land including the land under buildings. Following this resolution, special commissions measured and cut off private plots to the benefit of the collective farms. See the resolution "O priusadebnykh uchastkakh rabochikh i sluzhashchikh, sel'skikh uchitelei, agronomov, i drugikh ne chlenov kolkhozov, prozhivaiushchikh v sel'skoi mestnosti," in *Resheniia partii i pravitel'stva po khoziaistvennym voprosam*, vol. 2 (Moscow, 1967), pp. 719–20.

[10] The most recent study on the policy of cooperation is V. V. Kabanov, *Krest'ianskaia obshchina i kooperatsiia Rossii XX veka (Problemno-istoriograficheskie ocherki)* (Moscow, 1997).

[11] See Sheila Fitzpatrick, *Everyday Stalinism: Ordinary Life in Extraordinary Times: Soviet Russia in the 1930s* (New York: Oxford University Press, 1999), pp. 44–45; Hessler, "A Postwar Perestroika?" 519; and Osokina, *Our Daily Bread*, pp. 113–14.

Legal Forms of Private Activity in the Sphere of Trade and Distribution

Trade in collective-farm or secondhand markets (*barakholki, tolkuchki, bazary*), artisans' sales of their own products, and small-scale trade in manufactured goods were the only legal forms of private trade during the 1930s.

The so-called collective-farm market represented the most substantial form of legal private trade in this period. The peasant market was never officially prohibited during the repressive campaign against the private sector in 1929–30, although local authorities frequently implemented antimarket measures and the central government enacted piecemeal legislation against private activities. The state began to stimulate peasant trade only in 1932 in response to an acute supply crisis and the approach of famine.[12] This was a forced measure, one that did not coexist easily with Bolshevik political economy. Special decrees were issued to create better conditions for the development of peasant trade: state procurement plans decreased marginally, and peasant trade was tax-exempt. Moreover, peasant trade received the biggest economic privilege of the 1930s: it was the only form of private trade officially permitted to charge real market prices based on supply and demand.[13] Peasant trade in the collective-farm market was to provide one of the main sources of peasant livelihood.

Peasant trade had three main sources of supply: collective farms, independent peasant households (edinolichniki), and the personal plots of collective farmers. The latter two were the most crucial in supplying the collective-farm market. They provided the lion's share of sales, while the collective farms themselves had very little, sometimes nothing, to offer for sale after ever-increasing state procurements emptied their storehouses. Meat, dairy products, potatoes, and other vegetables went to the collective-farm market almost entirely from individual peasant plots. For that reason, perhaps, "peasant market" would be a better label for the collec-

[12] The main resolution on the development of collective-farm-market trade was adopted by the Central Soviet Executive Committee and the Council of People's Commissars of the USSR on 20 May 1932. See *Sobranie zakonov,* no. 38 (1932), pp. 356–57.

[13] Permission for peasants to sell at market prices constituted a large and important change in the Politburo's stimulation of the collective-farm market. Before the May resolution, collective farms were required to sell their produce in the market at the fixed prices of the cooperative stores. Thus, the Politburo resolution of April 1932 allowed only the collective farms located within a 100-kilometer zone around Moscow and Leningrad to sell their produce "at prices a little bit higher than those of the cooperatives," while all other collective farms had to sell at the fixed prices. See Rossiiskii gosudarstvennyi arkhiv sotsial'no-politicheskoi istorii (henceforth, RGASPI), f. 17, op. 3, d. 879, l. 5.

tive-farm market. However, the state would never accept the private nature of the collective-farm market—its peasant aspect—because that contradicted the allegedly public character of the socialist economy.

Legal peasant trade had its limits. Collective farms could bring their products to the market only after they fulfilled state procurement plans, and collective farmers and independent peasants only after they paid the agricultural tax. Sales were halted seasonally in the markets as soon as the harvest and state procurements began. The Politburo tried to control and direct all peasant trade. As soon as a region fulfilled the state procurement plan, the Politburo issued a special decree that allowed its collective farms and peasants to bring the rest of their produce (grain and potatoes were under special control) to the peasant market. Otherwise, peasant trade was considered illegal and defined as "speculation."

Workers' budgets show that during the time of rationing, from 1931 to 1935, peasant markets provided 50 to 80 percent of workers' (and their families') potatoes, dairy products, eggs, and oil and 20 to 30 percent of their meat, flour, vegetables, and fruits.[14] For those who did not receive state supplies during the years of rationing or were supplied poorly by the state, peasant markets were the main, and sometimes the only, source of food. During the second half of the 1930s, after the food crisis was alleviated, the peasant market flourished. It continued to play an important role, accounting for one-fifth of the country's domestic food sales.[15]

Secondhand markets represented another form of legal private trade in the 1930s. The state permitted certain urban neighborhoods to have secondhand markets where, usually on the weekends, people could sell their personal belongings. However, the law prohibited the sale of any items that were not secondhand, considering the sale of new products to be "speculation." The secondhand markets were extremely crowded. They not only took up their assigned space but often expanded into nearby streets, dead ends, and squares. The Smolensk market at the corner of Arbat Street and the Garden Ring in Moscow was famous. Foreigners would go there to sightsee. The assortment of goods at the Smolensk market during the first half of the 1930s varied from simple combs, boxes, toothbrushes, and the like to luxury furniture, carpets, jewelry, and art from the former estates of the Russian nobility and other prerevolutionary economic elites.[16]

[14] Rossiiskii gosudarstvennyi arkhiv ekonomiki (henceforth, RGAE), f. 1562, op. 329, d. 62, ll. 2, 8, 10.

[15] G. L. Rubinshtein, *Razvitiie vnutrennei torgovli v SSSR* (Leningrad, 1964), pp. 358–59.

[16] For a colorful description of the Smolensk secondhand market, see E. Ashmead-Bartlett, *The Riddle of Russia* (London: Cassell, 1929), pp. 207–9.

A crowded market in the Central Black Earth Region, 1933. Courtesy Rossiiskii gosudarstvennyi arkhiv kinofotodokumentov (RGAKFD).

"Soviet bazaar. Entry is forbidden to speculators and resellers," says the banner at the entrance to this market in Ivanovo, 1932. Courtesy Rossiiskii gosudarstvennyi arkhiv kinofotodokumentov (RGAKFD).

During the famine of 1932–33, secondhand markets played a crucial role in the survival of *lishentsy* (people deprived of their civil rights, including members of the privileged classes of prerevolutionary Russia and private entrepreneurs from the days of the New Economic Policy). Lishentsy did not receive state rations in the first half of the 1930s. They could provide for themselves only by selling their belongings. The secondhand markets were also important in the lives of workers and government employees, who were able not only to buy necessary items inexpensively but to sell or exchange their personal belongings and a part of their rations there. In fact, it became a normal and widespread practice for industrial workers with relatively high bread rations to sell bread at the markets. The state had no choice but to accept this practice, in which virtually every industrial worker was involved, by issuing a special decree saying that it did not consider this activity speculation.[17] Workers' budgets show that during the winter and spring of 1933—the high point of the famine—

[17] Gosudarstvennyi arkhiv Rossiiskoi Federatsii (henceforth, GARF), f. 5446, op. 15a, d. 1071, ll. 30–31.

sales and exchange at the secondhand markets provided about 9 percent of the income of workers' families. In the second half of the 1930s, secondhand markets did not disappear, although their role changed. They no longer existed primarily to save starving people but instead represented the normal way of obtaining goods in an economy of shortages, where store shelves were at least partly empty all the time.[18]

During the first half of the 1930s, artisans were also allowed by law to sell their products through cooperatives or in the market, either secondhand or collective-farm markets (which, in fact, were often combined). However, the prices that artisans could legally ask for their products were fixed at the level of equivalent products sold through state and cooperative trade. Otherwise, the law labeled such sales as speculation (even if the producers were selling their own products). In the midst of a supply crisis and high consumer demand, when goods could have been sold at the market for a huge profit, the low level of the fixed legal prices deprived artisans of an equitable level of exchange.

In the 1930s, the state also allowed small, private trade of manufactured goods by individuals who were not artisans. Such individuals had to buy a license and pay a tax. They were not allowed to open shops, stores, or even kiosks and had to sell their goods "out of hand" (*prodavat' s ruk*, that is, to sell only what they could, literally, hold in their hands) or on trays. The legal assortment of such trade was strictly defined by the state. A special 1934 instruction allowed private trade only in petty goods, such as notions (needles, thread, etc.), putty, baking soda, bleach, small metal items, shoe polish, toys, fruits, nonalcoholic beverages, sweets, and old clothes. Once again, the state prohibited the sale of new clothes.[19] During the 1939–41 supply crisis, private petty trade was further restricted. A Council of People's Commissars–Central Committee decree prohibited sales "out of hand" in the Moscow markets.[20]

Thus, the state left very little room for private activity in the sphere of production and trade. Obviously, the scope of legal private activity was not

[18] On the peculiar character of the secondhand market in the socialist economy, see V. Treml, "A Coping Mechanism: Redistribution of Assets in Soviet and Post-Soviet History," paper presented at the Annual Meeting of the Southern Conference on Slavic Studies, Asheville, N.C., April 1996.

[19] GARF, f. 5446, op. 15a, d. 1071, l. 14.

[20] The decree "O likvidatsii ruchnoi torgovli promyshlennymi tovarami na rynkakh goroda Moskvy" was issued on 25 July 1940. The decree affected not only the trade of individually manufactured goods but also the trade of secondhand goods. RGASPI, f. 17, op. 3, d. 1026, l. 17.

large enough to eliminate shortages and satisfy consumer needs. In this situation, private activity in production and trade surpassed by far the limits allowed by law, creating an immense black market.

Factors behind the Development of the Black Market in the 1930s

Despite official proclamations, the socialist sector of the economy (state enterprises and collective-farm production) failed to provide enough food and goods to supply the population. The conditions of acute shortage and permanent supply crisis characteristic of the insufficient and overly hierarchical state supply system, in conjunction with a narrow legal private sector, could not but have resulted in the development of a black market in the 1930s.

The state acquired considerable resources from the destruction of the private sector and the seizure of private properties and other assets, but it directed them mostly toward the development of heavy industry, military production, and other state needs.[21] Food and light industry had low priority. Thus, with the decline of a private sector that worked almost entirely to satisfy consumer needs and the increase of a socialist sector that focused almost exclusively on industrialization and the needs of the state bureaucratic apparatus, the supply of food and goods for the population dropped drastically.

Furthermore, the state's trade network was undeveloped and regionally uneven. It could not compete in efficiency with the private trade of the NEP period. State and cooperative stores depended heavily on bureaucratic planning, a chaotic supply system from centralized state stocks, and a poor transportation system that had to transfer large amounts of goods over a huge country. As a result, socialist trade featured stoppages, poor and insufficient assortments, long lines, and large losses.

It is no wonder, then, that the repression of the private sector led to a supply crisis in the USSR. Ration cards, issued first for bread and spontaneously at the initiative of local leaders, appeared in 1928.[22] With every new attack on the private sector, the supply situation worsened. Beginning at the end of 1929, forced collectivization had a major impact on the nation's supplies. In 1931, the state officially introduced a rationing sys-

[21] For special research on the development of heavy and military industries in the USSR, see N. S. Simonov, *Voenno-promyshlennyi kompleks SSSR v 1920–50-e gody: Tempy ekonomicheskogo rosta, struktura, organizatsiia proizvodstva, i upravlenie* (Moscow, 1996).

[22] That was not the first time Russia used rationing. Ration cards were introduced during World War I and the Civil War. For more on international and Russian experiences with state-regulated supply, see Osokina, *Our Daily Bread*, pp. 195–203.

tem for all major food products and goods, an unprecedented phenomenon in peacetime. The ration system was abolished only in 1935 for food and in 1936 for manufactured goods.[23]

The introduction of rationing, however, did not improve the supply situation, since it was not supplemented by an increase in the amount of food and goods available for domestic consumption. Under conditions of approaching famine, the main goal of the rationing system was to secure the food supply of the part of the urban population that worked in industrial production. In this endeavor, the state proved to be both selective and pragmatic. It refused to feed everyone and supplied only those whom it considered essential to the fulfillment of the industrialization plan.

Consequently, only those who worked in the state sector of the economy could receive rations. Industrial engineers and workers were the number one priority (after the small group of party-state, military, and intellectual elites, who received special and unrivaled amounts of supplies). Furthermore, people in the big industrial cities were supplied better than those who lived in small and nonindustrial towns. Those residents were assigned smaller rations and allotted an inferior assortment of goods. In fact, the state provided them only with trifling amounts of bread, sugar, and ce-reals.

Peasants—more than 80 percent of the population of the USSR at that time—did not receive rations at all. According to government plan, they had to supply themselves from the collective farm's reserves and their household plots. However, by increasing procurements, the state undermined the possibility of self-supply. The lishentsy was another group that did not receive state supplies.

The provision of state supplies during the 1931–35 era of rationing was not only hierarchical, but also quite clearly insufficient. In fact, it created a "hierarchy of poverty."[24] In the whole country, only the small body of official elites received sufficient supplies. Even the next group in this hierarchy—industrial workers and engineers—was supplied with a minimum standard of living. Others, especially groups with no rations, were left by the state to the mercy of fate. People had to count on themselves.

In the context of famine, this selective and insufficient state supply system made the development of private activity in production and trade necessary, if not inevitable. No force could have prevented private initia-

[23] On the introduction and abolition of the rationing system of 1931–35, see R. W. Davies and O. V. Khlevniuk, "Otmena kartochnoi systemy v SSSR 1934–1935 gody," *Otechestvennaia istoriia*, 1999, no. 5: 87–108; Osokina, *Our Daily Bread*, pp. 35–58, 133–44.

[24] On the hierarchy of state supply and ration norms, see Osokina, *Ierarkhiia potrebleniia;* and Osokina, *Our Daily Bread*, pp. 61–101.

tive under such circumstances. For the majority of the Soviet people, it was a question of physical survival; for some, it was a chance to earn good money in a situation of high consumer demand and acute shortage. Since the legal economic space that the state allowed for private activity was narrow, private economic activity flowed into illegal forms. The black market grew rapidly and broadly during the period of rationing.

By the mid-1930s, the situation had improved. The supply crisis was alleviated and the state abolished rations. As Stalin said, "Life has become better, comrades, life has become more cheerful." However, it would be a mistake to overestimate the improvement. The same factors that encouraged the development of illegal private production and trade during the first half of the 1930s remained.

During the second half of the 1930s, as before, heavy industry and military production received the lion's share of state resources, while light industry, though growing, did not develop enough to satisfy consumer demand.[25] After the relatively good years of the Second Five-Year Plan (1933–37), a new wave of forced industrialization and militarization on the eve of World War II made the disparity between heavy and light industry sharper and the shortage of food and consumer goods more acute.

Following the turmoil of collectivization and famine, life began to stabilize in the countryside by the mid-1930s. However, the lack of material stimuli in collective-farm work and exorbitant state procurements at low, purely symbolic prices made the collective-farm system ineffective and perpetuated food shortages.[26]

As a result of continuing shortages, purchases in state and cooperative stores were limited by norms even after the abolition of rations.[27] Twice in the second half of the 1930s, in 1936–37 and 1939–41, the population ex-

[25] By the end of the Third Five-Year Plan in 1940, light industry produced only sixteen meters of cotton fabric, ninety centimeters of wool, forty centimeters of silk fabric, less than three pairs of socks and stockings, one pair of leather shoes, and less than one pair of underwear per person. See Dikhtiar, *Sovetskaia torgovlia v period sotsializma*, p. 101. Per capita indicators were calculated based on a population of 171 million people.

[26] The state food industry produced only thirteen kilograms of sugar, eight to nine kilograms of meat and fish, about forty kilograms of dairy products, and four kilograms of soap per person in 1940. Ibid.

[27] Purchase limits established by the Council of People's Commissars in 1936–39 were two kilograms of meat, sausage, bread, macaroni, groats, and sugar; three kilograms of fish; five hundred grams of butter; one hundred grams of tea; two hundred cigarettes; two bars of soap; and half a liter of kerosene. The situation deteriorated in 1940 when purchase limits were decreased and restrictions were set on products which had been sold earlier without purchase limits. See RGAE, f. 7971, op. 16, d. 63, l. 55; d. 81, l. 78.

perienced supply crises with unofficial rationing systems spontaneously revived from below. Moreover, these crises were accompanied by local famine.[28]

Other factors that influenced the development of private activity during rationing also continued to exist in the second half of the 1930s. The networks of state and cooperative trade remained underdeveloped and concentrated in the big cities.[29] As before, state trade was based on a slow, chaotic, and bureaucratic centralized distribution system.[30] The hierarchical and selective character of state supply also persisted. Population density in a region failed to play a major role in state distribution of food and manufactured goods, and the most important industrial cities still had priorities in supply. And despite its much larger share of the population, the countryside received substantially less from the state supply system than the urban sector.

No wonder, then, that the private sector in production and trade continued to be an important and necessary part of the economy and of everyday life. Because the legal economic space for private activity remained as narrow as it had been during rationing, a considerable proportion of private initiatives developed in illegal, underground form. However, there were some changes in the portrait of the black market, influenced largely by a general improvement in living standards during the second half of the 1930s. Strategies of survival, which were crucial for

[28] On the supply crises, see Roberta T. Manning, "The Soviet Economic Crisis of 1936–40 and the Great Purges," in *Stalinist Terror: New Perspectives*, ed. J. Arch Getty and Roberta T. Manning (New York: Cambridge University Press, 1993), pp. 117–23; Osokina, *Our Daily Bread*, pp. 155–77.

[29] On average, by the end of the 1930s, every ten thousand people were served by twenty-one shops—only three shops more than under rationing. Most shops were small, earning only 100 to 200 rubles per day. See Dikhtiar, *Sovetskaia torgovlia v period sotsializma*, pp. 131, 133; and Rubinshtein, *Razvitie vnutrennei torgovli v SSSR*, p. 364.

[30] During the second half of the 1930s, in comparison with the rationing system of 1931–35, the centralization of trade even increased. The trade plans now not only determined the amount of goods in circulation and served as indicators of republic, regional, urban, and rural supply but also of the amount of reserves, turnover, number of stores, number of workers in trade, overhead costs, and profit. The plans were usually quarterly, but plans for flour and groats were monthly. In the prewar years, centralized planning and distribution encompassed over 70 percent of the commodities produced in the country, including not only the production of major enterprises but also those of local industry and artisanal cooperatives. Even such "nonstrategic" goods as wooden spoons and toys fell under centralized distribution. Price fixing provides another example of the increasing centralization. As a result of the two price reforms of 1935 and 1939, the central government determined not only wholesale industrial prices and trade surcharges, as before, but also retail prices for practically everything.

the disastrous First Five-Year Plan, no longer dominated. Entrepreneurial strategies of enrichment began to play more and more of a role for those who could provide food and goods for sale on the market.

Illegal Forms of Private Activity That Increased the Amount of Goods and Services in the Domestic Market

As a defense against the state's administrative measures and repression, black marketeers disguised their illegal practices to resemble forms of legal socialist production and trade.[31] Private capital hid under the cover of collective farms, state and even party organizations, and licensed handicraft work. This phenomenon calls to mind the biological forms of mimicry that organisms use to conceal themselves from predators. The same occurred in social and economic life: illegal practices mimicked the socialist forms of production and trade.[32]

Illegal private peasant production that developed under the cover of the collective farms represented the most significant form of underground black-market activity in agriculture. Documents show that during the period from 1934 to 1939, collective farmers considerably extended

[31] Soviet official historiography did not accept the black market as a part of the socialist economy. Soviet historians considered the black market as an evil that had to be and was defeated under socialism. Research of illegal private activity in Soviet historiography is limited, therefore, to the period of the Civil War and the New Economic Policy. After that, with the centralization of the economy and the liquidation of the private sector, the market was considered "defeated" by the plan. Soviet historians viewed the future as a communism with a nonmarket economy and direct product exchange. Thus, according to their theoretical construction, even the legal socialist market had to go. For an analysis of the Soviet historiography on the plan and the market, see Elena Osokina, *Za fasadom "stalinskogo izobiliia": Raspredelenie i rynok v snabzhenii naseleniia v gody industrializatsii, 1927–1941* (Moscow, 1998), pp. 14–26.

In Western historiography there was a considerable literature on the Soviet black market, focusing mainly on the period of *zastoi* (stagnation), during the 1970s and 1980s. See Gregory Grossman, "The Second Economy in the USSR and Eastern Europe: A Bibliography," *Berkeley-Duke Occasional Papers on the Second Economy in the USSR*, no. 21 (1990). However, the study of the black market of the Stalin era has just begun. See Hessler, "A Postwar Perestroika?" and her dissertation, "Culture of Shortages: A Social History of Soviet Trade, 1917–1953," Ph.D. dissertation, University of Chicago, 1996; Kotkin, *Magnetic Mountain*, esp. pp. 238–79; and Osokina, *Our Daily Bread*, pp. 102–29, 178–94. In Sheila Fitzpatrick's most recent book, the legal and illegal market, although not the main subject of analysis, emerges as an important part of Soviet everyday life under Stalin. See Fitzpatrick, *Everyday Stalinism*, esp. pp. 40–66.

[32] For other examples of the socio-economic mimicry used by private enterprise under Stalin, see Hessler, "A Postwar Perestroika?" 520; Kotkin, *Magnetic Mountain*, pp. 272–74; and David R. Shearer, "Crime and Social Disorder in Stalin's Russia: A Reassessment of the Great Retreat and the Origins of Mass Repression," *Cahiers du monde russe* 39, 1–2 (1998): 124–26.

their individual gardens and plots over the legal limits allowed by the 1935 collective-farm statute at the expense of the collective farms. Several factors contributed to this phenomenon. At the beginning of the Second Five-Year Plan, the state relaxed somewhat its control of and pressure on society. It was forced to do this to stabilize the economy and overcome the socio-economic crisis caused by its policy of forced centralization.[33] As a result of weakened state control, private activity—including its illegal side—intensified.

Another factor that contributed to the illegal extension of individual households was the collective farms' own interest in decreasing the land they used. At this time, state procurement plans depended not on the collective farm's total landmass but only on the part under cultivation. A decrease in cultivated land consequently led to a decrease in the plan. For this reason, collective-farm administrations allowed peasants, in exchange for rent payments, to use land that according to law was not even the property of the collective farm but of the socialist state. After allocation for individual use, this land became available for rent or even quasi-purchase among peasants. The products received from the illegally extended individual households went to the market. The peasant market flourished, providing peasants with high earnings. Though barely distinguishable at the market from "legal" produce, such "illegal" produce became a mainstay of peasant trade.

The illegal extension of individual peasant plots became so widespread, and peasant income received from the illegal trade so significant, that the May 1939 Plenum of the Central Committee made special note of such activities. In its report, the Central Committee stated that during the Second Five-Year Plan collective farmlands decreased, while individual landholdings increased by 2.5 million hectares; moreover, individual livestock exceeded that of the collective farms, and a peasant's income from individual trade could reach as much as 15,000 to 20,000 rubles a year.[34] (For comparison, the first secretary of the Central Committee of the Komsomol, who belonged to the highest party elite, earned 24,000 rubles in 1940; the Soviet trade representative in France earned 16,000 rubles; and the head of a district [*raion*] soviet executive committee earned a maximum of 17,000 rubles a year.) Thus, masked under legal forms of agricultural production and trade, private activity overcame the barriers the state

[33] On the phases of the prewar economic development of the USSR, see R. W. Davies, Mark Harrison, and S. G. Wheatcroft, eds., *The Economic Transformation of the Soviet Union, 1913–1945* (Cambridge: Cambridge University Press, 1994), pp. 14–18.

[34] *Istoriia sotsialisticheskoi ekonomiki SSSR* (Moscow, 1978), vol. 4, p. 386; vol. 5, pp. 131–32.

put in its way. By this time, moreover, it was not simply a question of survival for peasants but of profitability as well.

The Politburo was outraged by the illegal growth of individual households and soon implemented a series of administrative measures. In the fall of 1939, following the decision of the May Plenum, lands in the collective farms were measured; individual landholdings were reduced, to the benefit of the collective farms; and individual livestock that exceeded the legal limits were expropriated and given to the collective farms. Furthermore, state procurement plans from then on were based on the collective farm's total land allotment, not the amount of land under cultivation. The agricultural tax that peasants paid on behalf of their individual households also increased. The results of these policies were disastrous, leading directly to the new supply crisis of 1939–41.

Illegal private peasant activity also developed in other, smaller forms. Despite the law that allowed the collective farms and peasants to sell only after fulfillment of the state procurement plans and payment of individual agricultural taxes, peasants often brought their produce to the market "on the sly." From time to time, organs of the militia (regular police) and local OGPU/NKVD (Ob"edinennoe gosudarstvennoe politicheskoe upravlenie/Narodnyi komissariat vnutrennikh del—in short, the secret police) made raids on the markets, blocked the roads, and searched peasant carts. When agricultural products were found during periods of prohibition, they were confiscated and counted toward procurement plans or individual taxes. Those who were caught repeatedly or with large quantities of produce were punished as speculators. These sporadic measures, however, could not stop illegal private peasant trade.

Illegal private activity also developed widely in artisanal production under cover of licenses and cooperatives. While the law demanded that artisans sell their products at fixed prices, almost all of them brought their products to the black market where prices were higher. For example, according to the report of the Party Control Commission in 1935, only 4 to 5 percent of the eight thousand artisans registered in Moscow sold their products through cooperatives at fixed prices. The others sold their products either wholesale to middlemen or directly in the market "at high, speculative prices."[35] The law considered this an economic crime even though the artisans sold only goods they had manufactured themselves. Some artisans, despite the prohibition, hired one or two workers to increase their production. Since cooperatives could not provide artisans with sufficient raw materials to produce goods, they bought them illegally

[35] "O spekuliatsii promtovarami na bazarakh," GARF, f. 5446, op. 16a, d. 404, ll. 13–14.

at state enterprises from employees who had usually stolen them. Since the law prohibited any large, profitable private activity, artisans hid their real incomes. Thus, the state did not receive taxes and lost resources. Theoretically, the state could have legalized this activity and controlled the situation, which would have enabled it to impose taxes. Instead it prohibited such activity and punished it as speculation. In the end, high black-market prices and profit proved to be a stronger motivation than punishment.

Several examples of the illegal activities of artisans provide illustration. A machinist from the Lubertsy factory, Ianbaev, had a license that allowed him to produce skirts. He sold his products illegally in the market, earning about 20,000 rubles per year, while his annual salary as a machinist brought him only 3,600 rubles. Another craftsman, Konkin, produced clothes and sold them in the market. His annual income reached 11,000 rubles, while his pension yielded only about 2,000 rubles per year.[36] Thus, the income received from illegal trade was extremely high in comparison to most official salaries.[37]

In addition to individual artisans, entire underground craft "firms" operated on the black market. Their organization resembled the cottage industries of prerevolutionary Russia. This form of organization, in which hired workers labored separately in their homes, required less investment and was easier to mask than a stationary factory. Archival materials allow us to determine how the cottage industries of Stalin's time functioned. Usually there was a group of organizers who invested money in a firm. As a rule, they had artisans' licenses to manufacture goods individually. They paid tax on some of their income, but neither their licenses nor their taxes corresponded to the actual scale of their activity. In reality, they did not produce goods themselves but hired workers in the towns and countryside to make consumer goods at home. Organizers provided the workers with raw materials, which they usually bought illegally from the administrations of state factories or collective farms. Periodically, the organizers or their agents picked up the manufactured products from hired workers and took them to the big cities to sell. There they rented apartments to store the goods and bribed market administrators to look the other way.

NKVD documents provide several striking examples of such phenomena. A group called the "Kievan craftsmen" operated a private cottage industry in the 1930s. They hired workers, who made women's shoes in their

[36] Ibid.

[37] For example, the annual salary of a general designer at a big plant during those years was about 19,000 rubles.

homes. The organizers then transported the finished products to Leningrad, quickly sold them at the market, and just as quickly left the city, later returning with another stock of shoes. In another case, citizens Ilievskii, Shchedrovskii, and Fel'shtein had artisans' licenses to produce felt hats and berets. In reality, they had organized a firm with twelve hired workers who manufactured goods at home. In 1936, the NKVD uncovered a private underground firm that produced gloves. The firm consisted of sixteen organizers who had licenses for individual craftwork and about forty hired workers without licenses. During the arrest, the NKVD confiscated two thousand kid gloves and a quantity of leather with a total value of 70,000 rubles. The NKVD also reported the liquidation of two other private firms. One produced elegant shoes. Twenty people were arrested. The NKVD confiscated 50,000 rubles in cash, 100 pairs of shoes, 130 kilograms of imported caoutchouc (a crude form of rubber), leather, and other stocks. The other liquidated firm mentioned in this NKVD report produced caps. Organizers of this firm bought wool fabric from the state stores and supplied hired workers who produced the caps at home. During the arrest, the NKVD confiscated 3,000 caps and 250 bolts of fabric with a total value of 170,000 rubles.[38]

There were other, even more sophisticated underground firms. In the Koopkustar' cooperative in the Khar'kov region, all the members had licenses as individual artisans. In reality, under the cover of the cooperative, several firms with hired workers functioned. Each of them had its own business. One group consisted of eight people who bought fabric waste from textile factories. After being sorted by hired workers, the fabric was sold to state enterprises to use as rags for cleaning and drying. The firm bought the waste for 800 rubles a ton and resold it for 1,800 rubles a ton. Another group in this cooperative bought metal waste for 200 rubles a ton and, after sorting, sold it for 790 rubles a ton as a material to strengthen boxes. People made money out of air! The third group in this cooperative consisted of thirteen people who bought cattle from individuals in the market, made sausage, and then sold it. In eighteen months, this group used 39 tons of meat and 5.5 tons of bacon. Their income reached 552,000 rubles. Under the cover of this cooperative, other groups produced waffles, gelatin, mushrooms, pepper, fabric dye, and so on. Another cooperative, Gumkhimprom, whose members, according to their licenses, specialized in producing chemical materials, illegally manufactured candy and notions while also earning money by packing coffee, vanillin, and pepper.[39]

[38] GARF, f. 5446, op. 18a, d. 309, ll. 304–13.
[39] GARF, f. 5446, op. 16a, d. 404, ll. 13–14.

Underground firms not only produced food and goods but also provided services. An example is the Transport cooperative. Organizers of this cooperative had six horses and three carts. They hired workers to provide transportation services. The cooperative consisted of thirty-three people, and in one and half years it earned about 400,000 rubles. The organizers annually received 20,000 to 30,000 rubles each from this business.[40]

Private entrepreneurs also used state organizations as cover. Besides performing their normal duties as state employees, there were workers in, for example, state bakeries who bought flour with their own money and made bread that they sold privately, either through these bakeries or on the market. The people who worked at state kiosks selling mineral water also sold their own products, financed with their own money and often made with the aid of a few hired workers. Barbers, photographers, and the like in state services also worked part-time illegally. Income from such businesses reached into the thousands of rubles.

Artisans used state kiosks and small shops to sell their goods for a healthy profit. They made illegal, verbal agreements with a state employee to sell their products, for a fee, alongside state and cooperative goods. Naturally, the goods that were sold privately and the income thus generated were not registered in the store's documents. Artisans also used state commission stores (i.e., state stores that sold people's used [or new] goods for a commission) as cover. Thus, in 1934, Commission Store No. 23, in the Krasnaia Presnia region of Moscow, sold 150,000 rubles' worth of electrical appliances. All these appliances were made by a craftsman, Kamenev, who had his own small shop in the store's yard. The store gave him documents that made it possible for him to legally buy materials from state organizations (private purchases were prohibited at that time). Kamenev received a cut of the income that the store earned selling his products. The commission store was a state organization, but this particular activity was undertaken through an illegal agreement between the store administration and the craftsman. Documents on this case also noted that Kamenev was exempt from taxes because he managed to secure a medical certificate proving that he was mentally ill.[41]

Private business in the 1930s developed even under the cover of party and soviet organizations such as district party committees, the Red Cross, the "liquidation of illiteracy" committees (*likbezy*), and the societies of "Red Partisans." Documents show that these organizations often had canteens, snack bars, bakeries, and confectioner's, barber's, and mechanic's

[40] Ibid.

[41] GARF, f. 5446, op. 16a, d. 402, ll. 1–13.

shops that were operated on a private basis by an individual or a group of individuals who had invested their own money in the business. Such entrepreneurs paid a monthly fee to the organization at which they worked. The organization received money and services and in exchange provided a cover and documents that facilitated the private entrepreneurs' legal purchase of materials and products needed to provide the services.

Examples from the documents of the People's Commissariat of Finance from 1934 illustrate such cases. At the Ukrainian Red Cross organization, in the village of Lukashevka in the Kiev region, thirteen entrepreneurs used their own money to open a complex of services (*kombinat*) consisting of a bakery, a snack bar, a barber shop, a confectionery shop, and a small factory that produced mineral water. In Cherniakhov, the citizen Boriatinskii organized a snack bar at the Committee of the Red Partisans. He invested 3,600 rubles into his business, a rather large sum for that time. Officially, Boriatinskii was registered as the director of the snack bar, but in fact he was not a state employee at all. He used his own money to buy food for the snack bar on the private market or at Torgsin (Vsesoiuznoe ob"edinenie po torgovle s inostrantsami) stores;[42] and his income came not from state sources but from the pockets of the employees of the Red Cross organization for whom he provided lunches and dinners. He paid a monthly fee to the administration of the Red Cross organization to keep his business in operation.[43]

Private production of food and goods also developed under the cover of the collective farms. The pattern was pretty much the same. A collective farm made an unofficial agreement—usually oral—with an individual or a group. The collective farm then provided a legal cover and all necessary documents for the entrepreneurs to purchase materials and sell their produce. In this way, such entrepreneurs appeared to the finance agencies and police officials as representatives of the collective farm, buying materials for the farm and selling its produce. For this legal cover, entrepreneurs paid a fee to the collective-farm administration. Thus, in the Vinnitsa region in Ukraine, at the Voroshilov Collective Farm, a craftsman, Shriftelikh, allegedly on behalf of the farm, bought raw materials and produced and sold jam. He paid 8 percent of his income to the collective-

[42] Torgsin stores were state-owned stores, existing throughout the nation. They sold food and goods to foreigners for hard currency and to Soviet people in exchange for hard currency, gemstones, or precious metals.

[43] See the report prepared by the People's Commissariat of Finance for the Council of People's Commissars in November 1934: "Material o vyiavlennykh sluchaiakh proniknoveniia chastnika v gosudarstvennye i kooperativnye predpriiatiia." GARF, f. 5446, op. 15a, d. 1071, ll. 40–57.

farm administration. During 1933, Shriftelikh sold more than 70,000 rubles worth of jam. However, he was unfortunate enough to be caught by a financial inspector, who visited the collective farm and found that the farm did not produce jam. All the participants in this illegal business were arrested and brought to court.[44]

It is not possible to estimate the actual scale of underground private production during the 1930s. Information about licenses issued or taxes paid does not help, since it shows only the visible part of the iceberg and does not correspond to the actual size of illegal business. Archival documents provide information only about the firms or individuals that were discovered by finance agencies or the police.

Nonetheless, documents about illegal private production allow us to draw some conclusions and compose a portrait of the Soviet businessperson of the 1930s. Artisans working alone or with one or two hired workers dominated black-market production. Usually the producer was also the seller of the product. Despite the small scale of private production, earnings were relatively high during the 1930s because of exceedingly high consumer demand. The underground firms that existed on the black market could not be too large. Their average size was two to three organizers and about a dozen hired workers. The maximum size that documents reveal is about two dozen organizers with licenses and around thirty to forty hired workers. The larger a firm grew, the easier it was for the finance agencies and the police to discover it and punish its members. Thus, private business was doomed to be small and its production insufficient to satisfy high consumer demand. In limiting private production, the state in fact helped to maintain shortages in the domestic market and complicate daily existence, while leaving people no choice but to buy on the black market.

Illegal Forms of Private Activity That Redistributed State Funds

Besides the illegal private activities that produced and consequently increased goods and services available in the domestic market, other activities did not produce anything new but simply redistributed existing, mostly state, stocks. Although they did not contribute to the elimination of general shortages, these activities played an important role in overall supply. They broke the social and geographical hierarchy of state supply and created a new one, based not on state priorities but on consumers' purchasing capacity, personal abilities, and luck. By redistributing state

[44] Ibid.

stocks, these activities also diminished the selective character of state distribution, evening out the system of supply.

So-called speculation represented the main channel of redistribution. The laws and official practices of the 1930s interpreted this term (and crime) very broadly.[45] Any illegal type of trade could be considered speculation: the sale of stolen goods; the resale of goods received on ration cards or bought in state stores, cooperatives, collective farms, and markets or from the peasantry; the sale of artisans' products at market prices; and the sale of agricultural produce during times of prohibition or by middlemen. According to the law, high prices and profit represented the main indicators of speculation. As noted above, exceptions were made only for peasants and collective farms, which were allowed to sell their produce in certain seasons at regular market prices.

It is no wonder, then, that with such a broad official interpretation, speculation became one of the most widespread economic crimes of the 1930s. Its scale, especially during the hungry years of the First Five-Year Plan, suggests that practically every Soviet citizen was involved at some level in "speculation" and could therefore be labeled a "speculator." The Politburo and the People's Council of Commissars issued menacing decrees and organized special commissions to fight speculation (one of them headed by Ia. E. Rudzutak in 1934). Financial inspectors, the militia, and the OGPU/NKVD fined, arrested, and even shot speculators. However, people's needs and the high prices on the black market proved to be more powerful incentives. In an economy of acute shortages, where the private production of food and goods was limited by law and could not develop normally because of financial and repressive controls, resale inevitably flourished.

Speculation surrounded and engulfed all legal forms of distribution and trade, and all forms of production in the USSR contributed to speculation. During the first half of the 1930s, food and goods leaked (better, flooded) to the black market to be illegally sold there from the rationing system, state commercial stores, Torgsin stores, state enterprises, artisanal cooperatives, collective farms, and peasant households. During the second half of the 1930s, when the rationing system was abolished and so-called open socialist trade was proclaimed, this leakage did not stop. And with

[45] The main resolutions of the 1930s on speculation are the decrees of the Council of People's Commissars and the Central Committee, "O bor'be so spekuliatsiei," issued on 22 August 1932, and "O torgovle tovarami shirpotreba i bor'be so spekuliatsiei i ocherediami," issued on 19 July 1936. See Hessler, "A Postwar Perestroika?" 521; and Osokina, *Za fasadom "stalinskogo izobiliia,"* pp. 153, 223.

the improvement in living conditions, the black market changed its "face"—its assortment of goods became more varied and was no worse than that of a model Soviet store.

What made this leakage of goods to the black market inevitable and widespread was the high prices that customers were ready to pay to obtain goods in an economy of shortages. Thus, in 1935, men's shoes—which in the state commercial stores (where prices were already several times higher than on ration cards) cost 77 rubles but were rarely available—sold in the market for 130 rubles. The cost of a man's suit was 130 rubles in the commercial stores, if available, and 320 rubles in the market; a bicycle cost 250 rubles, as compared with 650 to 800 rubles in the market. According to the reports of finance inspectors, individual earnings from speculation could reach anywhere from 200 to 300 and even 1,000 or more rubles per day.[46]

There were several ways for goods to leak onto the black market from the legal sphere of the economy. As noted above, artisans individually or in firms manufactured goods and sold them illegally at market prices. Legal purchases in state stores, cooperatives, and peasant markets followed by illegal resale represented another avenue of speculation. Most people occasionally sold, at a profit, goods purchased from a state store, cooperative, or peasant market. Special militia and OGPU/NKVD raids at markets in the big cities and towns showed that, among arrested "speculators," the ordinary citizen—the worker, peasant, artisan, and white-collar employee—dominated. Thus, in 1934, one-third of the speculators arrested in Leningrad were workers; another third, housewives; and 10 percent, employees. In Kiev about 30 percent of those arrested were collective farmers and 10 percent, artisans. In Moscow, the two largest groups among the arrested were housewives and artisans.[47] For most Soviet citizens, buying and selling goods on the black market became an everyday way to obtain supplies.

Besides ordinary people involved occasionally in illegal trade, there were professionals who made speculation their main source of living, though they usually had some kind of cover—that is, an official place of employment. Those who had access to state stocks were hugely privileged materially within the economy of shortages. No wonder that, as NKVD materials demonstrate, the administrators of the big state stores were the richest people involved in the black market. Their wealth was not less, and

[46] GARF, f. 5446, op. 16a, d. 404, l. 12.
[47] GARF, f. 5446, op. 15a, d. 1071, ll. 16–20.

often was even more, than that of the party and government elites who received their privileges legally from the state.[48]

Other professional speculators were ordinary employees who worked in state stores, cooperatives, and warehouses or who had access through friends, relatives, or bribery to legal stocks of goods. And some just stood in lines day and night to buy goods, which they resold at a profit in the market. They were easy to identify by their weather-beaten faces.

Perekupshchiki—those who bought wholesale agricultural produce from collective farms or peasants and then resold it for a profit—made up another group of so-called speculators in the 1930s. The geographic area of their activity could be quite varied: some perekupshchiki bought from peasants on the road heading to town to sell their produce and then resold it at the nearest market; others bought cheaply in the main agricultural regions, like Ukraine and the Transcaucasian republics, then transported and sold the produce at the most expensive markets of Moscow and Leningrad, thus making an even larger profit. Here, too, "economic mimicry" was at play, as perekupshchiki made use of forged documents and disguised themselves as genuine producers (collective farmers or individual peasants). Some of the collective farms for which perekupshchiki allegedly sold fruit did not have a single fruit tree.[49]

Speculation flourished in the context of continuing shortages. Archival documents from the second half of the 1930s speak of "organized speculation." This type of speculation had a more complex structure, and it included organizers and agents who bought and transported goods as well as state store administrators and employees who provided information about the arrival of goods and facilitated their purchases. The so-called Syndicate of Entrepreneurs (labeled thus by the NKVD) provides an example of organized speculation. In the Syndicate, pseudo-craftsmen bribed the administration of large stores in Moscow and Leningrad to obtain deficit goods (fabrics, shoes, clothes, and so on). Then they transported the goods to Ukraine and sold them at high prices. The Syndicate included a financial group, a group in charge of raw materials, and groups in charge of purchases and trade. The Syndicate pumped more than 2.5 million rubles of goods from state trade onto the black market. The income of some of its members reached more than 30,000 rubles *a month,* at a time when the official salary of People's Commissar of Internal Affairs L.

[48] On the "millionaires" of Soviet trade, see Osokina, *Our Daily Bread,* pp. 178–86.

[49] On such activity, see, for example, the report "O spekuliatsii na bazarakh," GARF, f. 5446, op. 16a, d. 404, ll. 13–14.

Beria was only 36,000 *a year.*[50] In the end, the NKVD arrested fifty members of the Syndicate.

Theft was another channel through which goods leaked onto the black market. During the first half of the 1930s, theft was taking place on a massive scale.[51] Petty larceny made up the largest share of all thefts. Such theft was generally not a question of armed gangs robbing state enterprises, organizations, stores, warehouses, or trains; instead, theft was most often committed by ordinary workers, employees, and collective farmers who stole what they produced or what they could carry. This type of theft was so widespread that a special term was created to label its adherents: *nesuny* (from the Russian verb *vynosit'*, which means "to carry off").

During the hungry years of the First Five-Year Plan and later supply crises, petty larceny was a way of life for most Soviet people. It is no wonder that a huge surge in this type of crime occurred during the difficult years between 1929 and 1933. The annual numbers convicted in the Russian Federation (RSFSR) alone exceeded one million at this time.[52] In 1932, even Mikoian, the people's commissar of supply, said in a speech: "Everyone steals, including communists."[53] In April 1932, the Politburo created a special commission to prepare between five and ten show trials in different regions of the USSR, and—in the words of the Politburo's pronouncement—"considering the organizers of thefts to be enemies of the people, to give them death sentences, especially if they were communists. Other thieves, all over the USSR, must be sentenced to long terms of imprisonment in concentration camps. The punishment for communist thieves must be increased."[54] As the economic situation normalized, the statistics returned to the precrisis level—in the Russian Federation, about 700,000 convictions a year. (The war, combined with a worsening of the economic situation, would bring about a new increase in this crime.)[55] However, even during good years, petty larceny continued on a large scale, because any trifle could be used, sold, or exchanged at a profit within the context of an economy of shortages and unsatisfied consumer demand.

[50] GARF, f. 5446, op. 18a, d. 309, l. 298.

[51] For analysis of the statistics of crime see Shearer, "Crime and Social Disorder in Stalin's Russia," pp. 119–48.

[52] GARF, f. 9492, op. 2, d. 42, l. 125.

[53] RGAE, f. 8043, op. 1, d. 72, l. 1.

[54] The antitheft commission consisted of A. Ia. Vyshinskii, N. V. Krylenko, G. G. Iagoda, I. A. Akulov, and Ia. S. Agranov. See RGASPI, f. 17, op. 3, d. 880, l. 6.

[55] GARF, f. 9492, op. 2, d. 42, l. 125.

Barter, an important part of black-market dealings, represents another facet of illegal redistribution. Barter was not limited to exchanges of goods and services among individuals. State enterprises, organizations, and collective and state farms were widely involved in barter. Despite a strict prohibition on barter, enterprises illegally scrapped part of their production, often registering it as "defective," to prevent the state from taking it. They then exchanged such "scraps" for industrial products from other enterprises or agricultural produce (at the expense of state procurement plans). The enterprises then used the exchanged goods and food to supply their workers and employees. Barter is difficult to find in archival documents because such agreements, being illegal, were usually made in private or over the phone. However, official antibarter decrees illustrate that this illegal practice existed, continued, and, like a cobweb, enveloped the entire economy.

In addition to illegal resale, theft, and barter, there were many other channels through which goods found their way to the black market and contributed to the redistribution of state supplies. Several examples from the first half of the 1930s of what clearly must remain a nonexhaustive list will suffice to demonstrate.

During the years of rationing, the state strictly defined (by decree) the hierarchy of supply: different groups of customers were assigned to certain special, closed cooperatives and stores (*zakrytye raspredeliteli*) to receive their rations. Reality, however, was often different. Through personal relations, bribes, or an exchange of favors,[56] people could go into almost any special cooperative or store. It was even possible, though difficult, to gain access to the closed distributors that supplied the party and government elite. These illegal consumers were called *prikhlebateli*—that is, parasites.

"Dead souls" (*mertvye dushi*) made up another group of illegal consumers at closed cooperatives and stores in the years of rationing and, consequently, created another path for the redistribution of state supplies. According to the law, after changing their place of work, employees were to receive rations at their new place of employment. Administrators at their previous place of work and the individuals in charge of supply at the cooperative to which they were previously assigned were to strike them from the list of consumers. In reality, this did not always happen. Instead,

[56] The exchange of favors, in Russian terminology *blat*, played an extremely important role in the economy of shortages. For more on this phenomenon, see Fitzpatrick, *Everyday Stalinism*, pp. 62–65; and Alena V. Ledeneva, *Russia's Economy of Favours:* Blat, *Networking, and Informal Exchange* (Cambridge: Cambridge University Press, 1998).

administrators and cooperatives tried to keep the names of former employees and customers on their lists of consumers so as to make use of their rations. Employee turnover was extremely high during the rationing period, and the number of "dead souls" at enterprises and cooperatives grew accordingly.

People also forged ration cards and bought, sold, or exchanged them on the market. In this way, a person could end up with several official ration cards. There are documented examples of people having up to twenty ration cards for their personal use. Rationed products, too, were subject to illegal trade and exchange. The state tried to halt speculation developing in and around the rationing system. The Council of People's Commissars issued threatening decrees, demanding that the state rationing system be wiped clean of "parasites" and "dead souls"; special commissions repeatedly inspected supply systems at factories, construction sites, and institutions; and even the supply for official elites was more severely controlled. Nonetheless, illegal practices continued, allowing some people to survive and others to improve their existence to greatly varying degrees.

Conclusion

The first five-year plans of the 1930s, accompanied by the establishment of a planned centralized economy, introduced important changes in the life of Soviet society. Popular reaction to the new economic conditions took two main, apparently incompatible forms: disobedience and submission.

Economic disobedience revealed itself in illegal, private, black-market activities. It developed a number of quite distinct forms. Under the circumscribed conditions of economic freedom in the 1930s, entrepreneurial activities grew mostly in illegal ways. The application of administrative measures and repression—attempts to force private activity to fit the Procrustean bed of the socialist political economy—doomed it to develop in small, dispersed, and temporary forms. Long-term, stable, growing businesses were not possible under such circumstances. Furthermore, it was not only difficult to develop private business, it was dangerous: one could easily lose one's life along with one's business. To protect themselves and adapt to existing conditions, entrepreneurs disguised themselves using pseudosocialist forms and the techniques of socio-economic mimicry.

State policies caused further deviation in private activity. In an economy where production cannot develop normally and consumer demand is high, resale can bring huge profits. Not surprisingly, in the USSR during the 1930s, the main players in the black market were not those who produced but those who engaged in resale. So-called speculation represented one of the most common economic practices and crimes of the 1930s. As a result of this hypertrophy of resale, the black market pumped goods and raw materials from the legal socialist economy and, to some extent, acted as its parasite in what could be viewed as a kind of ironic revenge. The state experienced huge losses from the existence of the black market through theft, unpaid taxes, and the expense of all its antimarket campaigns. The state was trapped by its own policy: on the basis of ideology and politics, it refused to sanction the growth of private economic activity, but at the same time it was also unable to eradicate illegal business.

The illegal economic activities of the 1930s, however, should not be construed as a form of conscious resistance to the state. The major forces pushing the development of private activity were acute shortages and insatiable consumer demand. Within an economy of shortages, these factors clearly made the development of illegal private activity inevitable. In this sense, the very existence of the black market was a simple and objective manifestation of the universal law of supply and demand.

Turning from commonsense economic laws to the everyday perspective of Soviet people, it is clear that survival and profit served as the two most important motivations for illegal economic activities. Both motivations were probably no more than uneradicated characteristics of human nature. They suggest that the people who engaged in black-market activities did not consciously intend to undermine the state.[57]

The illegal and "rebellious" character of the black market in the 1930s was relative. Almost all the illegal activities described above, with the exception of theft and the sale of stolen goods, would not be considered illegal or rebellious in countries with a market economy (or even in a mod-

[57] Stephen Kotkin, for example, in *Magnetic Mountain,* analyzed black-market activities in Magnitogorsk during the 1930s, arriving at conclusions similar in many respects to those expressed in this essay and in my book *Our Daily Bread.* He believed that the main factor influencing the development of the legal and illegal markets was shortages. The main motivations for black-market activities, in his opinion, were survival and personal gain. It was the regime that viewed illegal economic activities as political opposition and "economic counterrevolution." This opposition revealed itself objectively in the existence of an economic sphere that lay beyond state control. The allegedly nonmarket nature of the Soviet economy turned markets and marketing into "resistance" (*Magnetic Mountain,* pp. 277–78).

The discussion provoked by David Shearer's essay on economic crimes in the 1930s at the Sixth Meeting of the Seminar on Russian and Soviet History in Paris in May 1996 is significant for understanding current thinking on the nature of the black market under Stalin. Seminar participants expressed a variety of views on the issues presented in Shearer's essay: were economic crimes under Stalin, especially theft and speculation, forms of resistance or not? As a result of this discussion, Shearer chose to label economic crime as "social disorder" or "social disobedience" in the final version of his essay published in *Cahiers du monde russe.*

ern communist regime that allows economic freedom, such as China). The Soviet people did not invent anything new. As far as the situation allowed, they simply continued to do what generations had done before: they privately produced, bought, sold, resold, exchanged, and stole. What made most private activity in the 1930s illegal was the official ideology, a utopian political economy, and a political system that left an extremely narrow space for legal private initiatives.

Most black-market activities of the 1930s were, in fact, not crimes at all from the point of view of a market economy. It was the Stalinist state that labeled the black market as a form of resistance and a crime against the socialist economy. From a scholarly point of view, it would be a mistake to accept at face value the highly ideological and politicized language of this oppressive regime. While prohibiting private activity even in its most moderate forms, the socialist state itself engaged in large-scale for-profit ventures that by its own definition could just as easily be labeled speculation. For example, by exploiting high consumer demand in the years of shortage and mass famine, the state drained the people of their possessions and savings through its Torgsin stores, where needy Soviet people exchanged their last remaining valuables for food and other necessary goods.[58]

Soviet people defended their most basic social and economic needs in their struggles to survive or improve their material conditions within the various illegal spheres of the economy. In so doing, they fought and overcame barriers and obstacles that the state erected in their path. In this limited respect, illegal private activity represented a form of opposition to contemporary economic policies, even if it was not the direct goal of most Soviet people. Such behavior is best defined as "economic disobedience" (*economicheskoie nepovinoveniie)* rather than as "resistance" (*soprotivleniie*)—a term that is far too strong in its implication of active and conscious activity aimed against the current social, political, and economic order. Within the context of the black market of the 1930s, terms such as the "art of survival" or the "art of enrichment" make more sense than James Scott's "art of resistance."[59]

It would, perhaps, be shortsighted if this analysis of the nature of the black market limited its interpretation of illegal activities to economic disobedience. Socio-economic phenomena are complicated and are always

[58] For more on state entrepreneurial activity in the 1930s, see Osokina, *Our Daily Bread*, pp. 121–29.

[59] See James Scott, *Domination and the Arts of Resistance* (New Haven, Conn.: Yale University Press, 1990).

composed of contradictory elements. In their present-day discussions about resistance in Stalin's Soviet Union, scholars concentrate mostly on one side of the argument—"opposition"—while neglecting the other side—"submission." Submission, and even support, revealed itself in the acceptance and development of the legal economic sphere of private activity: peasants did not refuse to sell at the collective-farm markets, artisans and petty traders did not abandon their licenses in a "rebellious" mood. Strategies of survival and enrichment by way of socio-economic mimicry were not only forms of disobedience but also forms of adjustment and adaptation. People endeavored to adapt themselves to the new economic situation—not to destroy it, but to survive within it.

Through adjustment and adaptation, the black market became an important part of the socialist economy. It not only fed off but also ironically aided the legal socialist sector of the economy by compensating for its failures. Both sides of the economy developed in symbiosis. (In my opinion, *symbiosis* is the best term to characterize the union of the legal and black market economies because it reflects a mutually influenced *development* rather than a static combination of legal and underground economies.) Legal and black-market economies fought, influenced, shaped, and compensated for each other, ultimately developing into a united socio-economic organism. "Unlikely bedfellows," they could neither reconcile nor live without each other.

CHAPTER SEVEN

Resisting the Plan in the Urals, 1928–1956

Or, Why Regional Officials Needed "Wreckers" and "Saboteurs"

JAMES HARRIS

The study of popular resistance has fundamentally challenged the image of Soviet society as passive and atomized, just as the study of the resistance of state and party institutions to central policy has undermined the image of a monolithic Soviet state.[1] These issues have long ceased to be controversial, and as Lynne Viola recently put it, "the significance of the topic [now] resides less in the fact of resistance as an object in itself than in the light the topic sheds on its historical surround-

The research for this article was funded by the British Academy.

[1] Over forty years ago, Merle Fainsod recognized that regional officials did not always do what the center wanted. In *Smolensk under Soviet Rule* (Cambridge, Mass.: Harvard University Press, 1958), he saw this as evidence that totalitarianism was "inefficient." More recently, historians have observed patterns of center–region interaction and conflict, at times influencing central policy. See for example, Lynne Viola, "The Campaign to Eliminate the Kulak as a Class, Winter 1929–1930: A Reevaluation of the Legislation," *Slavic Review* 45, 3 (1986): 650–72; J. Arch Getty, *Origins of the Great Purges: The Soviet Communist Party Reconsidered, 1933–1938* (Cambridge: Cambridge University Press, 1988); Catherine Merridale, *Moscow Politics and the Rise of Stalin: The Communist Party in the Capital, 1925–1932* (London: Macmillan, 1990); James Hughes, *Stalin, Siberia, and the Crisis of the New Economic Policy* (Cambridge: Cambridge University Press, 1991); Gabor Tamas Rittersporn, *Stalinist Simplifications and Soviet Complications: Social Tensions and Political Conflicts in the USSR, 1933–1953* (Chur, Switzerland: Harwood, 1991); Hiroaki Kuromiya, *Freedom and Terror in the Donbas* (Cambridge: Cambridge University Press, 1998); James R. Harris, *The Great Urals: Regionalism and the Evolution of the Soviet System* (Ithaca, N.Y.: Cornell University Press, 1999); and Gerald Easter, *Reconstructing the State: Personal Networks and Elite Identity in Soviet Russia* (Cambridge: Cambridge University Press, 2000).

ings."[2] This essay is a study of the response of regional officials to plan pressures across three decades. It is not a study of resistance per se, but rather an analysis of the consequences of that resistance.

From the early 1930s, Moscow refused to accept anything less than 100-percent plan fulfillment or any discussion of the reality of the plan itself. In turn, regional officials resorted to a variety of tactics that allowed them to evade the pressures of the plan and to mask plan underfulfillment. These two dangerously incompatible behaviors on the part of center and region generated and reinforced one common image: that of the internal enemy of the regime, the "wrecker" or "saboteur" responsible for plan failures. It was always easy to find a wrecker—a scapegoat on whom to shift blame—and thus to avoid an investigation of the real causes of plan underfulfillment. Moreover, the frequency of breakdowns, fires, shortages, and other problems complicating plan fulfillment convinced both central and regional authorities that the wrecker did exist. From the emergence of the "command-administrative system" until years after the death of Stalin, resistance to the pressures of the plan, or perhaps more accurately, the recourse to adaptive strategies, significantly contributed to state terror in the Soviet Union.[3]

The First Five-Year Plan and the Great Terror in Sverdlovsk Region

In the quasi-market economy of the 1920s, the regions persistently pressed the center for high levels of production and investment in the local economy.[4] In the absence of a strong internal market, the local economies relied on state investment and demand for their economic health. This had been a familiar pattern for the regions for over two hundred years. Central investment under Peter the Great had created a metallurgy industry for the Urals, at one time the leading producer of

[2] Lynne Viola, "Popular Resistance in the Stalinist 1930s: Soliloquy of a Devil's Advocate," *Kritika* 1, 1 (2000): 45.

[3] It may be inappropriate to use the term *resistance* in this instance. Can high-ranking officials, some of them members of the Central Committee—at the very core of the "system"—be "resisters"? Or can resistance come only from subaltern groups? Given that almost all of society was employed by the state, how far does one have to go down the administrative hierarchy before a group can be labeled "subaltern"? On another level, regional officials were not opponents of the regime. Quite the contrary, most thought of themselves as stalwart Bolshevik-Stalinists. While their actions often involved blatant insubordination, they may be more aptly labeled as "adaptive strategies" or "strategies of self-protection" rather than resistance.

[4] The issues presented in this section are analyzed in much greater detail in Harris, *The Great Urals.*

iron in the world. Sergei Witte's industrialization program created a wealthy and powerful heavy industry in Ukraine. Regional leaders wanted high levels of state investment and pushed Moscow for more and more ambitious proposals as they competed with each other for First Five-Year Plan projects. The plan would determine the wealth and power of the regions.

The fantastic ambitions of the First Five-Year Plan drove the economy into a state of chaos. Almost no plan targets were fulfilled, and the center and regions bickered about who was at fault. Nevertheless, when by 1931 the attention of planning organs shifted to the Second Five-Year Plan, regional organs once again proposed vast programs of investment and construction.[5] But this time, the center did not bite. Three times the general plan was revised, each time reducing projected targets. Even more disturbing to the regions was the fact that the fulfillment of these reduced targets would be enforced. No excuses would be accepted for anything less than 100-percent fulfillment.

A more "moderate" plan was hardly of any solace to the regions. Targets for construction and production were reduced, but projected financing was reduced even further. Calls for "iron discipline before the budget of the proletarian state"[6] contrasted sharply with the free spending of the First Five-Year Plan. An even more serious problem for regional leaders was rooted in the details of their own first five-year plan. In their determination to increase central investment, Urals planners had been rather liberal in their calculations. For example, the lack of a local supply of cokeable coal had been the single greatest hindrance to the further development of the Urals as a metals and machine-building center. By the late 1920s, when the Urals version of the first five-year plan was under review in Moscow, regional leaders, fearing that central investment would go to Ukraine, exerted intense pressure on local geologists and metallurgists to produce favorable results. After a group of specialists was arrested for "criminally delaying the development" of the local coal industry, "conclusive" evidence of vast local supplies of cokeable coal was provided to

[5] For a statement of the Urals' ambitions for the Second Five-Year Plan, see Gosudarstvennyi arkhiv Sverdlovskoi oblasti (henceforth, GASO), f. 241–r (Oblplan), op. 1 (Sektsiia promyshlennaia), d. 827 (Perspektivnyi plan UKK [Ural'skoi chasti] na 1931–1937), ll. 33–35. Gosplan criticized the Urals region for pushing "fantastical tempos." See Rossiiskii gosudarstvennyi arkhiv ekonomiki (henceforth, RGAE), f. 4372 (Gosplan), op. 30 (1932), d. 784 (Pervaia konferentsiia po razmeshcheniiu proizvoditel'nykh sil v UKK), l. 3.

[6] Rossiiskii gosudarstvennyi arkhiv sotsial'no-politicheskoi istorii (henceforth, RGASPI), f. 17 (Tsentral'nyi komitet), op. 2 (Plenumy), d. 514 (Ob"edinennyi plenum TsK i TsKK VKP(b), 7–12 ianvaria 1933), l. 93.

central authorities.[7] The exaggeration of reserves was not limited to coal. Similar scenarios were played out in plans for the Urals copper and chemicals industries.[8] What this meant was that as new plants were brought into production, as they were to account for an ever larger share of production, and as ever-greater efficiency was demanded of them, the plan became progressively more difficult to fulfill. Urals officials knew they were in trouble. Plan targets could not be fulfilled.

The resistance to these impossible targets involved a variety of strategies of self-protection. Most important of these was the careful control of Moscow's access to information on the state of the regional economy. Regional officials cultivated an image of themselves as aggressively active in their loyalty to the central leadership and the "Central Committee line," while at the same time they tried to reduce plan responsibilities and simplify tasks.[9] A slush fund was run out of the economic administration of the regional soviet executive committee, which ensured that every key member of the regional leadership would have a substantial income, a large apartment, a government car, a country home, and so on.[10] Their professional reputations were systematically promoted at state and party meetings, in public forums, and in the press. If it was discovered that damaging information had been leaked to Moscow, however, or complaints about the local situation had been aired, the offending party was removed, disgraced, and, in some cases, put on trial.

Scapegoating was a key strategy of self-protection. In cases of local scandals or problems of plan fulfillment that caught the attention of Moscow, the regional leadership conveniently found an "enemy of the people," often a former oppositionist or some other vulnerable official, to take the blame. The idea of internal enemies that so excited Stalin's mind was by no means discouraged in the regions. On the contrary, Sverdlovsk

[7] On the actions of the OGPU, and the regional party committee in promoting a trial of specialists, see Tsentr dokumentatsii obshchestvennykh organizatsii Sverdlovskoi oblasti (henceforth, TsDOO SO), f. 4 (Obkom), op. 8 (1930), d. 102 (Spravki, protokoly rassledovanii organov OGPU po Uralu, raikomov i gorkomov VKP(b) o faktakh klassovoi bor'by i vreditel'stva na predpriatiiakh oblasti), l. 54.

[8] Gosudarstvennyi arkhiv administrativnykh organov Sverdlovskoi oblasti (henceforth, GAAO SO), f. 1, op. 2 (Lichnye dela), d. 22861 (Delo Sedasheva, Konstantina Gavrilovicha), l. 33; and d. 22329 (Delo Davydova, Andreia Aleksandrovicha), l. 5.

[9] In *Factory and Manager in the USSR* (Cambridge, Mass.: Harvard University Press, 1957), Joseph Berliner wrote about this sort of behavior among factory managers. The collusion of leading regional party officials—some of them members of the Central Committee—is less well known. See Harris, *The Great Urals*, chap. 5.

[10] GAAO SO, f. 1, op. 2 (Lichnye dela), d. 17368 (Delo Kabakova, Ivana Dmitrievicha), l. 68; and d. 22861 (Delo Sedasheva), ll. 63–64, 174.

Urals Regional Party First Secretary I. D. Kabakov (second from left) at the Seventeenth Party Congress (1934). Courtesy Tsentr dokumentatsii obshchestvennykh organizatsii Sverdlovskoi oblasti (TsDOO SO).

region and several other regions developed a reputation for holding large numbers of show trials. In 1936, the Commission for Party Control singled out Sverdlovsk and Saratov regions for having "completely baselessly arrested and convicted people and undertaken mass repression for minor problems."[11]

The labeling of enemies was not necessarily cynical. Many local cadres believed in a diffuse, hidden "conspiracy" against the regime.[12] It was not difficult to find "enemies" in the context of super-pressurized plans. Officials were not likely to see their own behavior as "wrecking," but they perceived it everywhere in that of others. For example, a factory director might underfulfill his plan, but he would almost invariably lay the blame at the door of suppliers who were late with deliveries, builders who had

[11] Tsentral'noe khranenie sovremennoi dokumentatsii (henceforth, TsKhSD), f. 6 (KPK), op. 1 (Protokoly), d. 59 (Zasedanii biuro, 29 fevralia–3 marta 1936), ll. 184–86.

[12] For examples of unsolicited letters to the local OGPU, see TsDOO SO, f. 4 (Obkom), op. 8 (1930), d. 102 (Spravki, protokoly rassledovaniia organov OGPU po Uralu, raikomov i gorkomov VKP(b) o faktakh klassovoi bor'by i vreditel'stva na predpriiatiiakh oblasti). The popularity of conspiracy theories is described and analyzed in detail in Gabor T. Rittersporn, "The Omnipresent Conspiracy: On Soviet Imagery of Politics and Social Relations in the 1930s," in *Stalinist Terror: New Perpectives,* ed. J. Arch Getty and Roberta Manning (Cambridge: Cambridge University Press, 1993), pp. 99–115.

failed to install new equipment on time, workers who damaged expensive equipment, or warehouse staff who allowed the spoilage of inputs. It was not easy to distinguish incompetence from antistate behavior. It seems likely that a genuine and deep-seated belief in the existence of a hidden conspiracy against the regime coexisted with a willingness to scapegoat "unmasked enemies" for the problems in one's own factory or administrative department.[13]

Through the mid-1930s, the search for wreckers and saboteurs, whether it was motivated by a genuine belief in enemies of the regime or mere scapegoating, was controlled by the regional party leadership, but it could be dangerously excited by aggressive signals from the center. For example, the Sverdlovsk regional party committee had not enthusiastically promoted the Stakhanovite movement, given that it raised production targets and increased administrative tasks without providing clear local benefits.[14] But when evidence of resistance to Stakhanovism came to the attention of the Politburo and a purge of regional party committee department heads was threatened, the regional party committee bureau directed the regional legal organs to find cases of "sabotage and resistance" to Stakhanovism in the factory. In the spring of 1936, there were 236 trials in Sverdlovsk region related to accusations of wrecking in the Stakhanovite movement.[15]

The situation in the region was unstable. As production targets increased, it became more difficult to fulfill the plan and hide problems. Industrial accidents were increasingly common. Ill-trained workers often damaged new and expensive equipment. Incomplete or low-quality products were frequently shipped despite prohibitions. Several other factors combined to make 1936 a particularly difficult year. After three years of tolerating unplanned expenditures within industry, the center imposed tough cost-cutting measures to deal with inter-enterprise debt. In addition, the disastrous 1936 harvest put a further strain on the economy.[16]

[13] For a more detailed discussion of this phenomenon, see Stephen Kotkin, *Magnetic Mountain: Stalinism as a Civilization* (Berkeley: University of California Press, 1995), pp. 298–332.

[14] In 1935, Aleksei Stakhanov, a coal worker in the Donbass, set a record in coal hewing in a shock labor extravaganza arranged by the local party organization. The central party leadership then capitalized on this feat, urging other workers to follow Stakhanov's example. The "Stakhanovite movement" was used not only to push up output norms but to pressure industrial managers and engineers to increase the pace of production and to establish more efficient work patterns. Those in management who declined or failed to respond were often the targets of political invective. The campaign subsequently set the stage for the repression of industrial leaders that took place during the Great Purges.

[15] TsKhSD, f. 6, op. 1, d. 59, ll. 184–86.

[16] Roberta Manning, "The Soviet Economic Crisis of 1936–1940 and the Great Purges," in *Stalinist Terror*, pp. 129–33.

The increasingly desperate state of plan fulfillment accelerated the propensity to scapegoat. In response to the doubling of the accident rate in the Urals nonferrous metals industry since 1935, Glavtsvetmet (Glavnoe upravlenie tsvetnoi metallurgii, or Main Administration of Nonferrous Metals) recommended educational measures for workers and engineers, but a local trust director insisted that only show trials would reduce the number of accidents.[17]

Meanwhile, cracks had begun to develop within the leadership group. The directors of mining enterprises resented the regional machine builders for the shortage of mining equipment. The directors of the machine-building trusts were upset that they were not getting the metals they needed. Similarly, the directors of the metal works were angry at the mining enterprises for not supplying them with enough fuels and ores. And state and party leaders were not happy with the directors. The regional leadership was a tinderbox of tensions to which the center set a spark in the summer of 1936 with the trial of the so-called Trotskyist–Zinovievite Bloc. Associated with the trial was a central campaign designed to rout the "last remnants of the Trotskyist–Zinovievite band." It uncovered far more "enemies" than anyone expected. The campaign provoked a firestorm of denunciations beyond the ability of the regional leadership to control. After the trial of the Trotskyist–Zinovievite Bloc, tensions within the factories exploded as various groups accused others of "oppositionist activity" by way of assessing blame for poor economic performance. Workers denounced Stakhanovites, Stakhanovites denounced engineers and technical specialists. District and factory party committees traded accusations that the other was protecting counterrevolutionaries.

Of course, the spread of denunciations was also driven by the NKVD (Narodnyi komissariat vnutrennykh del—the People's Commissariat of Internal Affairs, or the secret police). In September 1936, when N. I. Ezhov took over the NKVD, he replaced almost every regional NKVD plenipotentiary. In Sverdlovsk region, this meant that the local leadership lost a key ally for controlling the use of repression. Suddenly, everyone arrested for "counterrevolutionary activity" was forced to "name names." Every arrest potentially resulted in a host of others. Nevertheless, the denunciations most damaging to the regional leadership were unsolicited. In November 1936, V. A. Riabov, a sector head in the administration of local industry, leveled a detailed denunciation against the regional state administration. Local industry was perennially underfunded and unable to

[17] RGAE, f. 8034 (Glavtsvetmet), op. 1, d. 938 (Stenogramma soveshchanii aktiva trestov "Uraltsvetmet" i "Uralmedruda" po voprosam okhrany truda i tekhniki bezopasnosti na predpriiatiiakh trestov, 10 oktiabria 1936 g.), l. 7.

fulfill its plans, and Riabov did not want to have to answer for it. His twenty-seven-page denunciation contained copies of correspondence between the head of the regional planning commission and the regional executive committee chairman indicating that the two had known about problems in local industry but had taken no action. The correspondence also showed how they had deliberately exaggerated production figures. The two were arrested within days. It was the thin edge of the wedge. Information such as this encouraged the NKVD to investigate other members of the regional leadership, in the process of which they uncovered further details of misbehavior. It is not difficult to see how the NKVD and the central leadership could interpret these discoveries as evidence of a conspiracy against the regime. By the fall of 1937, almost the entire regional leadership had been arrested and executed, and in the course of the following year, the swath of terror only grew wider.

The Devolution of Authority to the Regions, 1938–45: An Incomplete Experiment

What conclusions did the central leadership draw from the experience of the terror? The investigations of the NKVD had revealed that the patterns of resistance of the regional leaderships—the subversion of central directives and campaigns, the falsification of plan results, and so on—had been provoked by pressurized plans, but still the notion of internal enemies had a powerful grip on central and regional leaders. As the center slowly moved to bring the terror to a close, criticizing mass arrests, it continued to demand a vigilant watch for "spies" and "wreckers."[18] Meanwhile, plan pressures showed no signs of easing. As war approached, the needs of national defense only intensified the demands placed on heavy industry. The Third Five-Year Plan, adopted at the Eighteenth Party Congress in 1939, projected a 92-percent increase in industrial production, as well as growth of 58 percent in the production of steel and 129 percent in machine building.[19]

On the heels of the arrest and execution of the previous two regional party committee first secretaries, the Sverdlovsk regional leadership was desperate to set a distance between itself and its predecessors. When faced

[18] See for example, "Ob oshibkakh partorganizatsii pri iskliuchenii kommunistov iz partii, o formal'no-biurokraticheskom otnoshenii k appeliatsiiam iskliuchennykh iz VKP(b) i o merakh po ustraneniiu etikh nedostatkov" (Plenum TsK VKP(b), 11, 14, 18, 20 ianvaria 1938 g.), in *KPSS v rezoliutsiiakh i resheniiakh s''ezdov, konferentsii, i plenumov TsK*, 9th ed., vol. 7 (Moscow, 1984), pp. 8–17.

[19] Alec Nove, *An Economic History of the Soviet Union* (London: Penguin, 1986), p. 256.

with evidence of underfulfillment, the new first secretary V. M. Andrianov told his department heads and enterprise directors to "work twenty-four hours a day" if they had to, "but fulfill the directives of the Central Committee completely and unconditionally."[20] At the same time, the regional leadership was at pains to explain the shift in tasks from the "struggle against wrecking" to the "struggle against the consequences of wrecking." In their speeches, the "consequences of wrecking" referred to their predecessors' resistance to central directives. Passing incomplete or faulty production, cutting corners on production safety, and other measures of self-protection had facilitated an impression of plan fulfillment while making further consistent advances in production more difficult. At a regional party committee plenum in late 1939, directors and department heads were told not to look for wreckers but to take more responsibility for the state of affairs where they worked. The message met with resistance. It was no easier to meet the plan now than it had been in the mid-1930s, and they still needed to cut corners. Accidents, breakdowns, and other "suspicious" events continued to be very common. The specter of wrecking presented an invaluable opportunity to pass the blame for problems of production. At party and state meetings, factory directors and local party officials continued to assess accidents and breakdowns as the work of wreckers and saboteurs.[21]

Did they believe in an immanent threat from wreckers? One local assistant plenipotentiary of the NKVD wrote to People's Commissar of Internal Affairs L. P. Beria asking for clarification. On one hand, he wrote, his bosses continued baselessly to arrest innocent people. On the other hand, many others "on whom there was weighty compromising material" were being set free.[22] No clarification was forthcoming. The center discouraged mass arrests, but continued to demand vigilance against wreckers, spies, and saboteurs. While regional officials were responsible for total plan fulfillment in the absence of any input to the plan or flexibility in the means by which they met plan targets, the continued evasion of central directives

[20] TsDOO SO, f. 4, op. 34 (1939), d. 9 (Stenogramma XI plenuma Sverdlovskogo oblastnogo komiteta VKP(b), 29 noiabria–2 dekabria 1939 g.), ll. 249–50.

[21] TsDOO SO, f. 4, op. 33 (1938), d. 19 (Stenogramma III plenuma Sverdlovskogo oblastnogo komiteta VKP(b), 15–18 dekabria 1938 g.), ll. 30, 34; op. 34 (1939), d. 151 (Stenogrammy soveshchanii rabotnikov apparata obkoma, zaveduiushchikh otdelami, sekretarei gorkomov i raikomov partii po voprosu o perestroike partiinogo apparata), ll. 30–31.

[22] TsDOO SO, f. 4, op. 35 (1940), d. 300 (Dokladnye zapiski, spravki o rabote s kadrami v oblastnoi prokurature, ob itogakh i nedostatkakh v rabote sudebno-prokuraturskikh organov i rukovoditelei predpriiatii po vypolneniiu ukaza Verkhovnogo Soveta SSSR ot 26 iiulia 1940), ll. 47–51.

and scapegoating—the specific local impetus to the search for "enemies"—seemed likely. They continued to believe that enemies were complicating their work, but at the same time they needed them. The existence of masked enemies saved them from coming to terms with the fact that while their plans could not be achieved, they could not be challenged either.

Paradoxically, the terror itself presented an opportunity for the devolution of administrative authority to the regions, as well as a way out of the situation. The very scale of arrests and executions had affected economic performance. As arrested managers, technicians, planners, foremen, and others were replaced with less experienced cadres, established lines of authority and patterns of decision making broke down. The Third Five-Year Plan was under threat from the start. When central leaders took their first steps to deal with the administrative confusion, it was in terms of combating a conspiracy against the regime. "Trotskyist–Bukharinite agents of fascism" were accused of attempting to "disorganize the economy, upset defense capabilities, and undermine the system of socialist planning."[23] In early 1938, the administrative authority of the commissariats was downgraded and shifted to a network of regional plenipotentiaries under Viacheslav Molotov.[24] An article in the Gosplan (State Planning Commission) journal *Planovoe khoziaistvo* remarked, "enemies of the people have fixed a system of planning work in which regional planning commissions were in reality removed from participation in the compilation of economic plans, and in which the needs of the regions were ignored."[25]

The article reflected an unfortunate reality of economic life in the later stages of the terror. Once mass repression had crippled the central economic apparatus, it was necessary to rely more heavily on the regions to manage the economy.[26] But the article also expressed concerns, which regional leaders had harbored since the early 1930s, when the center had ceased to consult them in matters of economic policy. Regional leaders had resented Gosplan and the commissariats for their control over industry. They believed that the practice of planning and administering each industry separately (the "branch principle") created disproportions among interconnected regional enterprises and complicated plan fulfill-

[23] "Rabotu Gosplana—na uroven' novykh zadach," *Planovoe khoziaistvo*, 1938, no. 2: 20.

[24] Postanovlenie SNK SSSR, 2 fevralia 1938, "O Gosudarstvennoi Planovoi Komissii pri Sovete Narodnykh Komissarov Soiuza SSR," *Sobranie postanovlenii i rasporiazhenii pravitel'stva Soiuza SSR*, vol. 7 (1938), pp. 111–14.

[25] "Rabotu Gosplana," *Planovoe khoziaistvo*, 1938, no. 2: 26.

[26] On the increased role of the regions, see A. Korobov, "Raionnyi razrez narodno-khoziaistvennogo plana," *Planovoe khoziaistvo*, 1938, no. 12: 58–66.

ment. When regional leaders knew that they were allowed to criticize the existing system of economic administration, they wasted no time. They observed that although they bore the largest responsibility for plan fulfillment, they were almost never consulted and were often the last to see the plans. Furthermore, they argued that Gosplan was largely ignorant of local economic conditions.[27] They pointed out that the commissariats' habit of frequently revising plan targets complicated fulfillment and that changes were generally made without requisite alterations to the assortment of supplies. Requests for assistance were often lost in the tangle of commissariat bureaucracy.[28] Regional leaders were pleased to see the status of the commissariats lowered and their own involvement in economic management strengthened.

Even more promising were the discussions of the "complex development of the regional economies." Complex development was defined as the "the satisfaction of the main production requirements of a given region out of local output."[29] On its surface, the idea was to cut down on the costs of unnecessary shipments between regions, though the (rarely discussed) strategic implications were obvious. If the sole supplier of a given commodity were lost to an occupying army, many branches of the economy could be affected. For the regions, a different, very concrete benefit was foreseen. The less they were dependent on other regions for inputs, the more easily they could meet the plan. Combined with increased regional participation in economic administration, the direction of change held out the promise of a relaxation of the pressures of plan fulfillment.

At the same time, neither the commissariats nor Gosplan were pleased by the changes. Both acted to frustrate any shift in responsibilities to the regions. Regional proposals for the Third Five-Year Plan were ignored. Ten months after the authority of the commissariats had been downgraded, Gosplan was criticized for failing to give sufficient priority to regional planning, which was called "the only way to put an end to disproportions (in the economy)."[30] In his speech to the Eighteenth Party

[27] RGAE, f. 4372 (Gosplan), op. 37 (1939), d. 93 (Materialy k soveshchaniiu s predsedatel'iami respublikanskikh i oblastnykh planovykh komissii a takzhe nachal'nikov UNKhU v Gosplane pri SNK SSSR, 20 avgusta 1939).

[28] RGASPI, f. 476 (XVIII konferentsii VKP(b), fevral' 1941), op. 1, d. 10 (Preniia po dokladu o zadachakh partiinykh organizatsii v oblasti promyshlennosti i transporta), ll. 14–16, 31–33, 62–63.

[29] RGAE, f. 4372 (Gosplan), op. 41 (1941), d. 185 (Materialy k sostavleniiu general'nogo plana razvitiia narodnogo khoziaistva SSSR na 15 let [1943–1957]. Tezisy i doklady po razvitiiu ekonomicheskikh raionov SSSR), l. 4.

[30] Korobkov, "Raionnyi razrez," 65. See also Korobkov, "Zadachi kompleksnogo territorial'nogo planirovaniia," *Planovoe khoziaistvo,* 1940, no. 11: 42.

Congress in March 1939, Molotov emphasized the importance of regional planning and took a jab at the commissariats by promoting the transfer to the regions of control over local supplies of food, fuel, and construction materials.[31] Gosplan was also reprimanded, and the structure of the organization was shuffled to expand the status and size of the regional planning departments.[32] At the Eighteenth Party Conference in February 1941, the authority of the regions received a further boost at the expense of the commissariats. The conference resolutions stated: "The work of the commissariats suffers from bureaucratism. To this day, their reach does not extend to the individual enterprise. Rather, they 'lead' by means of paper communications." In contrast, it was asserted that regional leaders, "particularly of the city committees, regional committees, and the central committees of the republics have the potential to get to the bottom of problems at the factory most directly and objectively and without getting tied up in narrowly institutional interests. They can determine the source of failures and help factory administrators and the commissariats overcome them."[33] The central party leadership was now looking sympathetically at the idea of transferring operational control of the economy to the regions.

This is precisely what happened shortly after the Nazis launched their invasion of the Soviet Union in the summer of 1941. The demands of war required the maximum simplification of the command structure to speed policy implementation and reduce bureaucratic red tape. This involved, on one hand, an extreme concentration of all central leadership into a single "war cabinet" called the State Defense Committee (GKO). On the other hand, it involved the devolution of operational decision making to the regions. The decision to rely on the regions followed in part from the bad reputation that the commissariats had developed prior to the war, but it was also strongly influenced by the necessity of evacuating central agencies in the face of the German advance on Moscow.[34] In any case, the wartime structures appealed to regional leaders. Though they worked

[31] *Vosemnadtsatyi s''ezd Vsesoiuznoi Kommunisticheskoi Partii (bol'shevikov). Stenograficheskii otchet, 10–13 marta 1939 g.* (Moscow, 1939), p. 301. See also the resolution of the congress, "Tretii piatiletnii plan razvitiia narodnogo khoziaistva SSSR (1938–1942 gg.)," in *KPSS v rezoliutsiiakh,* vol. 7, pp. 68–69.

[32] "Ob organizatsii v sostave Gosudarstvennoi Planovoi Komissii pri Sovarkome SSSR territorial'nykh otdelov" (SNK SSSR, 31 October 1940), *Sobranie postanovlenii,* no. 28 (1940), pp. 941–42.

[33] "O zadachakh partiinykh organizatsii v oblasti promyshlennosti i transporta" (Vosemnadtsataia konferentsiia VKP(b), 15–20 February 1941 g.), in *KPSS v rezoliutsiiakh,* vol. 7, pp. 195–96.

[34] "Partiinye organizatsii v usloviiakh otechestvennoi voiny," *Bolshevik,* 1941, no. 14: 1–6; Alexander Werth, *Russia at War, 1941–45* (New York: Barrie and Rockliff, 1964), p. 217.

with a variety of central plenipotentiaries, they enjoyed unprecedented discretionary powers in their domains. They faced little interference from Gosplan or the commissariats, and they did not have to deal with plans based on the branch principle or, for that matter, with fixed plan targets in general. As one recent study put it, "the important thing, the thing which brought recognition and medals and privileges, became simply to work as hard and produce as much as possible, not to secure mechanistic fulfillment of the plan."[35]

Despite the devolution, the atmosphere of regional administration did not change fundamentally. While the pressures of the "plan" eased, in wartime conditions the pressure to increase production did not. Civilian plants had to be converted to military production. The evacuation of factories (and populations) from the south and west of the country massively increased regional responsibilities, and the task of bringing these plants on line was daunting. Meanwhile, almost one-half of regional party officials were drafted to the front, as were a large percentage of experienced (*kvalifitsirovannye*) workers, engineers, and other specialists.[36] As a result, the quality of administration declined. The frequency of breakdowns and serious accidents increased radically.[37] Once again, the extraordinary pressures on regional officials provoked measures of self-protection. Regional party committee first secretary Andrianov gained a reputation for destroying those regional officials who crossed him and generously protecting those who supported his "cult of personality." The same applied to many leaders in the district and city party committees.[38] Notably, scapegoating was much less common. Though local leaders were warned to investigate all accidents and breakdowns for evidence of sabotage—the work of "fascist agents,"[39] specifically—arrests on such charges were rela-

[35] John Barber and Mark Harrison, *The Soviet Home Front: A Social and Economic History of the USSR in World War II* (London: Longman, 1991), p. 42. Many of the local plenipotentiaries did not even know what the local plan targets were at a given time. RGAE, f. 4372 (Gosplan), op. 45 (1944), d. 58 (Stenogrammy soveshchanii u zamestitelia predsedatelia Gosplana SSSR po dokladam upolnomochennykh Gosplana SSSR, aprel'–dekabr' 1944), l. 47.

[36] TsDOO SO, f. 4, op. 37 (1942), d. 107 (Stenogramma soveshchaniia zaveduiushchikh org-instruktorskimi otdelami raikomov i gorkomov VKP(b), 16/IX/1942), l. 2.

[37] In the local coal industry, the number of fatal accidents more than doubled between 1942 and 1943. TsDOO SO, f. 4, op. 39 (1944), d. 108 (Dokladnye zapiski, spravki, i otchety ob avariiakh i neschastnykh sluchaiakh na predpriiatiiakh ugol'noi promyshlennosti, mart 1943–iiun' 1944), ll. 6–8.

[38] The subject of the "local variants of Stalin's cult of personality" arose at party meetings following the Twentieth Congress in 1956. TsDOO SO, f. 4, op. 55 (1956), d. 105 (Informatsii Obkoma v TsK KPSS o provedenii organizatsionno-partiinoi raboty v oblasti, ianvar'–oktiabr' 1956), ll. 161–75.

[39] RGASPI, f. 17, op. 122 (Organizatsionno-instruktorskii otdel TsK VKP(b)), d. 18 (Spravki otdela, dokladnye zapiski i pis'ma obkomov partii, TsSU, Gosplana SSSR, NKPS SSSR i dr. o

tively infrequent. The center appears to have made some effort to prevent baseless arrests,[40] but the shortages of experienced officials played an even larger role in restraining the most extreme forms of repression. While the number of arrests and expulsions from the party remained relatively low, the number of party punishments short of expulsion (*vzyskanii* and *vygovora*—official party reprimands) seems to have substantially increased.[41] However, the threat of repression was most severe for workers and peasants. Violations of work discipline were punished severely, and beatings of workers and peasants were not uncommon.[42]

"Mature Stalinism" and the Center-Region Relationship

As the war drew to a close, regional leaders hoped to retain autonomy in decision making. Their preference for devolved administrative authority was very strongly felt. Almost two decades later, at a meeting of a Central Committee commission discussing the structure of economic administration, a secretary of the Cheliabinsk regional party committee, B. A. Abramov, observed:

> Many of those present here worked in the Urals and in Siberia during the war. They know how the economy was structured in wartime. Regional party organs and soviets resolved many issues and we produced excellent equipment [*tekhnika*]. In any case, we defeated the fascists with that equipment.

---

sostoianii i nedostatkakh v rabote mestnykh partiinykh organizatsii, ianvar'–oktiabr' 1942), ll. 105–8.

[40] TsDOO SO, f. 4, op. 41 (1946), d. 161 (Spravki, informatsii, dokladnye zapiski gorkomov i raikomov VKP(b) o sostoianii partiinogo khoziaistva, uplaty chlenskikh vznosov, o roste riadov partii i nalozhenii partvzyskanii), l. 101: Spravka o vypolnenii Sverdlovskoi oblastoi partorganizatsiei postanovleniia TsK VKP(b) ot 29 dekabria 1943 g. "O nedostatkakh v rabote obkomov, kraikomov, TsK Kompartii soiuznykh respublikakh pri rassmotrenii reshenii raikomov i gorkomov partii ob iskliuchenii iz riadov VKP(b) i appeliatsii chlenov i kandidatov v chleny VKP(b)."

[41] For complaints against regional officials for the excessive issuance of party reprimands, see RGASPI, f. 17, op. 122 (Organizatsionno-instruktorskii otdel TsK VKP(b)), d. 18 (Spravki otdela, dokladnye zapiski i pis'ma obkomov partii, TsSU, Gosplana SSSR, NKPS SSSR, i dr. o sostoianii i nedostatkakh v rabote mestnykh partiinykh organizatsii), ll. 109–10; d. 30 (Spravki i dokladnye zapiski Upravleniia propagandy i agitatsii, org-instruktorskogo otdela i otdela shkol TsK VKP(b), otchety i informatsii oblastnykh komitetov i TsK VLKSM o khode vypolneniiapostanovleniia TsK VKP(b) "O rabote obkomov i o sostoianii del v oblastiakh," mart 1943–ianvar' 1944), l. 302.

[42] TsDOO SO, f. 4, op. 40 (1945), d. 117 (Spravki, perepiska o sostoianii partiino-sledstvennykh del, perepiska po komprometiruiushchim materialam na rukovodiashchikh rabotnikov), l. 83.

Voices: It's true!

M. V. Laptev (also from Cheliabinsk): We didn't even have any contact with the ministries [commissariats] . . . the experiment was successful.[43]

Unfortunately for the regions, this "experiment" did not last long, in no small part because it was not as successful as many leaders later remembered. The shortcomings were not always the regional leaders' fault. The massive wartime evacuation of industry from west to east was an extraordinarily complex task. While the evacuation itself was a stunning success, the relocation of people and production and the conversion of industry from civilian to military needs were bound to create imbalances in the economy. By 1942, supporting industries and essential services—among them transport, food production, and the output of electricity—were lagging badly. Regional leaders tried to blame many of their failings on the shortage of experienced officials, but they were not able to escape a reputation for "leadership on paper," that is, for issuing resolutions from the regional center instead of heading out to trouble spots.[44] More fundamentally, the center showed a growing concern that regional administrations were slipping from its control. The center began to doubt the veracity of regional reports on the fulfillment of decisions,[45] and criticized Gosplan's regional plenipotentiaries for becoming servants (*poruchentsy*) of local officials.[46] The center's suspicions were confirmed in the aftermath of war, when leading officials in many regions attempted to resist the center's targets for grain collections.[47]

While the center did not openly reject the wartime regional, or "territorial," basis of planning and administration, the previous system of branch administration and central planning was gradually restored. Quarterly and annual central planning had already been reinstituted at the end

[43] TsKhSD, f. 5 (Otdely TsK KPSS), op. 5 (Obshchii otdel), d. 196 (Stenogrammy zasedaniia komissii TsK KPSS po reorganizatsii promyshlennosti i stroitel'stva i soveshchaniia s predsedatel'iami sovnarkhozov i sekretariami obkomov i kraikomov RSFSR, 4 fevralia 1957), l. 92.

[44] RGASPI, f. 17, op. 122, d. 30 (Spravki i dokladnye zapiski upravleniia propagandy i agitatsii, Organizatsionno-instruktorskogo otdela i Otdela shkol TsK VKP(b), otchety i informatsii oblastnykh komitetov i TsK VLKSM o khode vypolnenii postanovleniia TsK VKP(b) o rabote obkomov i o sostoianii del v oblastiakh, mart 1943–ianvar' 1944), ll. 2–4 (Arkhangel'sk), 40–43 (Voronezh), 205–9 (Voronezh), 289–302 (Tambov).

[45] RGAE, f. 4372 (Gosplan), op. 45 (1944), d. 58 (Stenogramma soveshchanii u zamestitelia predsedatelia Gosplana SSSR po dokladam upolnomochennykh Gosplana SSSR, aprel'–dekabr' 1944), l. 8.

[46] Ibid., l. 29.

[47] RGASPI, f. 17, op. 116 (Orgbiuro i Sekretariat TsK VKP(b)), d. 238 (Zasedanie Orgbiuro TsK VKP(b) ot 27 oktiabria 1945 g.).

of 1942.[48] The decentralization of administration did not begin until the war was coming to a close, when the task of reconstruction created new pressures for unified economic policy. The regions could not be left with the task of managing the economy of a country split between an eastern half focused on the conversion of military industries and a western half rebuilding its economy from the ground up. As it was, regional leaders in the two halves of the country were engaged in a bitter struggle over their respective shares of central investment. The commissariats were restored to the level of power they had enjoyed before the terror, and regional party organs were reduced to the role of "dispatcher" at the call of the ministries and factories in their purview.[49] Once again, the regions were made to answer for plan fulfillment without any compensating influence over the construction of plan targets.

On 19 August 1945, a decree of the Central Committee and the Council of People's Commissars directed Gosplan and the commissariats to draft a five-year plan for 1946–50. Facing the devastation of areas under occupation, the loss of millions of citizens, and the need to relocate and reconvert much of the industrial capital stock, the leadership hoped to return to the growth rates characteristic of the first two five-year plans. Gosplan did discuss targets with its regional counterparts, but, as could be expected, the regions requested far more investment than Gosplan was prepared to provide and offered far lower production targets than Gosplan was prepared to accept. Gosplan showed very little flexibility, largely imposing its own figures for investment efficiency.[50] Objections were immediately rebuffed. Moscow refused to consider revisions to grain collection targets despite a terrible drought in 1946. Party leaders in many regions were threatened with expulsion if foot-dragging in grain collections did not stop.[51] Amid the tensions, by a decision of the Politburo, twelve regional party secretaries were transferred to the apparatus of the Orgburo.

[48] Mark Harrison, *Soviet Planning in Peace and War, 1938–1945* (Cambridge: Cambridge University Press, 1985), p. 98; Eugene Zaleski, *Stalinist Planning for Economic Growth, 1933–1952* (Chapel Hill: University of North Carolina Press, 1980), pp. 300–301.

[49] Timothy Dunmore, *The Stalinist Command Economy: The Soviet State Apparatus and Economic Policy, 1945–1953* (London: Macmillan, 1980), p. 19; "Ob agitatsionno-propagandistskoi rabote partiinykh organizatsii v sviazi s priniatiem zakona o piatiletnem plane vosstanovleniia i razvitiia narodnogo khoziaistva SSSR na 1946–1950 gg." (Party Central Committee, 27 March 1946), *Resheniia partii i pravitel'stva po khoziaistvennym voprosam*, vol. 3 (Moscow, 1968), pp. 320–23.

[50] RGAE, f. 4372 (Gosplan), op. 46 (1946), d. 171 (O raznoglasiiakh po obsuzhdeniiu proekta plana vosstanovleniia i razvitiia narodnogo khoziaistva na 1946–1950 gg., fevral' 1946). See also Zaleski, *Stalinist Planning for Economic Growth*, pp. 352–54.

[51] RGAE, f. 4372 (Gosplan), op. 45 (1944), d. 58 (Stenogramma soveshchanii u zamestitelia predsedatelia Gosplana SSSR po dokladam upolnomochennykh Gosplana SSSR, aprel'–dekabr' 1944), l. 8.

According to N. S. Patolichev (one of those transferred), Stalin directed them to "correct" the work of local party organs. He quoted Stalin as saying: "We need to restore the right of the Central Committee to monitor [*kontrolirovat'*] the activity of party organizations."[52]

Regional leaders shifted the pressure to local party and state officials. In a speech to the Sverdlovsk regional party committee plenum discussing the Fourth Five-Year Plan, party secretary S. Pustovalov addressed himself to those "who calmly view failures at work . . . who try to justify, legalize, and perpetuate them. . . . Such extremists, such carriers of rotten opportunistic attitudes one cannot correct [except to fire them and remove them from the party]."[53] The pronouncement echoed Stalin's warning to party leaders at the Seventeenth Congress in 1934: "Reference to so-called objective conditions cannot serve as justification" for underfulfillment of the plan.[54] The response was much the same, too. Local party leaders and enterprise directors simply lied about the state of plan fulfillment. Reports on plan fulfillment almost invariably were set in ruble terms, which allowed directors to hide shortcomings in production by inflating costs. Furthermore, they exaggerated their needs for inputs and did not report unused plant capacities. Overfulfillment in any given month was unreported and applied against subsequent shortfalls.[55] Such strategies may have fooled the center for a time in the 1930s, but not anymore—not merely because Moscow was better equipped in detection, but also because regional leaders did not cooperate with the city, district, and factory party secretaries and factory directors who used these strategies. This is not to say that regional leaders were on Moscow's side. Their reports also consistently and falsely claimed plan fulfillment on the basis of vague, ruble-based figures and misleading comparisons. In contrast to the 1930s, the regional party "clique" did not have the same power to dominate politics in the region. The party was much larger now, with many more positions of independent authority. Officials were better educated and much less inclined to be in awe of the regional party secretary and his membership on the Central Committee. In place of a single, dominant regional clique or "family group" to provide patronage and protection, local officials were more likely to be a part of smaller city-, district-, or factory-level cliques that managed their presentation to the outside world.

All this made regional politics more tense and conflictual than it had

[52] N. S. Patolichev, *Ispytanie na zrelost'* (Moscow, 1977), pp. 279–83.

[53] TsDOO SO, f. 4, op. 41 (1946), d. 2 (Stenogramma XXVI plenuma Sverdlovskogo obkoma VKP(b), 26–28 marta 1946 g.), l. 49.

[54] *XVII s''ezd Vsesoiuznyi Kommunisticheskoi Partii (b): stenograficheskii otchet* (Moscow, 1934), p. 33.

[55] Berliner, *Factory and Manager in the USSR.*

been in the 1930s. Then, regional leaders had kept a lid on local tensions (at least until 1936). Now that was no longer possible. When production problems grew to the point where masking them was impossible, there was no group that could prevent or control the process of scapegoating. For example, when the Uralmash plant was unable to hide serious plan underfulfillment in 1949, the Industry and Transport Department of the Sverdlovsk city party committee together with local representatives of the secret police revealed the "antistate practice of plan falsification [*pripiski k planu*]" at the factory.[56] In that way, Uralmash officials would have to answer for the mess. Similarly, when the regional coal industry was criticized by Moscow, the regional leadership accused the party secretaries of the coal-producing districts of suppressing local criticism and hiding production problems from them.[57]

The conflict between the regional party committee, on one hand, and district and city party committees, on the other, was particularly severe and consequential. In his tenure as regional party first secretary (1946–52), Viktor Nedosekin never managed to create the impression of plan fulfillment. While his reports to Moscow spoke of the great advances of Urals industry, other sources of information painted a far less flattering picture.[58] In 1948, Nedosekin was hauled into the Orgburo and told that if he failed to turn things around he would be removed.[59] In turn, he tried to lay the blame for problems on the district and city party committees and had their officials removed en masse. The annual rate of turnover of district and city party secretaries often exceeded 50 percent.[60] Like Andrianov before him, Nedosekin had a reputation for destroying the careers

[56] TsDOO SO, f. 4, op. 45 (1949), d. 196 (Dokladnye zapiski, spravki partiinykh rabotnikov, rukovoditelei khoziaistvennykh organisatsii v obkom partii o sostoianii i rabote predpriiatii tiazheloi i mashinostroitel'noi promyshlennosti oblasti, ianvar'–sentiabr' 1949 g.), ll. 47–56.

[57] TsDOO SO, f. 4, op. 45 (1949), d. 211 (Spravki, informatsii rabotnikov obkoma, gorkomov, raikomov VKP(b) v obkom partii o rasmotrenii zhalob i zaiavlenii na nepravil'nye deistviia rukovoditelei, zazhime kritiki, aprel'–oktiabr' 1949), ll. 26–29, 43–45.

[58] The sources include district and city party committees, regional plenipotentiaries, and the ministries. RGASPI, f. 17, op. 134 (Otdel tiazheloi promyshlennosti TsK VKP(b)), d. 8 (Proekty postanovlenii Sovmina SSSR, podgotovlennye Sverdlovskim obkomom VKP(b), spravki po nim otdela, zakliucheniia ministerstv i vedomstv, oktiabr' 1948–ianvar' 1949 g.), ll. 55–58.

[59] TsDOO SO, f. 4, op. 44 (1948), d. 14 (Stenogramma zasedaniia IV plenuma Sverdlovskogo obkoma VKP(b), 29–30 noiabria 1948 g.), ll. 120–32: Doklad tov. Prassa (inspektr TSK).

[60] TsDOO SO, f. 4, op. 52 (1954), d. 180 (Statisticheskie otchety, spravki o podbore, podgotovke, rasstanovke, i smeniaemosti rukovodiashchikh partiinykh, sovetskikh, komsomol'skikh, i khoziaistvennykh kadrov oblasti, ianvar' 1950–ianvar' 1954 g.), l. 64: Dannye o smeniaemosti sekretarei partorg i ikh zamestitelei po GK i RK.

of those who crossed him.[61] Even so, he succeeded only in provoking the ire of the local secretaries, who in turn relentlessly criticized the regional party committee in front of central officials for failing to give them appropriate assistance. In the summer of 1951, the Central Committee apparatus began to transfer regional party secretaries out of the region. By September, all mention of Nedosekin disappears from the local archives, though his replacement was named only in September 1952.

Was there a threat of a new terror against the regions on the eve of Stalin's death? The center had consistently failed to control the regions' behavior. Many of the types of corruption and other abuses of power revealed in the Mingrelian Affair were common to all the regions.[62] Certainly, the center was losing patience with regional organizations for misleading it about plan fulfillment and relying on "family groups" to protect their local authority.[63] The new party statutes passed at the Nineteenth Party Congress in 1952 made it clear that "hiding and perverting the truth from the party . . . was incompatible with membership in its ranks," as was anything less than the "active struggle for the fulfillment of party decisions."[64] More seriously, a decree of the Council of Ministers (successor to the Council of People's Commissars) earlier in the year had increased the punishment for some categories of plan falsification, equating them with wrecking.[65] Prosecutions did follow—on charges of counterrevolutionary crimes[66]—but the signals from Moscow were not strong enough or consistent enough to incite a broader wave of denunciations as in 1936–38.

There was, however, enough incendiary material. Plan pressures kept tensions among regional organizations high. Criticism of the plan itself was not permitted, so the temptation to blame others for production problems was great. There had never been a shortage of local officials who would have preferred to blame all their problems on counterrevolu-

[61] TsDOO SO, f. 4, op. 55 (1956), d. 105 (Informatsii Obkoma v TsK KPSS o provedenii organizatsionno-partiinoi raboty v oblasti), l. 168.

[62] In 1951–52, several leading officials (of Mingrelian nationality) in the Georgian Communist Party were accused of corruption and abuses of power. Hundreds of officials were subsequently arrested.

[63] See, for example, Khrushchev's speech to the Nineteenth Party Congress in October 1952: RGASPI, f. 592 (XIX s"ezd VKP(b) 5–14 oktiabria 1952 g.), op.1, d. 44 (Stenogramma desiatogo zasedaniia 10–go oktiabria. Doklad sekretaria TsK Khrushcheva, N. S., ob izmeneniiakh v ustave VKP(b)), ll. 16–19.

[64] *KPSS v rezoliutsiiakh*, 9th ed., vol. 8 (Moscow, 1985), p. 286.

[65] TsDOO SO, f. 4, op. 52 (1953), d. 112 (Stenogramma soveshchaniia rabotnikov promyshlennosti, stroitel'nykh organizatsii, i transporta Sverdlovskoi oblasti, 28–29 ianvaria 1953 g.), l. 181.

[66] Ibid., l. 178; TsDOO SO, f. 4, op. 52 (1953), d. 10 (Stenogramma ob"edinennogo plenuma oblastnoi i gorodskoi komitetov KPSS, 13 iiunia 1953 g.), ll. 74–78.

tionaries and other "enemies." Few regional party committee plenums passed without some official or officials expressing the idea that underfulfillment was the work of wreckers, despite the plaintive comment of one official in 1948 that "we have somehow lost the habit of seeing enemies."[67] In the same year, the regional organization was criticized by the center for the high numbers of baseless arrests of local officials.[68] If the center had chosen to send an unambiguous signal to seek out "enemies of the people" as they had in 1936, such "enemies" would almost certainly have been found, and in large numbers. As it was, the Politburo's new appointee to the post of Sverdlovsk regional party committee first secretary, Aleksei Kutyrev, immediately sought to ease tensions between the regional party committee and the city and district party committees, and he played a central role in reversing convictions for plan falsification in the summer of 1953.

De-Stalinization?

The arrival of Kutyrev did not, however, signal any sea change in local politics. Nor for that matter did the death of Stalin or the subsequent arrest of the Ministry of Internal Affairs (the NKVD's successor) chief Lavrentii Beria. In announcing Beria's arrest, the central party leaders observed that the party had an obligation to reassert its control over the Ministry of Internal Affairs, to restrain it and regulate its activity, but their message was not unambiguous in its criticism of "terror." There had been "excesses," but "vigilance in the struggle against enemies of the regime" was still needed. After all, Beria was accused of being an agent of foreign capital determined to overthrow Soviet power. The tactics of central party leaders continued to be classically Stalinist, preparing the party ranks to accept trumped-up charges against those they chose to oust. At the regional party committee plenum, which discussed the Central Committee resolution on the affair, almost every official who rose to speak demanded a severe punishment for the traitor Beria and asserted the need for continued vigilance against enemies of the regime in the region.[69] One exception, a secretary of the regional party committee, observed that the tendency to seek "wreckers" in the face of production difficulties had the

[67] TsDOO SO, f. 4, op. 44 (1948), d. 14 (Stenogramma zasedaniia IV plenuma Sverdlovskogo obkoma, 29–30 aprelia 1948 g.), l. 27.
[68] Ibid., d. 13 (Stenogramma zasedaniia IV plenuma Sverdlovskogo obkoma, 29–30 aprelia 1948 g.), l. 44.
[69] TsDOO SO, f. 4, op. 52 (1953), d. 10 (Stenogramma ob"edinennogo plenuma oblastnoi i gorodskoi komitetov KPSS, 13 iiunia 1953 g.), ll. 21, 24, 73, 125.

effect only of deepening production problems.[70] No one else picked up on the theme.

In the first few years after Stalin's death, little changed to relieve the pressures on regional officials. The Fourth Five-Year Plan (1951–55) had projected an increase in industrial production of 70 percent, and the decision of G. M. Malenkov, chairman of the Council of Ministers, in the autumn of 1953 to accelerate the production of consumer goods only intensified the pressures of the plan. All the measures of resistance to plan pressures remained—the "family circles," the tendency to send misleading and falsified reports of plan fulfillment, and the scapegoating of others if violations of state and party discipline were uncovered.

Enough of these *were* uncovered that in the autumn of 1955 the Central Committee apparatus again intervened to remove the regional party first secretary. His predecessor Nedosekin had been removed three years earlier, largely because of his persistent conflicts with the district and city party committees. Kutyrev had gone to the opposite extreme. The regional party committee bureau and department heads were accused of being "insufficiently demanding to [subordinate party organizations] that were negligent in execution of their duties."[71] For all that, the regional party committee bureau did not have a reputation for protecting local party officials. Rather, it had purged organizations only after their failures drew the center's attention. In the previous two years, 1,502 regional party members and candidates had been purged from the party, including 873 leading (*otvetstvennye*) officials.[72] The regional party committee plenum at which Kutyrev was formally removed was reminiscent of the February–March 1937 Central Committee plenum. One by one, the members of the bureau were forced to address the plenum and admit their mistakes.[73]

While the heavy atmosphere of Stalin-era politics continued to weigh on Sverdlovsk region, changes to the structure of economic administration promised to ease the burden. Regional leaders had never surrendered the hope for a return to the war-time "experiment" with territorial administration of the economy: a weakening of the centralized control of

[70] In his words, "no one should turn production problems, sometimes necessary production risks, into wrecking." Ibid., l. 75.

[71] TsDOO SO, f. 4, op. 55 (1956), d. 2 (Stenogramma X oblastnoi partiinoi konferentsii, 17–19 ianvaria 1956 g.), l. 71.

[72] Ibid., ll. 70–74.

[73] The attending representative of the Central Committee (Aristov) interrupted and criticized speakers who were not sufficiently self-critical. TsDOO SO, f. 4, op. 54 (1955), d. 6 (Stenogramma VIII plenuma Sverdlovskogo obkoma KPSS, 3 dekabria 1955 g.).

Gosplan and the ministries and a strengthening of local autonomy. Despite extensive support in the Politburo for an expanded role for the regions, resistance primarily from the ministries and Gosplan stalled implementation.[74] The latter did so through the newly established Council of Ministers, which they dominated. Under the chairmanship of Malenkov, the council functionally monopolized economic policy making.[75] In the late 1940s, several regions took the initiative to organize conferences "on the study of (local) productive forces" in order to promote regional planning. Following the lead of Kazakhstan and Western Siberia, the Sverdlovsk regional party committee proposed to hold one for the Urals region but was refused. In consultation with Gosplan and the ministries, Malenkov put an end to these conferences on the grounds that they encouraged the regions to assume that central organs would be bound by their resolutions.[76] Despite the persistent complaints of regional leaders, Gosplan continued to rubber-stamp the exaggerated plan projections of the ministries.[77]

The domination of the ministries and Gosplan over economic decision making was not seriously challenged until it became a central issue in the struggle for succession to Stalin. Following the death of the dictator, Malenkov remained at the helm of the Council of Ministers, and Nikita Khrushchev took over as head of the party Presidium (successor to the Politburo). At the time, the Council of Ministers was the locus of power, a situation reinforced by the fact that the power bases of most Presidium members were rooted in the ministerial system. Nevertheless, Khrushchev played an active role in economic policy through party structures, egregiously stepping into the territory of the Council of Ministers.

Khrushchev's ambitions were not limited to this sort of provocation. Towards the end of 1956, he moved to undermine ministerial power, and with it, the power of his rival Georgii Malenkov.[78] At the December 1956

[74] For a detailed study of this issue, see Dunmore, *Stalinist Command Economy*, chap. 3, pp. 26–63.

[75] By contrast, the Politburo had practically stopped meeting in the postwar period. Iu. N. Zhukov, "Bor'ba za vlast' v rukovodstve SSSR v 1945–1952 godakh," *Voprosy istorii*, 1995, no. 1: 39.

[76] RGASPI, f. 17, op. 134 (Otdel tiazheloi promyshlennosti TsK VKP(b)), d. 25 (Proekty postanovlenii Soveta Ministrov SSSR, zapiski sekretaria TsK VKP(b) P.K. Ponomarenko i otdela, pis'ma partiinykh organov, ministerstv, i vedomstv o provedenii konferentsii o proizvostvennkh sil oblastei i ekonomicheskikh raionov SSSR, fevral' 1949–noiabr' 1949 g.), ll. 21, 33.

[77] RGASPI, f. 17, op. 135 (Planovo-finansovo-torgovyi otdel), d. 16 (Zapiski, pis'ma i spravki otdela i sektora planovykh organov, mestnykh partiinykh organov, Gosplana, i ministerstv ob uluchshenii planirovanii narodnogo khoziaistva), ll. 1–4, 23–33, 41.

[78] For detailed descriptions of the power struggles, see William J. Tompson, *Khrushchev: A Political Life* (London: St. Martin's, 1995); Carl A. Linden, *Khrushchev and the Soviet Leadership*

Central Committee plenum, he proposed what appeared to be a minor reform decentralizing management of the economy in the union republics.[79] The issue itself was less important than that it opened the central economic apparatus to criticism: "Gosplan . . . and the ministries insufficiently study the condition of various branches of production. They are weakly connected with the union and autonomous republics, the regions, enterprises, and scientific institutions. They have permitted serious omissions and errors in the development of production plans, in capital construction, and in material-technical supply."[80] These were precisely the criticisms that had been raised persistently by regional leaders—not coincidentally, a key power base of Nikita Khrushchev. Shortly thereafter, Khrushchev convened a Central Committee commission to discuss the "reorganization of the administration of industry and construction" and invited regional party and state leaders to its sessions.[81] The latter did not hesitate to heap criticism on the central economic apparatus and propose ways to transfer control over the economy to the regions, up to and including the wholesale abolition of the ministries.[82]

The way was not entirely clear for an assault on ministerial power. Khrushchev had limited influence in the Council of Ministers, and much of the Presidium was sympathetic to the ministries' concerns. The results of the commission were the basis for a spirited discussion at the subsequent Central Committee plenum, but ministerial interests held the day. The plenum resolutions entrusted the Council of Ministers and the party Presidium to "work out concrete proposals" for reform.[83] Khrushchev did not surrender but instead presented the commission's results for public discussion without the approval of the party leadership. He was very direct, even with foreign journalists. To the *New York Herald Tribune*, he announced: "We mean to do away with the industrial ministries altogether, both in the center and the republics. Instead, all industrial enterprises . . .

(Baltimore, Md.: Johns Hopkins, 1966); and Robert Conquest, *Power and Policy in the USSR* (London: Macmillan, 1961).

79 Khrushchev had first raised the issue at the Twentieth Party Congress in February 1956. "Rezoliutsii po otchetnomu dokladu TsK KPSS (N. S. Khrushchev)," in *KPSS v rezoliutsiiakh*, 9th ed., vol. 9 (Moscow, 1986), p. 21.

80 Ibid., p. 151.

81 TsKhSD, f.5 (Otdely apparata TsK KPSS), op. 5 (Obshchii otdel), d. 196 (Stenogramma zasedaniia komissii TsK KPSS po reorganizatsiiu promyshlennosti i stroitel'stva i soveshchaniia s predsedatel'iami sovnarkhozov [*sic*] i sekretariami obkomov i kraikomov RSFSR, 4 fevralia 1957), l. 2.

82 Ibid.

83 Plenum TsK KPSS, 13–14 fevralia 1957 g., "O dal'neishem sovershenstvovanii organizatsii upravlenii promyshlennost'iu i stroitel'stvom," in *KPSS v rezoliutsiiakh*, 9th ed., vol. 4 (Moscow, 1984), pp. 167–74.

will be directed by territorial departments."[84] The regions proceeded to work out their own plans for the restructuring of local industrial administration.[85] The Leningrad and Gorkii regional party committees both created territorial departments before any central legislation had been passed.[86]

Malenkov and other members of the Presidium were livid over Khrushchev's usurpation of their authority and the violation of norms of political conduct, to say nothing of the blatant attack on their power. According to Presidium member Anastas Mikoian, the atmosphere of the party leadership was poisoned by an unspoken hostility.[87] It was unspoken because Malenkov, Molotov, and Kaganovich were surveying members of the Presidium for the support necessary to remove Khrushchev. In June 1957, when they were confident of a majority, they convened a meeting and demanded that he resign. But Khrushchev refused on the basis of party statutes. The Presidium was not authorized to elect or to remove its own members. This was the prerogative of the Central Committee—a body in which he had strong support, especially from among regional party secretaries, who constituted nearly half of its members. Khrushchev rejected the "illegal" decision of the Presidium and insisted that a Central Committee plenum be convened. The Presidium majority initially refused, but regional leaders, hearing of events in the Kremlin, rushed to Moscow and themselves demanded a plenum. The Presidium majority relented, not wanting to leave the impression that they were leading a coup against the will of the party. When the plenum was convened, regional leaders solidly backed Khrushchev and the reform of industrial administration. Members of the Central Committee from among the ministerial apparatus saw the correlation of forces and remained conspicuously silent.[88] Malenkov, Molotov, and Kaganovich were removed from their posts; and Khrushchev took over the chairmanship of the Council of Ministers.

With Khrushchev's victory, the reform proceeded apace. Most of the

[84] Quoted from Conquest, *Power and Policy*, p. 298.

[85] For the discussions in the Urals, see TsDOO SO, f. 4 (Obkom), op. 57 (1957), d. 7 (Stenogramma V plenuma obkoma KPSS, 10 aprelia 1957 g.), "O dal'neishem sovershenstvovanii organizatsii upravlenii promyshlennost'iu i stroitel'stvom Sverdlovskogo ekonomicheskogo raiona."

[86] Conquest, *Power and Policy*, p. 304.

[87] "Poslednaia anti-partiinaia gruppa: stenograficheskii otchet iiun'skogo (1957 g.) plenuma TsK KPSS," *Istoricheskii arkhiv*, 1993, no. 4: 22.

[88] The full stenogram of the meeting was published in *Istoricheskii arkhiv*, 1993, nos. 3–6, and 1994, nos. 1–2. For a comment on the reaction of ministerial officials see ibid., 1993, no. 5: 12.

ministries were abolished and their employees were sent to the regions. The day-to-day administration of the economy was transferred to regional "economic councils" (*sovnarkhozy*).[89] The regions were ultimately responsible to a supreme sovnarkhoz, but the permitted degree of functional regional autonomy remained to be explored. In this context, regional leaders steadily moved to increase their independence from other regions and especially from the center. The ministries had been criticized for failing to account for connections among the various branches of the economy. The regions, in contrast, linked the branches together with the object of establishing, as far as possible, a regionally autarkic economy, thus reducing the pressures of the plan. To this end, the leadership of Sverdlovsk region pushed to reunite the regions (*oblasti*) of the pre-1934 Urals into a "Urals economic zone" (*Ural'skii ekonomicheskii raion*).[90] Unification would accommodate a complete production cycle in heavy industry, combining sources of fuel, ores, metallurgy, and machine building. It would decrease the pressures exerted by central planners by increasing local control over all stages of the production cycle.[91] No longer would regional plan fulfillment be threatened by the failure of firms outside the region to supply inputs on time, by the unrealistic targets set by Gosplan, or by the interference of the ministries. Sverdlovsk leaders even pushed to have power over the creation of the plan shifted from Moscow to the regions.[92] In short, they sought the sort of local autonomy that they had envisioned when they proposed the Great Urals Plan in the late 1920s.[93]

While regional officials almost universally celebrated the sovnarkhoz reform, it was no panacea. As with the wartime "experiment" with region-based economic administration, no substantial improvement in the quality of administration was observed. Regional officials certainly appreciated their freedom from the tutelage of the ministries and increased local

[89] "Ob utverzhdenii Polozheniia o sovete narodnogo khoziaistva ekonomicheskogo adminstrativnogo raiona (26 sentiabria 1957 g.)," *Sobranie postanovlenii pravitel'stva SSSR*, vol. 12 (1957), pp. 408–29.

[90] According to Sverdlovsk regional party committee secretary Andrei Kirilenko, the Urals economic zone had been the subject of negotiation among Urals regions for many months before the subject was broached with the central leadership. TsKhSD, f. 5 (Otdely apparata TsK KPSS), op. 5 (Obshchii otdel), d. 196 (Stenogrammy zasedaniia Kommissii TsK KPSS po reorganizatsii upravleniia promyshlennost'iu i stroitel'stvom i soveshchaniia s predsedatel'iami sovnarkhozov i sekretariami obkomov i kraikomov RSFSR, fevral'–mai 1957 g.), ll. 77–78.

[91] TsDOO SO, f. 4 (Obkom), op. 57 (1957), d. 7 (Stenogramma V plenuma Obkoma KPSS, 10 aprelia 1957 g.), ll. 10–11: Rech' tov. Kirilenko.

[92] Ibid., ll. 7–8.

[93] See Harris, *The Great Urals*, for further details.

control over financial and material resources, but they did not achieve the level of local autarky to which they aspired, and fulfilling the plan continued to present considerable difficulties. While "family groups" remained, and some forms of plan falsification continued, scapegoating, arrests, expulsions, and other kinds of repressive measures became increasingly rare. Of course, this cannot be explained solely in terms of the devolution of administrative authority. The broader experience of "de-Stalinization," particularly Khrushchev's secret speech to the Twentieth Party Congress, served to reinforce the message that regional officials would no longer be subject to arrest or expulsion for shortcomings in their work. As such, scapegoating—a preemptive measure to protect oneself from punishment—no longer served the same purpose.

What had changed was the center's attitude toward the behavior of its regional officials. In the 1930s, Stalin accepted nothing less than the complete and unconditional fulfillment of all central directives. There was only "Bolshevik" leadership or "rotten" (*gniloe*) leadership. When it uncovered the practices by which regional officials had resisted the colossal pressures of the emerging "command-administrative system," the regime was surprised and frightened. A war with fascism was on the horizon, and there appeared to be a great internal conspiracy against its leadership. It responded by destroying the regional leaderships wholesale.

The experience of the terror and its "excesses" did not cure the central leadership of its belief in the existence of internal enemies of the regime. Even after the experience of regional administration during the war, Stalin kept a careful watch on the activities of the regional leaders. Their resistance—their violations of state and party discipline—were something of an open secret. Did the center see these regional responses as "wrecking" or merely as malfeasance? Regional leaders were never sure. The Leningrad Affair, the Mingrelian Affair, and other such murderous episodes aimed against regional leaderships demonstrated to regional leaders that their position was extremely vulnerable. The experience of 1936–38 was no distant memory, and they had reason to fear a repetition of those events. At all levels of the regional organization, scapegoating remained the favorite tactic of self-protection, and the notion that "wreckers and saboteurs" were at work in Sverdlovsk region served a valuable purpose. It had always been more acceptable to blame enemies for breakdowns and other sources of plan underfulfillment than to point to the real source of the problem: the plan itself was unrealistic.

In the end, there was never a return to full-fledged terror in Sverdlovsk region, though there were scares: in 1948, when Nedosekin was hauled into Moscow to explain the systematic failure to meet regional plans; in

1952, when the tensions between the regional party committee and local committees again drew the center's attention; and even in 1955, when Kutyrev was ousted and the regional party committee bureau was compelled to admit its "errors." For regional leaders, "de-Stalinization" began in earnest not only when the pressures of plan fulfillment eased, but also when they were certain that shortcomings of plan fulfillment were not a life-threatening issue. Under Khrushchev, and particularly under Leonid Brezhnev, the central leadership dropped Stalin's Manichean distinction between "Bolshevik" and "rotten" leadership. Moscow tolerated all but the most egregious forms of regional misbehavior, and only then, years after Stalin's death, did the hunt for "wreckers" and "saboteurs" come to a close.

Notes on Contributors

James Harris is lecturer in Modern European history at the School of History, University of Leeds, United Kingdom. His book *The Great Urals: Regionalism and the Evolution of the Soviet System* was published by Cornell University Press in 1999. He is currently writing a book on the Stalinist political system.

Dan Healey is lecturer in Russian history in the Department of History, University of Wales Swansea, United Kingdom. He is the author of the first book-length history of same-sex love in modern Russia, *Homosexual Desire in Revolutionary Russia: The Regulation of Sexual and Gender Dissent* (Chicago: University of Chicago Press, 2001). He is currently working on a monograph about early Soviet forensic medicine and the limits of sexual utopianism.

Tracy McDonald is assistant professor of history at the University of Utah. She carried out her graduate work at the University of Toronto, where she wrote her doctoral thesis, "Through the Window of Village Crime: Peasant and State in Riazan 1921–1930." She is coeditor (with Andrei Mel'nik, Lynne Viola, and Sergei Zhuravlev) of *Riazanskaia derevnia v 1929–1930 gg.: khronika golovokhruzheniia. Dokumenty i materialy* (Moscow, 1998).

Douglas Northrop is assistant professor of history at the University of Georgia. His forthcoming book, *Veiled Empire: Gender and Power in Stalinist Central Asia,* will appear with Cornell University Press. He is now at work on a study of everyday culture in Soviet Central Asia (1941–69) and is writing a book on natural disasters and earthquakes in the Soviet empire.

Elena A. Osokina is a senior researcher at the Russian Academy of Sciences and visiting professor at Oberlin College. She is the author of numerous articles and three books, including *Ierarkhiia potrebleniia* (Moscow: MGOU, 1993); *Za fasadom "stalinskogo izobiliia"* (Moscow: Rosspen, 1998); and *Our Daily Bread: Socialist Distribution and the Art of Survival in Stalin's Russia, 1927–1941* (Armonk, N.Y.: Sharpe, 2001). She is currently completing a book about the "extraordinary" financial sources of Soviet industrialization, including art exports and the Torgsin stores.

Jeffrey J. Rossman is assistant professor of history at the University of Virginia. He is currently revising a manuscript entitled "Worker Resistance under Stalin: Social Identity and the State in the USSR, 1928–1932" and is researching the social history of the Soviet home front during World War II.

Lynne Viola is professor of history at the University of Toronto. She is the author of *The Best Sons of the Fatherland: Workers in the Vanguard of Soviet Collectivization* (New York: Oxford, 1987) and *Peasant Rebels under Stalin: Collectivization and the Culture of Peasant Resistance* (New York: Oxford, 1996). She is currently working on a history of the kulak special settlements.

Index